"¡Mi Raza Primero!"
(My People First!)

"¡Mi Raza Primero!"
(My People First!)

Nationalism, Identity, and Insurgency in
the Chicano Movement in Los Angeles,
1966–1978

Ernesto Chávez

UNIVERSITY OF CALIFORNIA PRESS
Berkeley / Los Angeles / London

University of California Press
Berkeley and Los Angeles, California

University of California Press, Ltd.
London, England

© 2002 by the Regents of the University of California

Library of Congress Cataloging-in-Publication Data

Chávez, Ernesto, 1962–
   "¡Mi Raza Primero!" (My People First!) : nationalism, identity, and
insurgency in the Chicano movement in Los Angeles, 1966–1978 / by
Ernesto Chávez.
        p.   cm.
   Includes bibliographical references and index.
   ISBN 0-520-23017-5 (cloth : alk. paper). —
   ISBN 0-520-23018-3 (pbk. : alk. paper)
   1. Mexican Americans — California — Los Angeles — Politics and
government — 20th century.   2. Mexican Americans — California —
Los Angeles — Ethnic identity.   3. Mexican Americans — Civil rights —
California — Los Angeles — History — 20th Century.   4. Civil rights move-
ments — California — Los Angeles — History — 20th Century.   6. Los
Angeles (Calif.) — Ethnic relations.   I. Title.

F869.L89 M514   2002
979.4'940046872 — dc21   2002018880

Manufactured in the United States of America
10   09   08   07   06   05   04   03
10   9   8   7   6   5   4   3   2

The paper used in this publication is both acid-free and totally chlorine-free
(TCF). The paper used in this publication meets the minimum requirements
of ANSI/NISO Z39.48–1992 (R 1997) (*Permanence of Paper*). ♾

This book is dedicated to my parents,
Bertha González Chávez and Alberto Rodríguez Chávez

While many seem to the undiscerning eye to be alike it is only because collectively they are referred to as *chicanos*. But like *capirotada,* fixed in a thousand ways and served on a thousand tables, which can only be evaluated by individual taste, the *chicanos* must be so distinguished.

Mario Suárez, "El Hoyo"

Contents

List of Illustrations   xi

Acknowledgments   xiii

Introduction: "Those Times of Revolution"   1

1. "A Movable Object Meeting an Irresistible Force":   9
   Los Angeles's Ethnic Mexican Community in the 1950s
   and Early 1960s

2. "Birth of A New Symbol": The Brown Berets   42

3. "Chale No, We Won't Go!": The Chicano Moratorium   61
   Committee

4. "The Voice of the Chicano People": La Raza Unida Party   80

5. "Un Pueblo Sin Fronteras": The Centro de Acción Social   98
   Autónomo (CASA)

   Afterword: "Why Are We Not Marching Like in the '70s?"   117

   Notes   121

   Bibliography   149

   Index   159

Illustrations

1. "Mi Raza Primero!" poster   4
2. "Bato Loco Yesterday" illustration   58
3. "Brown Beret Today" illustration   58
4. "National Chicano Moratorium" poster   67
5. "Committee to Free Los Tres" poster   101
6. "¡Despierta Chicano, Defiende tu Hermano!" poster   105
7. Centro de Acción Social Autónomo (CASA) "¡Resistencia!" poster   111

Acknowledgments

The paradox of writing a book is that although it is a solitary experience, the author relies on the help of so many to produce it. The following is my attempt to thank those who made this study possible. Though I depended on the help of so many, in the end I accept full responsibility for any of this study's flaws.

I must start my long list of acknowledgments with the person who shepherded the manuscript to completion, Norris Hundley. Without Professor Hundley, my life would be quite different. From the start, as my advisor, and later as my doctoral committee co-chair, Professor Hundley took an interest in me like no one before. He made sure that my studies progressed by always making sure I had funding. In addition, his legendary editing skills turned my muddled words into pristine prose. Without his guidance, and the long hours he spent poring over every page of the manuscript, this book would not exist. Words cannot express how eternally grateful I am to him. The only way that I can ever repay him is by emulating him and serving my students with the same kindness, humility, humor, and love that he has given me.

George J. Sánchez, my other doctoral committee co-chair, insured that I completed the dissertation in a timely manner. I met George at a crucial juncture in my graduate career. From the start, he believed in my abilities and took time from his busy schedule to foster my intellectual growth.

Along with the help of individuals, ample fellowships funded the production of this book. As a graduate student at UCLA, I received the

University's Institute of American Cultures-Chicano Studies Research Center Pre-doctoral Fellowship and the Ortega Dissertation-Year Fellowship. In addition, while a doctoral candidate I was fortunate to be awarded the Ford Foundation's Dissertation Fellowship for Minorities. Two other generous grants freed me from teaching: the UC San Diego Chancellor's Postdoctoral Fellowship and the UC Santa Barbara Center for Chicano Studies Visiting Scholar Award.

I must also thank the many institutions and librarians that made retrieving documents much easier. The challenge of doing contemporary ethnic history is that the sources exist yet oftentimes are not in readily accessible repositories. The challenge for the historian doing this kind of work is to think creatively and work closely with librarians. Two people stand out among this group: Richard Chabrán, former librarian at the UCLA Chicano Studies Library, and Lily Castillo-Speed at the UC Berkeley Chicano Studies Library. Richard helped me find materials when I first began researching the topic, and Lily made her library accessible in the most helpful ways. She also went beyond her duties by making sure that copies of documents reached me in a timely manner. I must also thank Norma Corral at the UCLA University Research Library; Brigida Campos at the East Los Angeles Library Chicano Resources Center; John Vasi at the UCSB library; Raquel Quiroz-González at UCSB's Colección Tloque Nahuaque; David Sigler at the California State University at Los Angeles Special Collections Department; and the staffs of the Stanford University Department of Special Collections, the UCLA Department of Special Collections, the UCSB Department of Special Collections, and the Huntington Library.

Along with libraries, I am also grateful to the faculty and staffs at UCSD's Department of Ethnic Studies and the UCSB Center for Chicano Studies. At UCSD, George Lipsitz, Ross Frank, and Leland Saito provided intellectual and moral support at a crucial point in my career. UCSB's Center for Chicano Studies proved to be a productive place. Its director, Denise Segura, and the fine faculty affiliated with the center, Maria Herrera-Sobek and Don Luis Leal, provided guidance and camaraderie. The Center's administrative assistant, Patricia Richardson, made me feel welcomed and furnished encouragement and support throughout the year. The center also provided funds for a research assistant, in which capacity Alberto Herrera served well — doggedly pursuing hunches and finding amazing sources.

I am also grateful to those people who shared a bit of their lives with me in order to tell this story. These former activists are Victoria Castro,

Rosalio Muñoz, Carlos Chávez, Arturo Chávez, Jorge Rodríguez, Jacobo Rodríguez, Ramsés Noriega, Richard Santillán, Cruz (Olmeda) Becerra, Kathy Borunda, and Ernesto Vigil. My hope is that I have done justice to their experiences and that readers of this book will be as inspired as I was by their stories.

The history department at the University of Texas at El Paso has been supportive in so many ways. I arrived there as a newly minted Ph.D., both excited and scared, and the fine faculty took me in. I am especially grateful to Charles Ambler, Emma Pérez, and Michael Topp. Michael read early drafts of chapters and discussed my ideas in an intelligent and supportive manner, while Emma encouraged me to delve into theoretical works to better read my sources, plot my narrative, and analyze the events I write about. Her grasp of history and theory are a constant inspiration. My former colleague Sherry Smith also provided many hours of fruitful discussion on my work and on history in general.

Colleagues and friends at other institutions have also provided friendship and support during the writing of this book. Ramón Gutiérrez took an interest in my work and career while I was in graduate school. His guidance, encouragement, and conveyance of a strong work ethic made completing the dissertation possible. He also read the completed dissertation and gave me invaluable suggestions for revisions. George Lipsitz also provided guidance and inspiration. George read the dissertation and provided me with extensive comments that made me re-think my work and envision its deeper meaning. Two other historians have provided moral and intellectual support, along with deep and sustaining friendship: David G. Gutiérrez and Vicki L. Ruiz. In his distinctive and forceful way, Dave has made me think about my work in profound and meaningful ways. In addition, his friendship and support have been unwavering. I know that no matter what, Dave will always "have my back." Vicki has constantly believed in me and provided persistent support and inspiration. Since the day I met her, she has championed me and maintained the importance of the work I do.

I have also been fortunate to have the support of other senior Chicano historians, most notably Juan Gómez-Quiñones, Rudy Acuña, Al Camarillo, and Mario García. In their own special way, each has contributed to the completion of this book. Juan first told me that I should pursue this work, saying, "You know the city, you know these people, and you're not naive." Rudy cheered me on and lovingly teased me and ultimately honored me by including my work in *Occupied America*. Al has watched out for me from the day I met him. He has provided utmost support and has believed in my abilities. Mario, too, has been extremely supportive and encouraging.

My students at UTEP have provided inspiration and proved to be a great testing ground for my ideas. Among the students who have helped me think more clearly about my work and who have provided hours of interesting and enlightening conversation are: Karim Ley-Alarcón, Brad Cartwright, Monica Pérales, John Márquez, Matthew Powers, Ef Romero, Armando Alvarez, Irma Montelongo, Robert Fernández, Chrisopher Cázares, Julia Schiavone-Camacho, Hector Saenz, and Demetrio Medina.

I must also thank the many friends that I first met at UCLA. This *"colectiva"* has nourished me intellectually and provided lasting and unending friendship. First and foremost among them is Jeffrey Rangel, who helped me think about this project in deep and challenging ways. Jeff's creative suggestions are present throughout this book. In addition, I thank Omar Valerio-Jiménez, Miroslava Chávez-García, Cathy Komisaruk, Jaime Cárdenas, Brian O'Neil, Ned Blackhawk, Cathy Choy, Linda Nueva España Maram, Andy Smith, and Tony Iaccarino.

Other friends have also provided unending support while writing this book. Among them (in no particular order) are: Neil Foley, Zaragosa Vargas, Beth Haas, Dana Frank, Raúl Villa, Rita Alcalá Cano, Dionne Espinosa, Chris Friday, Josie Saldaña, Chela Sandoval, Bill Deverell, Bryant Simon, Chana Lee, Pablo Mitchell, Tom Romero, Natalia Molina, Jonathan Holloway, Raúl Coronado, Steve Pitti, Alicia Schmidt-Camacho, Ricky Rodríguez, Jason Ferreira, Scarlett Bowen, Francisco Barbosa, Adrian González, Michael Salman, Muriel McClendon, Ula Taylor, Raúl Ramos, Alexandra Stern, Gabriela Arredondo, Gregory Ramos, Laura Gómez, Rubén Martínez, and Gregory S. Rodríguez. I also thank Laura Pulido, who took time from her busy schedule to read and comment on an early draft of the introduction and first chapter. My dear friend Gloria Rodríguez also made time to read drafts of the introduction and conclusion, offering invaluable comments. Thanks also to Luis Alfaro who inspires me and makes me laugh like no other person I know, and to Joseph Aguilar who remains one of my true friends.

I must also thank two good friends whose support sustains me, Rafael Pérez-Torres and Beth Marchant. In the relatively short time I've known them, Rafa and Beth have become my best friends. They have believed in my work, offered me shelter at a crucial time, and they always provide wise counsel. My visits with them are filled with great conversations, intellectual musings, and all around fun.

At the University of California Press, I thank Monica McCormick for believing in this project from the start. I also thank the anonymous readers who provided excellent suggestions for revision.

Lastly, I must thank my family. My aunts Rosa G. Velasco and Guadalupe G. Barrios and my grandmother Refugio L. González shower me with unending love. My brothers Carlos, Arturo, Javier, and David have always provided unending support. My sisters-in-law Isabel, Elodia, Meghan, and Stella have also helped me in so many ways. Their children, my nieces and nephews Marisela, Arturo, David, Lori, Lisa, Yvonne, Evita, Lynnette, Elias, Micaela, Ashley, and Marcelo remind me that writing history is really about forging a better future. Finally, mere words cannot express the gratitude I owe my parents, Alberto Rodríguez Chávez and Bertha González Chávez, for the love and support they provide. The only way that I can begin to thank them is by dedicating this book to them.

"Those Times of Revolution"

Where did it go?
Can we say we know?
Those times of revolution.
Our time of revolution.
  Los Lobos, "Revolution"

More than thirty years after it began, the phenomenon known as the Chicano Movement remains an enigma in U.S. history. Was it a "revolution," as Los Lobos tell us, or was it more in line with the reformist activism pursued by the so-called Mexican-American generation? When compared to the Cuban Revolution, the African liberation struggles, student uprisings in France, Mexico and Czechoslovakia, and the Black Power movement, the Chicano insurgency pales. Rather than simply probing its revolutionary or reformist attributes, this study is guided by Frederick Jameson's suggestion to "situate the emergence of . . . new 'collective identities' or 'subjects of history' in the historical situation which made the emergence possible."[1]

The roots of the Chicano movement, indeed of all Mexican-American political and social experience can be found in the nineteenth century. Mexican Americans are a product of the U.S.–Mexico War of 1846–48. One of the key outcomes of that conflict was the granting of American citizenship to the residents of the ceded Mexican lands. Yet, as David G. Gutiérrez has argued in *Walls and Mirrors: Mexican Americans, Mexican Immigrants, and the Politics of Ethnicity,* this moment of inclusion created what can be called the Mexican-American dilemma. According to Gutiérrez, "In formally granting the ethnic Mexican population in the Southwest all the rights of American citizens in 1848, and yet denying them the possibility of exercising those rights, Americans planted the seeds of continuing ethnic discord in the region."[2] In addition, by granting them citizenship, the U.S. government, owing to the provisions of the 1790 naturalization act, made ethnic Mexicans legally white. However, socially, they were not given the privileges of whiteness and faced de facto segregation. Thus, Mexican Americans can be looked upon as "in-between" people.[3]

In addition to this in-between state, ethnic Mexicans' conquest and the manifestation of that subjugation has varied from region to region, with the result being an uneven racialization.[4] In some places, like present-day East and Central Texas, ethnic Mexicans, due to the large influx of whites, faced overt and institutional racism.[5] In other areas, New Mexico, for example, ethnic Mexicans remained the majority and therefore experienced a comparatively less-intense racism.[6] As opposed to other racialized U.S. minorities (Native Americans, African Americans, and Asian Americans), ethnic Mexicans have not encountered a unitary legal and social discrimination. These multiple occurrences of discrimination coupled with the "lure of whiteness" have ensured that Mexican Americans are (1) not a unified group, and, (2) have primarily waged battles for inclusion and parity.[7]

When viewed within this context, new light is shed upon Mexican-American reformist activism in the twentieth century. Perhaps the best example of this political mobilization is the League of United Latin American Citizens (LULAC). Founded in 1929 in Corpus Christi, Texas, LULAC's central concern was to empower Mexican Americans through assimilation. It stressed the notion that Mexican Americans were U.S. citizens and therefore should have all the rights of Americans. Thus, LULAC "pledged to promote and develop among [themselves] what they called the 'best and purest' form of Americanism."[8] Yet, in so doing, LULAC members limited who they sought to empower; they imagined a community composed of American citizens of Mexican descent.

Of course, other groups of the Mexican-American generation sought to empower both Mexican immigrants and Mexican Americans, but they did not have LULAC's longevity. Most prominent among these group were the Congress of Spanish-Speaking Peoples (El Congreso) and the Asociación Nacional Mexico-Americana (ANMA) of the 1930s and 1950s, respectively. Though leftist in orientation and advocating for the rights of all ethnic Mexicans, these two organizations did not survive more than a few years. The Second World War brought on Congreso's demise, whereas the Cold War ended ANMA. Thus, reform rather than radicalism has been long-lived in the Mexican-American community.[9] This is most evident, given the fact that the other perennial Mexican-American organizations are the American G.I. Forum, founded in 1948 by Hector García to address the grievances of his fellow World War II veterans, and the Mexican American Political Association (MAPA), established by California politicians in 1959 with the aim of electing more Mexican Americans to political office.[10]

Within the historical context of Mexican-American activism, the Chicano movement emerges as a moment — albeit an important one — rather than as a seminal event.[11] Yet, like all epochs, the insurgency was a complex phenomenon with unique traits. With that in mind, this study seeks to assess the goals, achievements, and failures of the various political groups that encompassed the Chicano movement in Los Angeles — the city, then and now, with the largest concentration of ethnic Mexicans outside of Mexico City. Such an inquiry probes not only local protests, but also, necessarily, the insurgency as it emerged in communities elsewhere that naturally looked to Los Angeles for leadership.

Los Angeles is also where I personally witnessed "those times of revolution." I am the son of Mexican immigrant parents who were born, raised, and married in Ciudad Juárez, Chihuahua, and who emigrated to Los Angeles in 1955. I was born in Boyle Heights, in East Los Angeles, and grew up in the adjacent City Terrace neighborhood, where I lived in a small two-bedroom house with my parents and four older brothers. My brother Carlos is twelve years my senior and began attending UCLA in 1968 when I was six. Though he was always *Carlos* at home, at school he was sometimes known as Chuck, but that changed when he got caught up in the burgeoning Chicano movement. Soon, he was no longer Chuck but *Carlos*. Our home was also transformed; prominently displayed on the walls of my brothers Arturo and Javier's room was a poster of a mustached man with his fist clenched in a power symbol and the words *MI RAZA PRIMERO!* (My People First!) scrawled on it (see figure 1). That was a great poster. In fact, my brother David, who was artistic and rebellious, liked it so much that he bought paints and poster board and created a colored version. A few years later, that poster was replaced with a large photograph of Cuban revolutionaries Fidel Castro and Ernesto "Ché" Guevara, with a caption that read "Somos Uno Porque América es Una" (We Are United Because America Is One Continent).

FIGURE 1. "Mi Raza Primero!"
poster, ca. 1970. Artist unknown.
This widely circulated poster expressed the fundamental message
of the Chicano movement.

The wall in my brothers' room reflected the change and continuity within the Chicano movement and also reflects the purpose of this study. I argue that the Chicano movement embraced nationalist and Marxist–Leninist ideas that gained popularity as a result of the social, economic, and political conditions in which ethnic Mexicans lived. Those ideas were not static, however, for numerous individuals and organizations were constantly adopting and refining them — just as my brother David did when he painted his own version of the "Mi Raza Primero!" poster.

Although my brothers enthusiastically participated in the Chicano movement, I, considerably their junior, remained in the background and away from the fray (because my mother feared for my safety). Nonetheless, my memories as a distant observer initially guided my research, until the weight of the evidence I uncovered compelled judgments that frequently — but not always — are at variance with those of the movement's participants, including the scholars who chronicled their experiences. I see myself in the middle of two groups of people who have studied the Chicano movement — scholar-participants and those who have no personal connection or understanding of the insurgency. As a bridge between the two camps, this study has a perspective of its own on the "revolution" of the 1960s and 1970s.

My inquiry is the first to examine the groups that encompassed the Chicano movement in one city. Unlike most previous work on the

Chicano insurgency, my approach assumes that understanding the Chicano movement in Los Angeles requires comprehending the conditions in which the ethnic Mexican community lived and which shaped the identities of its residents. Those circumstances were not new, for they had prompted earlier protests, but in the 1960s and 1970s they roused the community as nothing had before, producing calls for change voiced in a common anti-American language of *chicanismo* that emphasized *la raza* (the people), *huelga* (strike), *carnalismo* (brotherhood), *Chicano,* and *Aztlán* — the latter a call for the re-creation of the Aztec homeland that some believed had existed in the Southwest.[12] Beneath that common language, however, was great diversity in goals and strategies.

Chicanismo was the vehicle used to express Chicano nationalism, which is best understood as a "protonationalism" because, as Eric Hobsbawm has argued, it is based on "the consciousness of belonging to or having belonged to a lasting political entity" — in this case, Mexico.[13] Yet Chicano nationalism is more complicated because of the proximity of Mexico to the United States and the consequent reassertion of Mexican traditions through immigration.[14] Thus, Mexico acts as a safety valve for the often-harsh realities of the United States, just as the prosperity of the United States serves as a safety valve for those immigrants seeking escape from Mexico's poverty. In the United States, Mexican protonationalism took the form of a "residual culture" that Mexican Americans used to combat what they found distasteful in the larger American society. A residual culture, according to literary critic Raymond Williams, consists of those "experiences, meanings and values, which cannot be verified or cannot be expressed in terms of the dominant culture, [yet] are nevertheless lived and practiced on the basis of the residue — cultural as well as social — of some previous social formation."[15] Mexican nationalism became a Chicano nationalism created to confront the inequalities in American society during the Vietnam era.[16] Thus, in the protest atmosphere of the 1960s, the residual culture, Mexican protonationalism, was transformed into Chicano nationalism, an "emergent culture," which, according to Williams, embraces the "new meanings and values, new practices, new significances and experiences, [which] are continually being created."[17] Ultimately, Chicano nationalism, though unique, can also be looked upon as a truly American phenomenon that at times encompasses the tenets of American liberalism.

Chicano nationalism, as it emerged, privileged males and marginalized females. As Elleke Boehmer has observed about nationalism generally, the male role is usually "metonymic," that is, men are contiguous with each other and with the nation as a whole. Women, on the other hand, have only a "metaphoric or symbolic role."[18] Thus, carefully prescribed gender roles for both men and women characterized the Chicano movement and, as this study demonstrates, broaden our understanding of the insurgency's ideologies, tactics, and Chicano identity of the participants. The construction of Chicano identity is best understood, in the words of Stuart Hall, as a "process . . . that happens over time, that is never absolutely stable, that is subject to the play of history and difference."[19] Hence, my findings highlight the evolution of various Chicano identities within a fluid and constantly changing Chicano movement.

This study begins with ethnic Mexicans of Los Angeles in the 1950s as they develop a community — that is, a Mexican protonationalism — to counter their sense of powerlessness resulting from limited political representation, police brutality, and urban renewal that displaced their communities. This is not to say that ethnic Mexicans lacked agency, but, rather, that the Cold War atmosphere circumscribed the reach and power of their actions. Throughout this era there is sporadic evidence of public displays of Mexican pride but not in the dramatic scale that one would see in the 1960s and 1970s. The relatively small number of ethnic Mexicans in the city meant that ties and imaginings of Mexico remained in the private rather than the public sphere.

This situation changed in the 1960s as the ethnic Mexican population increased dramatically, which, within the protest atmosphere of the Vietnam War, allowed for the construction of a Chicano nationalism that fostered militant opposition to the inequalities of American society. The focus then shifts to four Chicano movement organizations — the Brown Berets, the Chicano Moratorium Committee, La Raza Unida Party, and the Centro de Acción Social Autónomo (CASA) — and how they imagined community and fashioned Chicano nationalism to fit their needs. For Brown Berets, the community groups most in need of help were the young street thugs, the *vatos locos*, who were being brutalized by the police. The Chicano Moratorium, on the other hand, viewed draft-age Chicanos as its core constituents. For La Raza Unida Party, the ballot box and Chicano voters were key to Chicano empowerment, whereas, for CASA, Mexican immigrant workers emerged as the crucial constituency. As opposed to other organizations, such as the Educational Issues Coordinating Committee (EICC), which was a multiethnic coalition, or El Movimiento Estudiantil Chicano de Aztlán (MEChA), which was not a single organization but rather had (and continues to have) chapters in various colleges and universities in the Southwest, or Católicos Por La

Raza, a short-lived organization that was primarily concerned with democratizing the Catholic Church, the groups that comprise the bulk of this study best represent the trajectory of nationalism in Los Angeles's ethnic Mexican community. For the most part, these organizations were male dominated. That is not to say that women are not depicted in this study. This study's strategy has been to discuss gender, and its various manifestations and complexities, within the organizations covered.

By focusing on the above groups, what emerges is a multifaceted Chicano movement that shared a sense of cultural nationalism, but differed in tactics and goals and in its appeal to different sectors of the community. The narrow conception of community among these militant groups was at odds with the vision of cultural nationalism that they shared. That conflict undermined their sense of nationalism and ultimately contributed to the demise of each group. Hence, the collapse of the Chicano movement resulted from the failure of its constituent parts to recognize the dynamic and heterogeneous nature of the ethnic Mexican community in Los Angeles and, indeed, the nation. The forging of a truly mass movement had become impossible. Yet it is the attempt, the process, which this study is most concerned with. In imagining community and attempting to empower ethnic Mexicans, the subjects of this study tried to change their, albeit narrow, worlds. That, in itself, was a great accomplishment and worth knowing about. Ultimately, this study affirms historian Van Gosse's notion that "the period from the late 1950s through the fall of Nixon [was] the beginning, not the end of struggle across the widest imaginable field of class, race, gender, and empire, a struggle no more resolved in the 1990s than it was in 1972 or 1981." As he has aptly observed, "The true significance of that era is a great legacy of unresolved civil, political and cultural divisions."[20]

The Chicano movement, like the other social movements of the Vietnam era, had the potential of redefining the nature of what American society was — and is. The Vietnam era can be looked upon as a historic moment in which the United States failed to constitute itself as a truly democratic society. It is an example in which, as the political philosopher Ernesto Laclau has argued, the "distance between the universal and the particular [became] unbridgeable" and burdened activists with the "impossible task of making democratic interaction achievable."[21] My hope is that this study presents a conversation between the present and the past, and that it inscribes history with a resonant meaning. Perhaps in this way we can begin to understand what became of those days of revolution and truly forge a just society.

This study rests on a wide range of sources, including interviews with participants, the papers of Chicano movement organizations, mainstream and movement newspapers, census reports, FBI reports obtained under the Freedom of Information Act, and ephemera like posters, pamphlets, and fliers. I have also consulted the works of previous scholars of the Chicano movement, who were, for the most part, participants in what they chronicled. Hence, their books and articles are not only frequently source materials, but they also have provided the scholarly foundation for subsequent research on this subject.[22] I owe a huge debt to this body of previous work. My study is the first book-length attempt to grasp how the Chicano movement emerged in the community of Los Angeles. Others are invited to build upon this work so as to enhance our vision of the Chicano insurgency.

On Terminology

Since this study deals with issues of identity, a few words on terminology are appropriate. For the most part, I have tried to identify the subjects of this study as they identified themselves. In the Chicano activists' vocabulary, the term *Mexican-American* meant someone who had assimilated — someone who had taken on an "American" outlook rather than a Mexican one. Chicanos also objected to being "hyphenated" Americans; they believed the term *Mexican-American* inferred that they were second-class citizens. The term *Chicano*, which to earlier generations was a label reserved for the "lower classes," denoted one's support of activism. In this study, only when *Mexican American* is used as a modifier does it contain a hyphen (e.g., *Mexican-American generation*). Yet, for clarity and variety, I go against the wishes of movement participants and use the terms *Mexican American* and *Chicano* interchangeably, to denote a resident or citizen of the United States. Those born in Mexico but who resided in the United States are called *Mexican immigrants*. When speaking of both Mexican Americans and Mexican immigrants, I use the phrase *ethnic Mexicans*.

I

"A Movable Object Meeting an Irresistible Force"

Los Angeles's Ethnic Mexican Community in the 1950s and Early 1960s

---

The roots of Chicano insurgency are found in the post–World War II era. The children of the 1950s and early 1960s — the so-called baby boomers — became the rebels of the later 1960s and 1970s. This generation reaped the benefits of prosperity but also faced discrimination. It was indoctrinated with a Cold War culture that stressed peacetime consensus yet ignored the racial strife that existed at the core of American society. Thus, the Chicano youths of the 1960s reached maturity with rising expectations of abundance, only to be confronted with the realization that they were not part of the tapestry of America. They reacted by constructing a Chicano protonationalism. Their mobilization in the 1960s and 1970s built upon the work of a prior generation of ethnic Mexican activists who in the 1950s and early 1960s employed a residual Mexican culture in their communities as a counterhegemonic tool. A residual culture, according to literary critic Raymond Williams, denotes "some experiences, meanings and values, which cannot be verified or cannot be expressed in terms of the dominant culture, [but which] are nevertheless lived and practiced on the basis of the residue — cultural as well as social — of some previous social formation."[1]

This residual culture emerged in part as a result of the substantial population growth of Los Angeles's ethnic Mexican community. At the beginning of the decade, according to the U.S. Census Bureau, the num-

9

ber of ethnic Mexicans in Los Angeles was 156,356, but by 1960 that number had grown to 291,959, a 51 percent increase.[2] In the same period, the number of Anglo residents increased an estimated 37 percent, whereas the total non-white population grew by 49 percent. Though immigration contributed to this growth, the major explanation was a higher ethnic Mexican birthrate — so high that the median age of ethnic Mexicans in 1960 was 20 compared to 30 for Anglos and 24 for non-whites.[3] The Los Angeles metropolitan area had more Mexican Americans than the southwestern states of Arizona, New Mexico, and Nevada combined. This growth prompted a group of social scientists to conclude that "the future of Mexican Americans [in the United States] depends largely on their progress in California."[4]

Such burgeoning numbers did not translate into economic and political power for ethnic Mexicans in California.[5] Census data reveal that their median income for 1959 was $5,700, well below the $7,213 of Anglo families. Mexican males also earned less than their Anglo counterparts, $4,275 as compared to $5,421.[6] The income disparities reflected occupational differences. Anglo men were four times more likely to be professionals than ethnic Mexican men (13.7 percent versus 3.9 percent), whereas ethnic Mexicans predominated as laborers and farm workers (30.4 percent), occupations held by fewer Asians and African Americans (24.8 percent) and only a handful of Anglos (6.8 percent).[7] Ethnic Mexican women, on the other hand, held many more professional jobs than Mexican men (32.4 percent versus 3.9 percent), but these were concentrated primarily in clerical/sales (23.9 percent), with relatively few in professional/technical and managerial/proprietor ranks (8.5 percent). The second largest category of jobs for women was as blue-collar workers (28.1 percent), where most were semiskilled operatives and very few were skilled (craft) or unskilled laborers (1.4 percent). In the same period, ethnic Mexican women made up 27.8 percent of all those employed in service industries in the Southwest, 6.3 percent of the farm workers, and a minuscule 0.3 percent of farm managers.[8]

Low economic and occupational status did not mean that ethnic Mexicans were utterly powerless. Two organizations of the immediate postwar era, the Community Service Organization and the Asociación Nacional México Americana, struggled vigorously on behalf of civil rights for ethnic Mexicans. Many of their members belonged to the so-called Mexican-American generation that came of age during the upheavals of the Great Depression, the Second World War, and the Cold War.[9] They not only shared these common historical experiences, but also held a deep commitment to American democracy while also advocating social reform. They did not constitute a monolithic community, however, for they differed in their partisan affiliations and in their strategies and tactics for eliminating society's ills.[10]

Their commitment to democracy derived at least in part from the Americanization campaigns they experienced during and after the First World War. This was a time when government at all levels, and many private groups as well, had sought to forge a national identity by emphasizing pledges of loyalty to the U.S. government, what it meant to be an American citizen, and the myriad benefits of the American way of life. So thoroughly indoctrinated did they become that they later felt compelled to couch their demands for equal rights and a greater share in the political process in the rhetoric of Americanization.[11]

The language of Americanism is best understood in terms of four overlapping dimensions: nationalist, democratic, progressive, and traditionalist. Nationalism demanded a devotion to American heroes, such as the Pilgrims, the Founding Fathers, and Abraham Lincoln. Closely linked was an emphasis on democracy, which encompassed not only the heroes but also the ideals for which they stood: "rule by the people," "liberty," "civil rights," "independence," and "freedom." To be progressive meant believing in the rational and ever-improving character of the world in general and of American society in particular. Americanism stressed the ability of "man" to transform the world through modern technology and create a free marketplace for consumer goods that would be within reach of every American. The emphasis on tradition was rooted in nostalgia for a mythic, simpler, and more virtuous past.[12] Such views formed a common bond among those of the Mexican-American generation, but they also allowed for a multiplicity of political visions, tactics, strategies, and, hence, organizations for improving society.

Though the Second World War and the draft led to a demise of two organizations founded in the late 1930s, El Congreso de Pueblos de Habla Español and the Mexican American Movement, the wartime experience encouraged activism among other Mexican Americans, especially those sharing the great fear of communism that soon permeated the national consciousness. The U.S. foreign policy of containment and its emphasis on stopping the growth of communism bred a strong anticommunist movement at home. Garnering support for the Cold War, the anticommunist crusade stifled domestic dissent, compromised civil liberties, and ensured that advocates of social reform risked being pilloried as agents of a foreign state.[13] To combat these threats, Mexican-American activists, like those earlier, couched their expectations in the language of Americanism, but that language now emphasized two themes only touched upon earlier: anticommunism and the virtues of free enterprise.[14] American democracy was also reconceptualized with an emphasis on the ways in which ethnic minorities embraced and deferred to "American" ways. All this was done in an attempt to avoid appearing "un-American," but that hope produced mixed results for Mexican-American activists in Los Angeles.

I

The Community Service Organization (CSO), created in September 1947, carefully used a Cold War variant of Americanism to press its demands. The CSO was an outgrowth of a political campaign: the unsuccessful bid of Edward Roybal for Los Angeles's 9th district council seat. The day after that election, he had received a telegram from Saul Alinsky, the noted community organizer and head of the Industrial Areas Foundation (IAF), who had led the crusade to create better living conditions in Chicago's destitute "Back of the Yards" ghetto. "What are you going to do next?" Alinsky asked Roybal, whom he had met in the early 1940s at a social workers' convention in Texas. Roybal replied that he would run again for the city council in 1949. With Alinsky's encouragement, Roybal and a group of former campaign workers then discussed ways to keep interest in his candidacy alive during the next two years. To accomplish that task, they created the CSO.[15]

The creation of the CSO occurred almost simultaneously with a meeting Alinsky had, while on a visit to California, with Fred Ross, who was a clerk for the American Council on Race Relations (ACRR), a Chicago-based group dedicated to easing racial tensions. Ross had been hired by ACRR to conduct community surveys but instead had begun organizing people to combat racial discrimination, a redirection of his efforts that displeased his employer. Alinsky, however, was impressed with Ross, who was then working in the citrus-belt communities of Belltown and Casa Blanca east of Los Angeles. The two agreed that Ross's organizing efforts would have greater effect if he joined the IAF and concentrated on the Boyle Heights area of Los Angeles with its large ethnic Mexican population.[16]

Ross realized from the outset that he had to adopt tactics different from those used by the IAF in Chicago. There, the approach had been to work through Catholic parishes, but the lack of a strong allegiance of the

Los Angeles ethnic Mexican community to the Catholic Church called for a new strategy. So, too, did the presence of only a few young activist priests. Ross found his vehicle for gaining access to the community in Edward Roybal, whom he met for the first time in September 1947 at the Eastside YMCA. Ross liked Roybal, but Roybal was at first unsure about this stranger who had a fondness for cowboy boots. "I said to myself," he later recalled, "What the hell is this guy doing with cowboy boots? He must be a Texan, and Texans don't like us."[17]

Slowly, Roybal grew to trust Ross, who found his way into the CSO's inner circle. Ross strongly endorsed the CSO's goals — stopping police brutality, ending gerrymandered school boundaries, and confronting other problems facing the ethnic Mexican community — and persuaded the leadership that the key to success lay in launching an education campaign directed at the entire community.[18] Thousands of Boyle Heights residents would have to be educated about not only the CSO but also how their hopes for the future depended on the community working together. To achieve this cooperation, CSO members went door-to-door spreading their message and winning new recruits to bring it to others. Modest membership fees (two dollars a year) helped underwrite costs. The efforts proved successful. By April 1948 the CSO had two hundred members, an increase of 80 percent in eight months.[19]

With a strong membership base, the CSO now shifted its preoccupation to voter registration as the 1949 city council election drew near. Some 125 men and women attended classes to become deputy registrars. Then two-person registrar teams, always comprised of a man and a woman so as to appeal to both genders, combed the East Side for potential voters. Since the CSO was officially a nonpartisan entity, the organization claimed that the registration drive was also nonpartisan. None of the registrars openly campaigned for Roybal. Eventually, the CSO registered seventeen thousand people, approximately fifteen thousand of whom had Spanish surnames.[20]

The new voters assured Roybal's victory in the summer 1949 city council election. He became the first Spanish-surnamed person to hold such a position since 1888, and he won handily, defeating his incumbent opponent, Parley Parker Christensen, by a vote of nearly two to one: 20,472 to 11,957.[21] Four years earlier, when Eduardo Quevedo sought the same seat, he had lost heavily: 17,683 to 2,277. Only 38.9 percent of the district's eligible voters had gone to the polls on that occasion, whereas in 1949, 82 percent did so. CSO was the reason for the dramatic turnabout.[22]

Though the registration drive and Roybal's campaign were aimed at

U.S. citizens of Mexican descent, the CSO also sought to serve resident aliens, a goal of most Mexican-American organizations. At the same time, CSO believed that resident aliens should become citizens and "actively participate in community programs and activities that are for the purpose of improving the general welfare."[23] To the CSO, Mexican aliens should not be merely sojourners in the North but participants in the struggle to advance the Mexican-American community.[24] "What makes a nation indivisible?" asked a CSO pamphlet. "What generates this goal of unity, of oneness, of togetherness that holds a people of a country steadfast?" The answer is "citizenship, with its assurance of protection of home and family when it assures justice and a voice in the government." This heightened interest in citizenship reflected CSO's deep concern with the rampant Cold War hysteria of the time.[25]

McCarthyism nonetheless clouded CSO's existence. Its organizers were vehemently anticommunist, so much so that Bert Corona believed that the CSO had been created solely to prevent "radicals" and "Communists" from gaining a foothold in the Mexican community.[26] This was an exaggeration, but Roybal was straightforward about his views: "We had been fighting communism and communists in Boyle Heights for many years. They did everything they possibly could to get us involved in the Communist Party. We fought them and we were trigger happy when it came to communism."[27] Such a strong stand helped the CSO survive a very difficult era.

II

The CSO was not the only group battling at the time for the rights of the Los Angeles ethnic Mexican community. Also active in the struggle was the Asociación Nacional México Americana (ANMA), a creation in 1949 of the Denver-based Union of Mine, Mill, and Smelter Workers (Mine Mill). Primarily composed of Mexicans and Mexican Americans in Arizona, California, Colorado, New Mexico, and Texas, the union envisioned ANMA as its political arm and the "new voice" for Mexicans in the United States. Membership in this self-proclaimed "national association for the protection of the civil, economic and political rights of the Mexican people in the United States as well as for the expansion of their education, culture and progress" was open to any person who was interested in advancing "*el pueblo mexicano*."[28] ANMA stressed popular-front tactics and found sponsors among a diverse group of liberals and radicals, including writer and civil rights advocate Carey McWilliams; former state attorney general Robert Kenny; the Reverend Oscar Lizárraga; state CIO president James Daugherty; Aaron Heist of the American Civil Liberties Union; Charlotta Bass of the African-American newspaper, the *California Eagle;* and William Elkonin of the United Electrical Workers.[29] Local chapters quickly sprang up around the nation, and by 1950 there were four thousand members and thirty-five chapters, with eight locals in the Los Angeles area.[30]

That same year, ANMA held its first national convention in October in Los Angeles, attracting eighty delegates and observers from five states. The delegates approved a constitution committing ANMA to the "struggle for the recognition, protection and full development of the human, civil, economic, educational, cultural, civic, and social rights of the Mexican people, and the Mexican-American, in the United States." Five specific goals were identified: the political unification of Mexicans in the United States, the achievement of democratic rights for all Americans, the development of ethnic and political awareness, the maintenance of ties of solidarity with Mexicans south of the border, and keeping ANMA a democratic organization. Transformed into policy, these goals targeted for action such areas as public housing, civil rights, and immigration.[31]

ANMA emerged as a radical voice in Mexican-American politics after establishing its national headquarters in Boyle Heights in 1951. Although a contemporary of the CSO, it was farther to the left and grounded its policies in its view of the Mexican-American past — a past commencing in violence, conquest, and the subjugation of the Mexican population of the Southwest. The Treaty of Guadalupe Hidalgo stipulated guarantees that were not honored, as the arriving Anglos had abused the Mexicans' culture, language, and political rights and took their property. The result was an underclass, *el pueblo olvidado* (the forgotten people), who remained in bondage into the twentieth century, when they were joined by an outpouring of Mexican immigrant laborers who shared their exploited status.[32]

ANMA stressed the need for unity among the largely working-class Mexican population in the United States. Ninety percent of the Mexicans north of the Rio Grande were unskilled laborers, a reality that helped shape ANMA's faith in the union movement. But it was the traditional labor movement with which ANMA identified and not the radicals calling for the overthrow of capitalism and the formation of a socialist state, a position reflecting in part the oppressive McCarthyism that was rampant at the time. Still, ANMA believed that the abuses of labor could be

ANMA
goals

traced to an economic elite who gained great profits through the exploitation of workers, and especially Mexicans.[33]

Ethnic Mexicans suffered disproportionately to others, ANMA
argued, because of racism. Like blacks, they had been singled out for discrimination in housing, education, political representation, public services, and other areas. This discrimination had tragic by-products, like the
creation of an inferiority mentality that caused some ethnic Mexicans to
pass themselves off as "Spanish Americans," or individuals of Spanish
descent. Just as with the abuse of labor, ANMA traced racism to the white
ruling class, not to all whites, and certainly not to the working class.
Indeed, ANMA found the solution to the ethnic Mexican population's
problems in class cooperation — in ethnic Mexicans joining with white
laborers to eradicate prejudice and improve working conditions. In
short, the liberation of ethnic Mexicans required liberating all laborers.[34]

Complementing ANMA's views on race and class were its attitudes
toward culture. Mexicans in the Southwest had been deprived of an
autonomous cultural development; nonetheless, they still possessed a distinct culture that needed protection and encouragement. That common
culture could also serve as a means for organizing people and reforming
society. At ANMA's second annual convention in El Paso in 1952, the delegates stressed that their fight was a "cultural struggle" being waged on
behalf of "cultural democracy" for the Mexican-American people. What
they did not quite appreciate was that the Cold War era was not a good
time to emphasize anything that could even remotely be construed as
denigrating or attacking "American democracy."[35]

ANMA first attracted public criticism when it urged Mexican
Americans to rediscover their cultural roots in both the Southwest and
Mexico. Contrary to the CSO, ANMA leaders told members to "never
completely integrate themselves in all aspects of the national life of this
country." Develop your own cultural forms, insisted the leaders, especially
the use of the Spanish language. Only by being proud of their culture and
promoting it could Mexican Americans not only achieve self-respect and
the respect of others but also enrich the cultural life of the United States.
Revitalization could occur only if the rejection of one's Mexican heritage
was replaced with a new cultural and ethnic awareness and pride. ANMA,
unlike later Chicano groups, never advocated a separate nationhood for
Mexican Americans. Instead, like El Congreso de Pueblos de Habla
Española (a Mexican-American civil rights organization of the late 1930s
and early '40s), it emphasized reform of the U.S. from within.[36]

Along with its emphasis on domestic reform, ANMA encouraged the strengthening of ties with Mexico and Latin America generally. The U.S. treatment of Mexican Americans as second-class citizens, according to ANMA, reflected America's attitude toward Latin America. Mexican Americans should cooperate with Latin Americans in combating such prejudiced views. The struggle for Mexican-American liberation was linked with a similar struggle for liberation throughout Latin America. As a beginning, Mexican Americans should establish ties of solidarity with Mexicans south of the border, with whom they had a common history and culture.[37]

In addition to its concern with Latin America, ANMA critiqued U.S. foreign policy as it affected other parts of the world, actively supporting the peace movement and opposing U.S. military intervention in Korea. Despite critics who questioned their loyalty, ANMA members in 1950 met in Los Angeles in a two-day mobilization of peace groups supporting the Stockholm Peace Appeal calling for an end to the Cold War. The Korean War also drew their criticism because of the disproportionate loss of Mexican-American lives. Mexican Americans in Colorado, for example, comprised 10 percent of the state's population yet they made up 28 percent of the state's casualties. In Arizona they were 20 percent of the population and 44 percent of the state's casualties; in New Mexico, 49 percent of the population and 56 percent of the deaths; and in Texas, 17 percent of the population and 30 percent of the casualties. ANMA urged Mexican Americans to protest this unfair burden by writing directly to President Harry S. Truman.[38]

[Margin note: Mex-Amer. fighting for democracy]

ANMA also linked the Korean War with conditions at home. While the U.S. was seeking to defend the "Free World" from communist aggression, it had victimized Mexicans through the application of the "anti-subversive" Smith and McCarran acts, the loss of economic benefits due to the anti-labor Taft-Hartley Act, and the loss of social services for the poor, aged, and the young. Ethnic Mexicans and other minority groups unjustly bore the cost of the war through excessive taxes, prices, and declining wages.[39] The war thereby intensified ANMA's emphasis on working-class solidarity and encouraged cooperation with the CIO in its unionizing efforts. It vigorously protested the deportation of Mexican immigrant workers, especially the undocumented, which climaxed with "Operation Wetback" in 1954 when hundreds of thousands were deported.[40]

To increase its community appeal and following, ANMA, like El Congreso earlier, sought to involve women in leadership roles. At its founding convention, members endorsed a resolution stressing the importance of women as steadfast partners and organizers who should be

[Margin note: women in leadership]

integrated into all levels of the organization as well as have their own special women's committee. Eventually, perhaps a third of the members in ANMA's Southern California chapter were women, but official resolutions notwithstanding, few women achieved leadership positions because of lingering resistance to having them in such roles.[41]

Despite ANMA's attempts to bring about change, its achievements were few and the opposition that it encountered was formidable. There was much harassment and political persecution because of its reputation as a "red-front group." The FBI believed that ANMA was affiliated with, if not controlled by, the Communist Party. FBI files reveal that agency informants infiltrated ANMA and carried out extensive surveillance of members. In 1952 the FBI, on the grounds that alleged communists belonged to ANMA, identified the organization as a security threat under the Internal Security (McCarran) Act of 1950. ANMA unsuccessfully appealed that designation to the U.S. Attorney General, who listed it as a subversive organization in 1954. The beating that ANMA now took in public opinion led to its demise in the same year.[42] Though accused of being "un-American," ANMA was the opposite, for it promoted reform of American society, not revolution, and the reform it sought was protection of the constitutional rights of all, including Mexican immigrants as well as Mexican Americans.[43]

III

Far more effective over the longer term than ANMA was Edward Roybal, whom CSO helped elect to the Los Angeles city council in 1949. He served in that capacity until he successfully ran for the U.S. House of Representatives in 1962. Roybal, as noted earlier, was the only Mexican-American city council member throughout the 1950s. Although his district was small, the lack of other Mexican-American representation on the city council ensured that he became the at-large representative for Mexican immigrants and Mexican Americans throughout the Los Angeles area.

During his city council tenure Roybal used a liberal Americanism to voice ethnic Mexicans' concerns. An early example of this approach was his September 1950 battle against the "Subversive Registration Ordinance," a city council measure stipulating that "communists and other subversives" must register with the police department. The ordinance was the first attempt at legalized witch-hunting by any major American city.

Though the measure was enacted overwhelmingly (thirteen to one) with Roybal as the lone opponent, the courts ultimately declared it unconstitutional. As a member of the Knights of Columbus, Roybal was obviously an anticommunist, yet he might have been committing political suicide with his action.[44] Instead, he stood firm against the measure that he believed could be used to persecute Mexican Americans, and thereby won the undying support among his constituents. The ordinance, he argued, "will not only fail to curb the Communist danger but it will push the door open for the entry of other dangers which may very well prove equally menacing to our way of life. . . . The doctrine implicit in the ordinance, carried to its logical conclusion, places every citizen and organization whose word or act resembles at any time those of the communists at the mercy of the biased crackpot who may decide to report the matter to the Police Department as subversive."[45] Thus Roybal feared that the legislation would be used against Mexican Americans, other minority organizations, and civil rights groups that could easily be targeted as un-American. His sensitivity derived from firsthand experience with how the Cold War climate placed a low priority on racial discrimination.

In September 1949, shortly after being elected to the city council, Roybal went to a housing tract posing as a potential home buyer in order to investigate reports that developers were refusing to sell to African Americans, Japanese Americans, Mexican Americans, and Jews. When asked if he was of "Mexican extraction," he said yes and was denied an opportunity to purchase.[46] Not long after, he introduced legislation, which was later enacted, to outlaw this discriminatory practice. Like Mexican-American activists before him who used the Second World War to push their civil rights agenda, Roybal employed the Korean War to leverage his fight against discrimination. "There is no room for discord based upon differences of race, nationality or religion in this crisis," he stated. "How ironical. We send billions of dollars and tens of thousands of men across the seas to prevent the spread of communism and at the same time allow destructive forces among us to subject these men to the humiliation and insult of being rejected when purchasing homes because their names or complexions differ from those of other applicants."[47]

paradox fighting for democracy

The housing discrimination that Roybal sought to eliminate worsened, especially for the poor and minority groups, during the postwar population surge and shortage of available homes. At the urging of Mayor Fletcher Bowron, Los Angeles took advantage of federal funds for public housing in August 1949, when the city council unanimously authorized the City Housing Authority (CHA) to build 10,000 low-rent, slum-clearance units. The housing measure ran into trouble when the national real estate lobby attacked it as communist-inspired. The anti-housing foes received reinforcement when Congress, in 1951, specified that federal funds could not be used for a project that was rejected by a city's governing body. Some members of the council now wanted to do just that, but Mayor Fletcher Bowron argued that, since Los Angeles had already spent a huge amount of federal money on public housing, to reject such an undertaking would constitute a breach of contract. In addition, the federal housing authority threatened to sue the city if it tried to sever the agreement.

Though Bowron stood firm, the city council did not and voted in late 1951, by a majority of one, to repudiate the housing contract.[48] When the California Supreme Court and the U.S. Supreme Court ordered the city to honor the contract, the city council arrogantly placed the issue on a citywide ballot. State Attorney General Gerald "Pat" Brown argued that the courts' decisions demanded that the city honor the contract, but the measure nonetheless passed by a 59 percent vote. Then, in July 1953, the city was allowed to abandon 5,700 of the originally planned 10,000 low-rent housing units when Congress passed legislation authorizing the government to take the loss for any expended sums on the Los Angeles project. In the end, the city squandered $4.5 million in federal funds and never solved its slum problem. After all the debates about the future of Los Angeles, there still remained 65,888 substandard dwellings.[49]

Roybal was in the midst of these battles for public housing, having sided with the mayor and other housing supporters. For this, he and his fellow dissident council members were labeled "Communists, anarchists, socialists."[50] Roybal was singled out for personal abuse by Edward Davenport, a staunch cold warrior on the city council. Shortly after arriving at the council chambers a bit disoriented, on June 4, 1952, Davenport had gone into a tirade against his opponents. When Roybal tried to help him to his seat, Davenport accused the Mexican-American councilman of threatening him with a knife. Disgusted with Davenport's accusation, the Mexican Chamber of Commerce subsequently adopted a resolution denouncing Davenport's "vile, false, and defamatory statements" against Roybal.[51] The rebuke served only to inflame Davenport further, and he delivered tirades against the city housing authority, which he said was "infiltrated with Communists and Communist principles," and against Roybal: "Repeatedly Roybal has voted sympathetically with organizations known to be Communist front outfits."

During the harangue, the council voted to adjourn and left the chamber, but Davenport stayed and continued denouncing his enemies. Even the arrival of doctors and Los Angeles police chief William Parker could not calm him. He finally left the chamber when he got a phone call from his wife. "Yes, my wife is concerned," he remarked on leaving. "Both of us have been frequently threatened by persons using the most powerful methods of intimidation against me."[52] The other liberal council members were never as vehemently attacked as Roybal by their colleagues in public, a clear indication of the racial overtones present and never doubted by the ethnic Mexican community. "Davenport made strikes out not only against the housing issue," noted a letter to the editor of the *Eastside Sun,* "but against the Mexican people and all the people who have put their faith in the fact that Councilman Roybal will represent their interests in the face of even such a powerful force as the real estate lobby."[53]

Throughout the 1950s Roybal was identified as the spokesperson for the ethnic Mexican community. Community and liberal newspapers and magazines continuously praised Roybal for the smallest accomplishments, including speaking Spanish in the city council chambers for the first time since the 1880s and funding sidewalk construction in Boyle Heights.[54] Joseph Kovner, editor of the *Eastside Sun* called him "the fighting liberal for people's rights."[55] He received correspondence from ethnic Mexicans asking for his help in a myriad of situations. His popularity ensured his nomination for California lieutenant governor in 1954, a post which he ran for unsuccessfully.[56] In 1958 Roybal's liberal politics and his pro-community activism ensured his defeat when he vied for a seat on the Los Angeles County Board of Supervisors. Controversy surrounded his upset. Though ahead in the early stages of vote counting, he lost the election after four recounts and allegations of fraud. His opponent, Ernest Debs, a pro-business Los Angeles city councilman, and Debs's colleagues subsequently gerrymandered the supervisorial districts to dilute Mexican-American political power. Mexican Americans remembered this election for decades.[57] Given the many political defeats that the ethnic Mexican community endured, Roybal remained one of its only resources, ensuring his presence in both its tragedies and triumphs.

IV

In addition to limited representation on the city council, the Los Angeles ethnic Mexican community also had to contend with violence at the hands of those who were supposed to protect them: the Los Angeles PD

violence

Police Department and the Los Angeles County Sheriffs Department. In the 1950s Mexicans and African Americans in Los Angeles, reported one journalist, "lived in utter fear of the Gestapo-like tactics of some members of the police department."[58] Three prominent events of the early 1950s exemplify the kind of violence inflicted by law enforcement officials on ethnic Mexicans: the "Santo Niño 7," "Ríos-Ulloa," and "Bloody Christmas" incidents. When viewed collectively, they underscore the powerlessness of the ethnic Mexican community.

PD violence

The Santo Niño 7 case involved members of a CYO (Catholic Youth Organization)-sponsored basketball team who were suspected of stealing auto parts and who were then beaten at the University Police Station in 1950. The CYO and the CSO took legal action that eventually led to the charges against the boys being dropped. Though a minor victory, as the CSO's newsletter reported, "The public was being reminded that a problem existed in East Los Angeles between the community and the law enforcement agencies, and that people on the Eastside deserved the same respect and confidence due to any other person, no matter in what part of the city they might live."[59]

A more prominent episode involved Anthony Ríos, the chair of the CSO, and a friend of his, Alfred Ulloa. On January 27, 1952, as the two were emerging from a café in Boyle Heights, they witnessed a struggle in which two men were beating a third. Ríos told the men to stop and then learned that they were vice-squad plainclothesmen F. J. Najera and G. W. Kellenberg. They were also obviously drunk and Ríos accused them of drunkenness. When additional police arrived, Ríos asked them to arrest Najera and Kellenberg, only to find himself and Ulloa taken to police headquarters at gunpoint. Ordered to strip to their underwear, the two men were then beaten by Najera and Kellenberger. "I guess this will teach you to keep your nose out of other people's business," Najera told them. The beating stopped only when Roybal, alerted by community members, called the station. The detainees were then taken to Lincoln Heights jail, booked on suspicion of interfering with officers, and released when friends posted $500 bail for each. A trial was set for February 26.[60]

At the trial, Najera and Kellenberger denied beating the men and accused them of interfering in police work — the arrest of a suspect named Joe Betance. According to Kellengerger, Ríos had grabbed him by the back of his coat and said, "Where do you think you're going? We are all American citizens, and in this country we can't be treated this way." The officers had identified themselves as policemen, but this had made no difference to Ríos and Ulloa whom the policemen then hauled to the station. As for asking the men to remove their clothes, that was necessary because they were suspected of using narcotics and the officers wanted to check their bodies for hypodermic needle marks. Ríos questioned the validity of the charge, pointing out that a witness to the incident, Alvaro Rodríguez, had also been taken to jail, charged with drunkenness, and booked on the count in municipal court.[61]

Ríos's prominence in the ethnic Mexican community and his connections with CSO and Roybal insured that the incident would be fully investigated. The Police Department assigned its internal affairs division to look into the matter, while the CSO assisted Ríos and Ulloa in their civil suit against the city and the two officers involved in the beating.[62] Though the police threatened them during the trial, the men stood their ground and a jury acquitted them of the charges. Their case served as a symbolic vindication for the countless others who had been involved in brutality but did not have the clout to win their lawsuits. The incident also spurred the CSO to intensify its civil liberties efforts, creating a legal-aid fund in order to assist residents. Another by-product was increased media attention on the police force's tactics. "We are disturbed and alarmed," announced the *Daily News,* "at the increasing reports of violent attacks on members of minority groups and brutality against persons held for trial."[63]

Still another infamous incident was the so-called "Bloody Christmas" episode in 1951. Though in some ways just another example of police brutality, the attention it garnered made it different. The case started out as a routine arrest on Christmas Eve 1951 of six men, Danny Rodela, Elias Rodela, Jack Wilson, William Wilson, Manuel Hernández, and Raymond Márquez, who ranged in age from 21 to 23, five of whom were former GIs, at a Riverside Drive tavern after participating in a brawl. Brought before Judge Joseph L. Call, they were charged with battery and disturbing the peace and convicted. However, during the course of the trial it was revealed that the police had beat the six (along with a seventh man, Eddie Nora, who was not arrested). Angered at the police abuse, which Judge Call described as "lawlessness" and "anarchy," the court overturned the convictions and the judge initiated a grand jury investigation.[64]

Occurring in the wake of the Ríos-Ulloa incident, the grand jury's inquiry was thorough and received a great deal of coverage from the press, especially the *Daily News.* After a little over a month, the grand jury produced findings that led to the indictment and convictions of eight officers for felonious assault. The grand jury heard seventy-nine witnesses, including Roybal, Ríos, and Geraldine Eaton, the secretary to Chief of Detectives

Thad Brown. Eaton testified that her boss told her of the beatings in a cavalier manner.[65] Perhaps the most damning testimony came from the victims themselves, who revealed that they were beaten repeatedly, with Nora suffering a ruptured kidney and less severe injuries for the others. One victim's words pointed to the mean-spiritedness of the police:

> They . . . were boozing and having a big party. They called us cop beaters and cop killers. They were climbing over each other to get at us, but only 10 to 20 of them actually participated in the beatings. They would holler "Merry Christmas" and then slug us. They would use their fist, elbows, and knees. When we were beaten again at Lincoln Heights jail some of the officers would strike us with big keys to the cellblocks. They cussed us and called us cop killers and told us to get out of the country.[66]

There were also subsequent threats. A police officer told Márquez's father that if he ever caught his son "on the street I'll shoot him down. I'll kill him."[67]

Following the trial, at least one anonymous police officer acknowledged being more careful when arresting citizens: "Since Bloody Christmas we've been afraid to so much as touch anybody."[68] Though the incident eventually led to convictions and seemingly showed a triumph of justice, it also reinforced the ethnic Mexican community's belief that it had been singled out for abuses in Los Angeles. Roybal affirmed that judgment by revealing during the grand jury investigation that he had received fifty complaints of police brutality, most of which, he believed, were valid. "It appears to be not only a problem in my eastside district but prevalent throughout the city. These cases have ranged from mere slapping around to hospitalization of victims with internal injuries by police officers who have over exerted their authority."[69]

The LAPD had no monopoly on brutality, as revealed in suits against Los Angeles County Sheriff Eugene W. Biscailuz and his department. In May 1953 Máximo Bustillos accused two deputy sheriffs of beating him en route to and in the East Los Angeles sheriff's substation. In September of the same year, David Hidalgo, a high school student, filed a civil suit against two deputies for an unprovoked beating.[70] Hildalgo's lawsuit resulted in the first instance of officers being found guilty of "police brutality." In a 1956 ruling, the judge also found the defendants financially liable for the beatings, fining them $8 each as part of an overall $1,016 settlement. The Hildalgo experience encouraged other Mexican immigrants and Mexican Americans to file suit when their civil rights were violated.[71]

Tension between law enforcement officials and the ethnic Mexican community continued into the future, but the battles of the 1950s brought into the open the hostility that existed between both parties. At the forefront of these struggles were the CSO, ANMA, and numerous individuals, including Roybal. Despite such challenges, hostility by law enforcement personnel against ethnic Mexicans continued and created a siege mentality among officers. "We can't tell the good Mexicans from the bad," confessed one policeman, "so we have to treat them all alike."[72] Chief Parker's testimony before the Federal Civil Rights Commission in January 1960 also reflected this view. "Some of these people were here before we were, but some of them are not far removed from the wild tribes of Mexico."[73] Sadly, this attitude remained dominant throughout the 1960s and perhaps continues in some form into the present.

V

Tense community relations were not limited to law enforcement officials, but also flared in dealings with the California Highway Commission, especially over freeway construction that became widespread in the 1950s, '60s, and '70s. In September 1953 the commission ignited protests when it proposed the Golden State Freeway, which would cut through the ethnic Mexican enclave of Boyle Heights. Civic and business leaders as well as residents denounced this disregard for the well-being of the city's ethnic Mexican population. Roybal, in whose district the new highway would be located, immediately went on record against the project, as did the nearby residents of Hollenbeck Heights. So too, did the Brooklyn Avenue Businessmen's Association when it realized that the highway "would eliminate several hundred families who are now customers and would create a barrier between the Los Angeles River and our business district."[74]

Led by longtime resident Marie Tubbs, these citizens, in October 1953, formed the "Boyle-Hollenbeck Anti-Golden State Freeway Committee" and invited Roybal to become chair, and he gladly accepted.[75] While the association sponsored protest rallies, Roybal secured passage of a city council resolution asking the California Highway Commission for a rehearing on the proposed route. Additional support came from Los Angeles County Supervisor John Anson Ford, California State Assemblyman Edward Elliott, and Congressman Chet Hollifield, who asked the California Highway Commission to delay the project until a new route could be found.[76] Over 350 Boyle–Hollenbeck Heights residents, property owners, clergymen, and merchants, along with Roybal and Elliott, attended the rehearing in Sacramento on December 15, 1953.[77]

Their efforts were to no avail. The commission persisted in its plan and, in March 1955, the Los Angeles city council, with Roybal dissenting, endorsed the freeway, despite the petitions containing the signatures of fifteen thousand opponents that Roybal presented.[78] When completed in 1956, the Golden State Freeway, according to the *Eastside Sun,* led to the "eradication, obliteration, razing, moving, ripping asunder, [and] demolishing of Eastside homes."[79] Though other freeways would be built in East Los Angeles, the ethnic Mexican community's opposition to them never achieved the magnitude of the fight against the Golden State Freeway. That defeat produced a sense of resignation and apathy captured by the *Eastside Sun* when the State Division of Highways announced plans for the Pomona Freeway, which would bisect the predominantly ethnic Mexican community of Belvedere in unincorporated East Los Angeles:

Again I am a movable object meeting an irresistible force
Again I am slaying dragons with toothpicks
Again I shall hear a mournful chorus of "You Can't Stop Progress"
And again another freeway called the Pomona Freeway is to slice through our
  homes, our businesses, and our lives
Again people will be told that they must sell their homes and again and again and
  again.[80]

VI

Having lost the battle against the state highway commission, ethnic Mexican neighborhoods also had to contend with the Community Redevelopment Agency and its efforts to "modernize" Los Angeles. These actions came in the guise of "urban renewal" and at the expense of the Bunker Hill, Boyle Heights, and Chávez Ravine districts, which had high concentrations of poor and ethnic Mexican people. Bunker Hill lay to the immediate west of the central business district. At the turn of the century it had been one of the city's fashionable residential areas, but by the 1950s its marginalized inhabitants and hilly terrain made it an impediment to the growth of the city's business interests. These characteristics ensured that the Community Redevelopment Agency (CRA) would target it for renewal. The initial renewal calls in 1948 were for "predominantly residential" land use. Under the provisions of the 1949 Housing Act, plans were initiated for 6,913 residential units, 43,000 square feet of office space, and 4 underground garages. The Bunker Hill plan also called for the building of bomb shelters in the civic center, a reflection of Cold War fears.[81]

With the defeat of public housing in 1953, and the subsequent election of Mayor Norris Poulson, the city council approved a new CRA plan for Bunker Hill. The design called for the purchase, clearance, and "improvement" of the area using public taxes, and the selling of the lots to private investors for less than the market value but more than the old-time and poor residents could afford. Private enterprise rather than the public were the beneficiaries. Downtown commercial and real estate interests — the same people who had so vehemently opposed public housing — championed Bunker Hill redevelopment. Support also came from newspapers that had earlier so effectively denounced public housing proponents as communist inspired.[82]

the establishment

Opponents to the plan included the residents of Bunker Hill and its surrounding neighborhoods, who viewed Bunker Hill redevelopment as a threat to their homes and their way of life. They created the Downtown Community Association as a vehicle to "protest, resist, and insist!"[83] Despite a campaign of letter writing, lawsuits, lobbying public officials, and receiving the support of Roybal and two other city council members, theirs was a lost cause. The council voted overwhelmingly for the plan and resistance dwindled as residents moved or died. The CRA began acquiring the property on the hill in 1961, followed by reselling of the property to private investors.[84]

The displacement caused by freeways and urban renewal efforts in Bunker Hill made Boyle Heights residents fear for their community when redevelopment proponents targeted it in 1958. Calling themselves the "Boyle Heights Urban Renewal Committee," a group of medical doctors asked the city to designate a large portion of Boyle Heights an "urban renewal district."[85] The group's reasoning was that "the central location and close proximity to established medical facilities makes this area ideal for an institution devoted to the study of nervous diseases."[86] Opponents countered that "Boyle Heights . . . has always been a place to live, . . . a residential area, . . . a district that did not put [on] any airs."[87] Senior citizens especially objected to being uprooted and made vulnerable to banks and other financial institutions. Tensions mounted when a second group, the College of Medical Evangelists of White Memorial Hospital, while claiming no association with the Boyle Heights Urban Renewal group, nonetheless also sought a "new" Boyle Heights. It advocated using the right of eminent domain to condemn property on behalf of institutions serving the public.

In response, the "Property Owners Committee for the Preservation of Boyle Heights" protested against being made "to suffer the fate of those who dwelt in [*sic*] Bunker Hill," and called on the city council and the mayor to save them from "displacement and dispersal."[88] That message was repeated in petitions and individual pleas to Roybal, who supported them. Typical was the letter from Francisco Martel of 1602 Bridge Street: "I and mi [*sic*] family live in this place since 1928. I spend plenty of money fixing this house and now I make additional rooms and I still owe $4,000 in [*sic*] this work so we don't want to move because I am too old to buy another house now. Please protect us."[89] The protests proved successful, for by the end of 1958 the urban renewal advocates had abandoned their plans.[90]

In addition to Boyle Heights, the forces of modernity also converged on Chávez Ravine. The two neighborhoods had much in common: a poor ethnic Mexican population, substandard housing, and little to no political clout in the city. Urban renewal worked its will on Chávez Ravine. When the public housing plan for the area was scrapped in 1953, the CRA sold the land to the City of Los Angeles, with the provision that the property must be put to public use. The nature of that "public use" became clear when Brooklyn Dodgers owner Walter O'Malley announced dissatisfaction with New York. Seeing an opportunity to lure baseball to Los Angeles, Mayor Norris Poulson and two members of the city council, Rosalind Wyman and Kenneth Hahn, approached O'Malley and offered him the 315-acre Chávez Ravine site in exchange for the 9-acre Dodger-owned Wrigley Field. The city council also offered to pay $2 million for site grading and $2.7 million for access roads. The obstacle that remained in this scheme was the mostly ethnic Mexicans who lived in the ravine. The plan was to remove them with the same mechanism used by the CRA to obtain Bunker Hill — eminent domain and subsidized land improvements.[91]

Opponents responded in October 1957 with the formation of the Committee to Save Chávez Ravine for the People. As a result of fliers, radio and TV broadcasts, and community newspapers — except for the powerful *Los Angeles Times,* which supported the city's efforts and offered little or no coverage of the opposition's activities — support came from throughout the city. The committee also used other tactics to gain attention: lawsuits, letter writing, and pressure on elected officials. Within thirty days of its founding, the organization had gathered more than 82,000 signatures and, with Roybal's help, placed a referendum on the June 1958 ballot to revoke the city's Chávez Ravine contract with the Dodgers. The voters went with the Dodgers, narrowly endorsing the project by a vote of 351,683 to 325,898. Following an unsuccessful appeal to the California Supreme Court, the Chávez Ravine residents, on March 9, 1959, were given thirty days to vacate their dwellings.[92]

Instead of complying with the order, an elderly couple, Manuel and Arvina Arechiga, along with their extended family, refused to leave. Although the City Housing Authority had purchased their home in 1951, when the public housing project targeted the area, the property had been resold to the city following the abandonment of the housing plans. In the interim era of uncertainty, the Arechigas had continued to live in their old home rent-free. On May 8, the Los Angeles Superior Court issued a writ of possession. As local stations televised the event and a throng of reporters and photographers watched the proceedings, sheriff's deputies forcibly evicted them from their home of thirty-six years and their possessions were put in storage. Even then, the Arechigas and their approximately forty supporters refused to leave the area and camped out on the property. "The eviction is the kind of thing you might expect in Nazi Germany or during the Spanish Inquisition," observed Roybal.[93]

The city council then scheduled an inquiry into the legality of the Arechiga eviction but was sidetracked when the family was accused of being wealthy landlords. After much fanfare, the Arechigas were revealed as owners of two rental properties, in addition to the Chávez Ravine home, but Mrs. Arechiga refused to move into one of the other properties. She preferred to stay at the Chávez Ravine homeplace, the reason being, as her daughter explained, "She wants to die" there, and she "just can't believe that anyone can throw her off her land."[94] Perhaps an indication of the limited residential areas in which Mexican immigrants and Mexican Americans could live, one of the Arechigas' houses was in Boyle Heights and had been condemned to make way for the Golden State Freeway.[95] The drama came to an end on May 14. After Roybal intervened, the Arechigas agreed to abandon the property when the city assured them that they would be able to keep their land rights in the ravine (what this exactly meant is unclear).[96] The Chávez Ravine removal would become part of the historical memory of Los Angeles's ethnic Mexicans, as an example of how the city's authorities looked upon them and poor people in general.[97]

The struggles against police brutality, freeways, and urban renewal underscore the precarious position of the ethnic Mexican population in Los Angeles. Those same battles, however, also reveal the community's resiliency in the face of hostile challenges. This is not to say that ethnic Mexicans, as historian Tracy Ainsworth has argued, won "all the cultural battles" and lost "the economic war."[98] Rather, their relatively little economic and political power enhanced cultural production in small, yet important, ways. Their experiences were not so much about winning or losing but about surviving and developing safe havens from an often cruel reality. It was in this light that ethnic Mexican cultural opposition emerged.

VII

A belief in the ideals of Americanism and efforts at assimilation characterized this era, but the Cold War atmosphere also engendered often-hidden gestures of Mexican protonationalism — a residual culture. Though not as pronounced as what was to come in the later 1960s, these "pockets" of ethnic nationalism nonetheless represented formidable signs of resistance.[99] Such pockets could take obscure forms, like the A9 Graduation brochure distributed at Belvedere Junior High in East Los Angeles. Though it resembled similar brochures distributed elsewhere in the city, it also differed in its use of the original full Spanish name for the city: "La Ciudad de Nuestra Señora La Reina de Los Angeles de Porciúncula." The program's counterhegemonic characteristics do not stop there. The table of contents reveals — along with the usual proceedings of processional, pledge of allegiance, invocation, and presentation of diplomas — a student performance entitled "The History of Los Angeles." The cast of characters included Indians, Father Junípero Serra, Governor Felipe de Neve, and Generals Andrés Pico and John Frémont. The performance began with Indians crossing the isthmus of Catalina and landing in what became Los Angeles to trade their pottery. It ended with Californians signing articles of surrender and, in turn, becoming U.S. citizens. The play resembled a didactic piece along the lines of the Mission Play so prevalent in the early part of the century. However, it was also a reaffirmation by these young Mexican Americans of their ethnic heritage and their place within the polity — conquered but not powerless, American but also Mexican.[100]

Another pocket of Mexican ethnic pride was John F. Mendez's writings in the *Eastside Sun*. Given the limited access to mainstream newspapers and other publications, this community periodical served as an important voice of resistance.[101] Mendez's regular column, "Pan-American Panorama," appeared from 1950 to 1954. Along with his coverage of the Latino club scene in Los Angeles ("Where there is nite life there is Mendez"), he also tackled cultural issues and commented on their political significance. Such was his essay "Significance of Cinco de Mayo to the Mexican American Community of the Eastside," which argued that "Benito Juárez, great Mexican patriot, was the one that inspired the people to greater efforts while still suffering under the yoke of the invaders." Mendez's message was straightforward: "There is some similarity in our present position here in our state and city. The Mexican-American people are awakening and are taking very active steps to improve themselves, socially, politically, and educationally."[102] Given the Cold War atmosphere at the time, Mendez's indirect identification of Americans as invaders was clearly oppositional.

A more direct appeal to Mexican Americans to take pride in their Mexican heritage appeared in Mendez's Panorama column on April 9, 1953. Here, he called on Mexican Americans not to be ashamed of their Mexican ancestry. "We will never be able to advance ourselves socially and economically if a large number of non-Latins believe that we are ashamed of our racial background," he wrote. "You can never gain respect that way."[103]

Mendez offered a potpourri of information and often buried an important comment in his column — yet that did not take out the bite. In a piece in which he showed his enthusiasm for the "Ram football team," he also included a "Hohum note: New mayor, Norris Poulson, as usual failed to name a qualified Mexican-American to the police commission just like his predecessors." In another place he commented, "Wish that restaurant on 11th and Western would change its present name of El Cholo to something else. Not too flattering to Mexican Americans."[104] Other Panorama installments criticized the Los Angeles Mirror's "feature story of a dope addict of Mexican ancestry," which the newspaper said should set "'an example' for other Eastside kids"; celebrated the exploits of Mexican-American boxer Art Aragon; and encouraged young ethnic Mexican men to "try for an appointment to West Point or Annapolis."[105]

Still another pocket of ethnic pride could be found in the annual celebration of Mexican Independence Day sponsored by the Comité de Festejivos Patrios.[106] That residents looked upon the festivities as much more than an excuse for a good time is evident in Eloy Durán's letter to the editor of the Eastside Sun:

In commemorating the "Grito de Dolores" we pay tribute to the heroic stature of Hidalgo and his aspirations for freedom for which he was soon to die. In these fear ridden times his call to action should inspire us with determination to continue the battle until man everywhere is free — free from persecution, from bigotry, from fear.[107]

Thus, knowledge of Mexican history served as much more than nostalgia. Perhaps others felt the fear that Durán acknowledged and looked to Mexican protonationalism as an antidote to the many ills that plagued Los Angeles's ethnic Mexican community.

VIII

The emergent cultural nationalism reflected in the writings of Durán and others, together with the discriminatory nature of American society, prompted many ethnic Mexicans in the 1950s and early 1960s to work on behalf of putting people like themselves into political office. Their initial efforts proved encouraging but also ultimately showed that something more was needed. This was nowhere more clearly demonstrated than in the campaigns of two prominent local Mexican Americans, Edward Roybal and Henry López, for state political office.

Because of his prominence on the Los Angeles city council, Roybal easily won nomination as the Democratic Party's 1954 candidate for lieutenant governor, but that victory produced disappointingly little funding from the party for his campaign. Instead, the party focused its money and efforts on unseating the Republican incumbent governor, Goodwin Knight.[108] Nor was Roybal helped by a party chair openly hostile to his candidacy. "You dare not run. You won't be good for the ticket," the chair bluntly told him. When Roybal asked "Why not?," the chair replied: "Because the people of California will not support two Catholics on the same ticket," a reference to Democratic gubernatorial candidate Richard Graves. To Roybal, the comment masked the chair's prejudice against Mexicans, a view shared by his close friend Bert Corona.[109] Roybal went on to lose the election, but in doing so he received more votes than Graves did. To Roybal, the lesson of the campaign was the tenuous relationship between the Democratic Party and the ethnic Mexican community, and the need to create a strong independent base from which to launch the bid of any Mexican American for public office.[110] That conviction received reinforcement four years

later when Henry López ran as a Democrat for California secretary of
state.[111]

As with Roybal earlier, López was the lone Mexican American running
for a statewide office, and he also faced hostility from members of his own
party. Speaker of the Assembly Jesse Unruh and Lieutenant Governor
Edmund G. "Pat" Brown believed that a Mexican American could not
gain the necessary support to win. To Roybal, this attitude toward his
friend was dismaying, for López "was the best qualified of all candidates:
Harvard graduate, top of his class, law review and everything."[112]
Nonetheless, López, like Roybal earlier, received little funding from the
Democratic Party and had to raise what he could on his own. That was
very little. He could not afford public relations agents, billboards, campaign literature, or radio and television ads. Reduced to canvassing the
state in an old automobile, he lost, but in a very close campaign.[113]

Now thoroughly convinced that ethnic Mexicans would never gain
office unless they found the means to raise money and organize effectively
on their own, Roybal set out to do just that.[114] He found a kindred spirit
in John Acevedo, who had been appointed to the board of the California
Youth Authority by newly elected Governor Brown. Acevedo's new job
required him to travel throughout the state, and he used that opportunity
to lobby Mexican-American leaders elsewhere for the creation of a political support group of their own.[115] He and those sharing his views envisioned an "independent electoral organization that could take up the
questions pertinent to the Mexican communities without having to
compromise itself with other groups inside the Democratic Party."[116]
Acevedo's contacts led to a small weekend meeting on March 28–29, 1959,
in Fresno, that led to a larger gathering in April and the formal creation
of the Mexican American Political Association (MAPA).[117]

One hundred and fifty-five delegates from communities throughout
the state attended the April meeting. Among them were Frank Paz, Julio
Castelan, Herman Gallegos, Fred Castro, Eduardo Quevedo, Ignacio
López, and Lucio Bernabé — all political activists in such groups as the
Spanish-Speaking Congress, the ANMA, and the CSO. These were pri-
marily men who had come of age during World War II and the Korean
War. Women were also in attendance, among them Mary Soto of Los
Angeles and Hortencia Solís of Bakersfield, who, like the men, were
mostly in their thirties and civil servants, professionals (attorneys, teach-
ers, and engineers), and trade unionists.[118]

MAPA emerged as an organization created and controlled by Mexican
Americans. Though the group's constitution allowed "all persons who

foster" MAPA's aims to "be members and vote and participate in activities, . . . only Mexican-Americans and other persons of Spanish-speaking origin" could "hold office on either the state or local levels." In addition, given its emphasis on electoral politics, the organization restricted membership to U.S. citizens.[119] MAPA's ethnic focus became abundantly clear when attempts to authorize coalitions with other non-white minorities such as African Americans, Asian Americans, and Native Americans were decisively rejected.[120] The need for allies and the conviction of many ethnic Mexicans that they were people of color led two years later to a reversal of this action, but MAPA's preeminent goal remained putting ethnic Mexicans into political office: "to bring the Mexican-American community to its place in the sun in all councils of government," so as to advance "the social, economic, cultural and civic betterment of Mexican-Americans and all other Spanish-speaking people through political action."[121]

MAPA members eschewed the militancy of El Congreso and ANMA, and had no desire to create a third party as La Raza Unida later did. Instead, they emphasized working within the Democratic Party while retaining their autonomy. They channeled their energies into creating strong MAPA chapters in every California Assembly District inhabited by Mexican Americans. To facilitate their activities, they divided the state into a northern and southern region, stipulating that the president had to come from a different region at each election and that the president and vice-president could not be from the same region.[122] Those initially responsible for organizing the chapters and attracting members were Mexican-American elected officials and appointees of the governor.[123]

Early success led members, at their second annual meeting in 1960, to authorize joining with other politically active Mexican-American groups to create a national bipartisan umbrella organization. The goal was to move fast enough to be a force in the presidential election later that year. Hector García, founder of the American G.I. Forum, at Roybal's urging sent out a call to the leaders of ethnic Mexican organizations throughout the Southwest to meet in Phoenix in April. The large turnout buoyed spirits, though everyone was soon bickering over what to call the new coalition. The New Mexico delegation preferred the Congress of Hispanic Peoples, Californians insisted on having "Mexican-American" in the name, and the Texas representatives opposed both suggestions — all of which demonstrated the diversity of the Spanish-speaking peoples of the Southwest. In a search for common ground, they agreed on Political Association of Spanish-Speaking Organizations (PASSO) and elected Albert Peña from San Antonio as president and Roybal as vice-president.[124]

PASSO and the organizations affiliated with it endorsed John F. Kennedy for president. To help ensure a November victory, Edward Kennedy oversaw efforts in the West, while a group of Mexican-American leaders — Texas state assemblyman Henry Gonzales, U.S. Senator Dennis Chávez of New Mexico, and Roybal — promoted "Viva Kennedy Clubs" throughout the Southwest, with Roybal in charge of efforts in California.[125]

The Viva Kennedy Clubs answered directly to Robert Kennedy and were independent of the state Democratic Party's campaign machinery. The goal was to associate the clubs directly with John Kennedy, thereby providing them a visibility they would otherwise not have as a part of state-run campaigns.[126] Responsible to Roybal for recruiting campaign workers in Los Angeles was Ralph Guzmán, who concentrated his efforts on local colleges and universities, especially East Los Angeles Junior College, Los Angeles State College, and UCLA. Thus, most of the recruits were students, with a smattering of faculty who were both Mexican American and white. Their task was not only to get Kennedy supporters to the polls, but also, in the tradition of the CSO, to register eligible voters. Guzmán appointed the volunteers as deputy registrars and instructed them on how to go successfully door-to-door. In the first weekend of these efforts, some 150 people registered to vote; later, from July 10 to the eve of the election, a single team of volunteers registered 1,500 citizens. The clubs became so successful that the Republicans imitated them by establishing "Arriba Nixon" groups.[127]

A by-product of the Viva Kennedy campaign was the encouragement of local communities to come out publicly on behalf of Democratic candidates. "We hope that after this election, the spirit, the enthusiasm and organization will be carried on," stated a young volunteer from East Los Angeles. "We Mexican Americans must make our needs felt. If we do a good job for Kennedy and they know about it, then they will have to say: 'Those Mexicans down in L.A. mean business.' I'm tired of MAPA being laughed at and called a 'paper bull' by even our own people. *Basta* — enough."[128]

Kennedy's victory in November 1960 delighted Mexican Americans but brought little change to their communities. When the new administration offered ambassadorships to Texas's Henry Gonzales and Hector García, they turned them down, explaining the need to remain at home and work for the betterment of their people.[129] Many ethnic Mexicans saw the appointments as tokenism — "some two-bit job that was mean-ingless," in the words of Bert Corona.[130] Not all Mexican Americans declined White House offers, however. University of Texas professor George I. Sánchez accepted posts with the National Advisory Council for the Peace Corps and the committee on "New Frontier Policy in the Americas," while Reynaldo Garza of Texas received an appointment to the federal bench. El Paso mayor Raymond Telles, in what historian Mario García calls "the ultimate expression of the politics of status," accepted Kennedy's offer to become ambassador to Costa Rica.[131] These rather minor posts offered to Mexican Americans, and the new administration's feeble efforts to improve life in the nation's barrios, left Spanish-speaking peoples, as Corona observed, with a "bad taste toward the Kennedy Administration."[132]

The end of the campaign brought the demise of the Viva Kennedy clubs and more attention by ethnic Mexicans to their own communities. As at the national level, this was in part due to disappointment with state leaders. Though Mexican Americans had worked more closely with the Kennedys than with the state Democratic candidates, they felt deeply disappointed by the Pat Brown administration's inattention to their problems and his failure to reward them for their efforts. Of the five thousand political appointments made by Brown in the early 1960s, only thirty went to Mexican Americans, a number that would grow to only forty-nine by the end of his second term.[133]

In Los Angeles in the wake of the 1960 election, the hot political issue became cityhood for East Los Angeles. MAPA saw it as a means to "reshape and control local political systems" and revived its earlier tactics of door-to-door campaigns, press releases, and pamphleteering efforts on behalf of incorporation.[134] Since East Los Angeles was predominantly an ethnic Mexican community, the proponents emphasized how cityhood would produce better municipal services and showcase the ability of local residents to govern themselves better than outsiders.[135] The opponents, however, proved themselves better campaigners, drawing on residents' fears of higher taxes (despite the counterclaims of MAPA and the incorporation committee) and attracting the support of the *Eastside Sun,* the East Los Angeles Property Owners Association headed by Art Montoya, and the Whittier Boulevard businessmen.[136] Defeat of cityhood in 1961, coming on the heels of the disappointments that followed the 1960 election, did nothing to strengthen MAPA's image in the community.[137]

MAPA sought to change this situation by turning with even greater energy to electioneering, announcing in 1962 that it planned to shatter "once and for all 100 years of almost complete exclusion from participation in state and national government."[138] It endorsed attorney Anthony G. Bueno's unsuccessful bid to represent East Los Angeles in the state assembly, and Municipal Judge Leopoldo Sánchez's successful quest for a seat on the Los Angeles County Superior Court bench. MAPA also worked vigorously for the election of John Moreno (from the 51st Assembly District in Pico Rivera) and Philip Soto (from La Puente's 50th Assembly District). They were the first two Mexican Americans to serve in that body in seventy-five years. But these achievements became short-lived when the districts were almost immediately reapportioned, leading to the defeat of Moreno and Soto in their reelection bids.[139]

MAPA's efforts received no help from the Democratic Party, a factor that only encouraged its tendency toward ethnocentrism and cultural nationalism. Mexican Americans, its leaders argued, had "unique political skills," a claim that did not go over well with outsiders, given the still prevalent assimilationist political climate of the early 1960s. On the other hand, MAPA flatly denied charges of cultural nationalism.

MAPA has been accused of being nationalistic. What does the term nationalism mean? The dictionary defines it in the following way . . . "devotion to the interests of glory of one's own country." We as Mexican-Americans do not identify with Mexico or Mexican politics. The members of MAPA are American, the problems are American, the solutions will definitely be American. As Mexicans we have made our marks in the American scene, our contributions are there for anyone who cares to look.[140]

Such protestations notwithstanding, MAPA's support of only Mexican-American political candidates and avoidance of involvement with white political groups underscored its ethnic allegiance, an emphasis that became even more pronounced in ethnic Mexican organizations of the Chicano movement era.

MAPA's weak record led to decline in its influence at the same time that Roybal's own popularity was on the increase, especially in 1962 when he won election to Congress. The downside of his victory was the Los Angeles ethnic Mexican community's loss of his expertise and close attention to local issues. Roybal's departure left his seat on the city council up for grabs. MAPA quickly, and unilaterally, selected a candidate for appointment to Roybal's unexpired term — Richard Tafoya, an aide to Mayor Samuel Yorty and Roybal's cousin. Roybal objected to Tafoya's selection as being out of harmony with the changing ethnic composition of the 9th district. By the early 1960s, it was approximately 50 percent

African American, 35 percent ethnic Mexican, and 15 percent Asian and Jewish, with a smattering of other ethnic groups. "This was the biggest mistake a Mexican American [organization] could have made," Roybal told the *Los Angeles Times*. "It [has] probably hurt Tafoya's chances to succeed me." He was particularly incensed that his advice had been ignored. "I told them that they should think of ways to select a liberal candidate to succeed me. I warned them against selecting a candidate unilaterally."[141]

The African-American majority in the 9th district opened the door for Gilbert Lindsay to campaign for Roybal's seat. Lindsay, a black deputy to Los Angeles County Supervisor Kenneth Hahn, benefited from the civil rights movement being at its height and the African-American community's lack of representation on the city council. Nor was he hurt by a confrontation between the LAPD and black Muslims on April 27, 1962, that reminded the city council of the potential for violent black protest. Moreover, Lindsay, with the backing from the powerful National Association for the Advancement of Colored People (NAACP), had a more effective support group than the ethnic Mexicans who were split over Tafoya's candidacy. Not surprisingly, the city council appointed Lindsay, once again associating MAPA with a losing cause.[142]

That experience repeated itself in June 1963 when the council seat came up for election. MAPA once more supported Tafoya's bid, but this time an internal split weakened its energies when a faction backed another candidate, Josefina Sánchez.[143] That weakness now allowed Lindsay to handily win the council seat. His victory left Los Angeles with no Mexican American in city government except for Tafoya, who soon lost his post as a Yorty aide when the city council slashed the mayor's budget.[144] Thus, by mid-1963 a power vacuum existed in Mexican-American political circles in Los Angeles. "Today," mourned the Mexican-American newsletter *Carta Editorial*, "the city founded by our ancestors does not have one Mexican American in official capacity. La Reina de Los Angeles weeps."[145]

The election results and Roybal's departure left MAPA in disarray. Dissidents took advantage of the situation to reverse completely the organization's liberal orientation by electing a new state chair, Eduardo Quevedo, who changed the constitution, centralizing power in his office, and then embarked on a McCarthy-like purge of leftists in the organization by limiting membership to "citizens of the United States who avowedly respect and uphold the tenets of the Constitution of the United States and who do not advocate the overthrow of our democratic form of government, other than through legal constitutional procedures."[146]

The abrupt change of direction did nothing to improve MAPA's success rate. Indeed, it led only to a rash of additional disappointments in 1964. First, the four candidates endorsed by MAPA in the southern California primaries met defeat.[147] Next, California's delegation to the Democratic National Convention that year included only five Mexican Americans, a pitifully small number in view of the 1.5 million ethnic Mexicans in the state. Then, another setback (this one shared by blacks) came with the failure in 1964 to defeat Proposition 14, which overturned the 1963 Rumford Act and reestablished discriminatory housing practices in California.[148] (Three years later, the California Supreme Court threw out Proposition 14 as unconstitutional, but that did little to assuage bitterness created by the earlier loss at the polls.[149])

Still another 1964 disappointment — and most unsettling of all — came when the Los Angeles city council redrew its district lines, making it virtually impossible for the ethnic Mexican population to gain a seat on the council.[150] As Mexicans were squeezed out, two more blacks joined Lindsay on the city council. Moreover, the 9th district, which Roybal had held for fourteen years, was redrawn to ensure that African Americans constituted 56 percent of the voters. These changes were all signs of blacks' success in gaining visibility and strength from the civil rights movement, something that Mexican Americans failed to do. Thus, the nation's largest ethnic Mexican community was without a voice on the city's governing board.[151] (Not until the 1980s, following court-ordered city redistricting, would a Mexican American serve again on the Los Angeles city council.)

The 1964 defeats led to further erosion of MAPA's standing in the ethnic Mexican community when its conservative leadership clashed with more activist groups now gaining statewide and national attention.[152] The most serious confrontation was with César Chávez's United Farm Workers Association (UFWA), which picketed MAPA's annual convention in 1965 because of its recruitment of Mexican immigrant workers on behalf of farmers.[153] Anger against MAPA also flared when state chair Quevedo was named a special consultant to the U.S. Department of Labor to aid in the securing of "Mexican American farm workers who have little or no knowledge of the English language."[154] Lack of English, charged the UFWA, undermined the workers' bargaining power. In an attempt to diffuse the situation, Quevedo asked UFWA official Dolores Huerta to speak to the convention. She used the opportunity to blast MAPA for contributing to the "*bracero* evil" and demanded that the organization leave farm workers alone so that they could bargain with agribusiness through groups like the UFWA.[155]

Only little more than a month later, MAPA further distanced itself from the ethnic Mexican community when it refused to take a stand on the Watts rebellion of August 1965, describing the uprising as "non-political." This explanation fell flat in the community, which believed that the three Mexican Americans killed in the revolt had been shot without justification by the authorities.[156] MAPA did join with other Mexican-American organizations in calling for the federal government to investigate "the causes of poverty and propose constructive programs of rehabilitation," but by then the damage to its already tarnished reputation had been done. By contrast, other Mexican-American groups took bolder action.[157] CSO called for an investigation of the charges of police brutality, and a group of thirty Mexican Americans acting as individuals rather than as members of an organization demanded a public inquiry into the social conditions that precipitated the violent outburst. They sent their message to Governor Brown through a delegation consisting of Congressman Roybal, Ralph Guzmán, Armando Morales, and Frank Muñoz. The delegation, however, was not allowed to participate in the hearings held by the McCone Commission into the causes of the "riots."[158]

MAPA's weak showing during the Watts violence was partially undone during the following year as it sought to mend its relations with UFWA by supporting Chávez's efforts to reverse a farm workers' vote selecting the Teamsters as their representative. UFWA believed that the growers had coerced the vote. The popularity of these actions in the community (and the lack of any competing strictly "political" organization) brought a large turnout, the biggest since MAPA's founding, to its annual meeting in Fresno in June 1966. Another reason for the impressive attendance was the upcoming state elections, especially the gubernatorial race between incumbent governor Brown and Republican challenger Ronald Reagan. Brown and most other major candidates (except Reagan) were present.[159]

With the exception of the candidacy of Ivy Baker Priest, a Republican and former U.S. Treasurer, the delegates endorsed the Democratic candidates. Priest got the nod for state treasurer because of her national visibility as a public servant and because she was a woman. The endorsement of Democrats, especially Brown, came with little enthusiasm.[160] As *Carta Editorial* observed, the governor's race entailed a "choice of two evils." The "slow progress of the Mexican American population under the Democratic Party administration of the past 8 years in California," stated the newsletter, "has caused many of the activists to feel a distinct lack of interest in the current gubernatorial campaign." The displeasure stemmed from Brown's reluctance to intervene in the farm workers' struggle for union recognition, his wavering in appointing Judge Leopold Sánchez to the Los Angeles Superior Court, and his appointment of only a handful of Mexican Americans to state offices. There was also resentment toward Democratic leaders for failing to include adequate Mexican-American representation in the party's internal structure.[161]

The endorsement of Democrats did not come entirely by default, however, for a Reagan victory would be a severe blow to ethnic Mexican interests. During the previous twenty years of Republican party rule, only three Mexican Americans had been appointed to state posts. Moreover, Reagan was calling for denial of state old-age pensions to non-citizens. "No activist who pretends to work for the interests of Mexican Americans," editorialized *Carta Editorial,* "can refuse to work for Brown or to remain neutral in the conflict."[162]

The 1966 elections turned out to be a replay of the earlier Los Angeles city council elections: not a single Mexican American remained in office at the state level. Congressman Roybal retained his seat by a huge majority, but state Attorney General Thomas Lynch was the only other Democratic victor. The party was in a shambles and so was MAPA. After seven years, it had failed in its major goal and was back where it started, only now it no longer had the earlier strong support of the ethnic Mexican community. The electoral losses could not be attributed solely to MAPA, for gerrymandered districts, machine politics, and Reagan's personal popularity with the voters played major roles. But MAPA could not escape its share of the blame. The allegiance of many residents, especially younger people, was shifting to other groups that were arguing for solutions outside the political process.[163] Still, MAPA's efforts had not been in vain. It had been the first organization to recognize the voting potential of Mexican Americans and to attempt to organize them effectively. As the new millennium approached, it remained active, yet by 1966 the torch had passed to others.

The 1950s and early '60s proved to be trying times, but the with the help of the CSO, ANMA, MAPA, and councilman Roybal, and through the activism of everyday people, Mexican Americans and Mexican immigrants defined and defended their place in the city. Though their efforts did not receive the recognition accorded the battles of their counterparts in the later 1960s and 1970s, their struggles and slow but steady gains during the Cold War era set the foundation for the more dramatic actions of the coming decade.

"Birth of a New Symbol"

The Brown Berets

In January 1967 *Time* magazine declared: "The Man of the Year 1966 is a generation: the man — and woman — of 25 and under."[1] The youth of the sixties, observed *Time,* are "well-educated, affluent, rebellious, responsible, pragmatic, idealistic, brave, 'alienated,' and hopeful."[2] People of color were not well educated and affluent, but their desire to be so and also to eliminate racial and ethnic discrimination in American society caused them to strike out at that society in ways that were both similar to and strikingly different from the efforts of earlier generations. For Mexican Americans, no group better illustrated the rebellious 1960s and 1970s than the Brown Berets.

As shown in the previous chapter, by 1966 the Mexican American Political Association's approach to empowering Mexican Americans had proved inadequate. This ineffectiveness combined with the general protest environment of the later 1960s to ensure a new style of politics known as the Chicano movement. The Mexican protonationalism that an older generation used as an oppositional tool was transformed into a Chicano nationalism when suffused with the anti-Americanism of the Vietnam era. Though the issues faced by the ethnic Mexican community were similar to those confronted earlier, the approach to them now differed. Instead of relying on the ballot box, Chicano activists took to the streets and demanded change through protest. This is not to say that protest was nonexistent in prior years, but, rather, that it now attracted mainstream attention, especially from the media and young people, the "baby boomers" who had come of age in the 1960s.

Like other ethnic groups in post–World War II America, the ethnic Mexican community experienced a population boom, its numbers almost doubling from 156,356 in 1950 to 291,959 in 1960.[3] The increase reflected a birth rate 50 percent higher than that of the general population, and resulted in a disproportionately large number of youths in the impoverished community, a fact not lost on the McCone Commission which investigated the causes of the 1965 Watts rebellion in south-central Los Angeles. "Recommendations regarding the Negro problem in Los Angeles," observed the commission, "apply with equal force to the Mexican-Americans . . . whose circumstances are similarly disadvantageous and demand equally urgent treatment."[4] The post-Watts atmosphere created a sense of urgency in the city and prompted the Los Angeles County Human Relations Commission, formed following the 1943 zoot-suit riots, to join with the Wilshire Boulevard Temple's Camp Hess Kramer in sponsoring a conference for Mexican-American young people in April 1966.[5]

This event, with the prosaic name of the Mexican-American Youth Leadership Conference, became the vehicle for igniting a new generation of Mexican-American reformers.[6] The conference's purpose was to "examine emotions, feelings, values, identity and the label 'Mexican American.'" Attendees were high-school leaders who were urged to discuss what they shared in common, in the hope that they would forge alliances to bring about positive changes in their neighborhoods.[7] The conference lasted only three days, but some of those present continued to talk about issues that troubled them. In May 1966 six of them — Vickie Castro, David Sánchez, Moctesuma Esparza, Ralph Ramírez, Rachel Ochoa, George Licón, and John Ortiz — created Young Citizens for Community Action (YCCA).[8] Far from being radicals, they believed in the principles of President Lyndon Johnson's "war on poverty" and had faith in the electoral process. With headstrong, eighteen-year-old Roosevelt High School senior Vickie Castro as president, they surveyed student needs, discussed school problems with education officials, and gathered information about candidates running for election to the Los Angeles Board of Education. They were convinced that the flaws in the school system could be remedied only through political action, and their first move was to support Julian Nava, a state-college professor in the San Fernando Valley, in what became his successful bid for a seat on the school board. They followed their "Youth for Nava" campaign with membership in Los Angeles Mayor Samuel Yorty's Youth Advisory Council. Later, some of them served on the California Governor's Youth Advisory Council during the administrations of Governors Gerald "Pat" Brown and Ronald Reagan.[9]

These youths gradually began focusing on issues other than schools, especially police brutality and the need to improve the quality of life in their communities. Particularly strong encouragement came from Father John B. Luce, rector of the Episcopal Church of the Epiphany in Lincoln Heights and before that a pastor in the poor neighborhoods of East Harlem in New York City and Jersey City, New Jersey. In October 1965 he relocated to Los Angeles at the request of the local Episcopal bishop who encouraged him, as well as others, "to try to reach out and work with all sorts of different groups and kids, drug addicts, people that had been troubled with the law."[10] The challenge excited Luce, who shared the bishop's conviction that "the support of indigenous organizations of the people themselves will build real democracy in this country."[11]

The church formed part of an ever-growing network of urban groups that encouraged the YCCA in its efforts. Across the street from the church was the California Center for Community Development's Social Action Training Program, an organization funded by the Southern California Council of Churches through the federal Office of Economic Opportunity. The Social Action Training Center, in turn, introduced the YCCA youths to a Community Service Organization young people's group — the Young Adult Leadership and Community Development Project — dedicated "to train[ing] young adults in East Los Angeles in community action by involving them in neighborhood improvement and community participation projects."[12] No longer actively involved in electoral politics, CSO now concentrated on providing much-needed community services, such as a credit union and a "buyers club" that provided opportunities to buy food, clothing, and other items in bulk and at reduced rates.[13] Through CSO the YCCA members met Richard Alatorre, who schooled them in the ways of practical politics and community organizing and who also introduced them to the now famed César Chávez.[14] These numerous contacts left them not only better informed but also with greater pride in their own ethnicity that was reflected in the new name they gave their organization: Young Chicanos for Community Action (YCCA).[15]

These energetic youth, in addition, became more visible in the community. With the financial help of Father Luce, in 1967 they opened "La Piranya," a coffeehouse located on East Olympic Boulevard in an industrial section of unincorporated East Los Angeles. La Piranya served as an office and meeting place, where prominent civil rights leaders expressed their views to an ever-increasing number of Chicano youth. Among those making appearances were César Chávez, Reies López Tijerina of New Mexico's Alianza Federal de Mercedes, and African-American leaders Hubert "Rap" Brown and Stokely Carmichael of the Student Non-Violent Coordinating Committee and Ron Karenga of United Slaves (US).[16] The coffeehouse also sponsored "Educational Happenings," designed to encourage youth to get a college education.[17] Usually present on these occasions were representatives from nearby colleges and universities as well as speakers from other community groups — for example, the United Council Community Organizations and the United Parents Council — and sometimes a political leader or representative from a congressional field office. The coffeehouse remained, however, a gathering place for young people run by young people, with little and only nominal adult supervision. As *La Raza,* a local Chicano newspaper, observed, "Many nights you will hear live music . . . but mostly you will find young Chicanos like yourself."[18]

The gatherings also attracted Los Angeles County sheriff's deputies, who harassed La Piranya patrons on the grounds that the coffeehouse was a hangout for Chicano "hoodlums." The deputies would frequently drive by and shine their lights into the windows, as well as question and illegally search customers as they left the building. Angered by such affronts, the YCCA organized protest demonstrations at the nearby East Los Angeles sheriff's station.[19]

These protests marked a change in the leadership of YCCA, for they occurred at a time when some members began their college studies and gradually drifted away because of the pressure of classes. Licón, Esparza, Ochoa, and the group's president, Vickie Castro, were among them. Now assuming leadership positions were people like David Sánchez, the new president, who had little patience with police harassment and urged a more militant stance. In January 1968 this attitude took the symbolic form of khaki military clothing and a name change to the Brown Berets. Law-enforcement abuses had transformed them from moderate reformers into visually distinctive and combative crusaders on behalf of justice for Chicanos. Residual Mexican cultural nationalism was becoming Chicano nationalism, the core value of the now-emerging Chicano movement.

Besides the khaki attire, the most revealing feature of their apparel was the beret and the emblem attached to it, depicting a yellow pentagon with two bayoneted rifles behind a cross and the words *La Causa* ("The

Cause") above them. The design originated with a new member, Johnny Parsons, but others instinctively shared the message he sought to convey.

We asked him why [are you designing an emblem]? He said, "Look, it's like an emblem for guerrillas, . . . a symbol of guerrillas, and in this case like urban guerrillas." He started telling us how there were green berets, how the French guerrillas and the Spanish guerrillas had worn it during the Spanish Civil War and that we should wear a brown beret. So, we thought it was a good idea. So we started wearing the brown beret and the khaki jacket — the bush jacket. But we didn't call ourselves the Brown Berets. [Those] who started calling us the Brown Berets were the East L.A. Sheriffs . . . and we got pissed off. We would hear it because every time they had us up against the wall we'd hear all the radio messages from the patrol cars, "Brown Berets here" and "Brown Berets over here," and so then it stuck. So, then we just stayed with it.[20]

A new member had proposed the group's outward symbols, but someone who had been with the organization from the outset, eighteen-year-old David Sánchez, expressed in writing the anger and goals shared by all the Berets. Following his arrest in February 1968 and a sixty-day jail term for participating in an unlawful assembly, Sánchez wrote "The Birth of a New Symbol" in a setting reminiscent of Martin Luther King Jr.'s imprisonment in 1963, when he wrote his "Letter from a Birmingham Jail." Instead of the nonviolent philosophy advocated by King, however, Sánchez, using words suggestive of Malcolm X, called on Brown Berets to use "any and all means necessary . . . to resolve the frustrations of our people."

"As a Brown Beret," he admonished his followers, "you are to be considered prophets of [a] disillusioned past" and a "symbol of hope" who should "preach hope. . . . By merely standing on a street corner, [and] wearing a Brown Beret . . . people [can] observe you and gather information and form an opinion about the Brown Berets." The Berets' mission was conversion: "Talk to every potential Chicano who crosses your path. Because every Chicano that you miss is a potential enemy." But avoid "Anglos," he cautioned. "DO NOT TALK TO THE ENEMY, FOR HE IS EITHER A DOG OR A DEVIL. . . . For over 120 years, the Chicano has suffered at the hands of the Anglo Establishment" and the only way to "stop discrimination and the many injustices against our people" demands "pressure." Sánchez outlined three escalating stages of pressure. The first was "communication," sending telegrams and letters and making telephone calls to elected officials and other authorities. The second was to "embarrass and expose those who are in the wrong." The final stage consisted of "alternatives," which he ambiguously described as "any and all means necessary." Similar statements coming from Malcolm X and the Black Panthers had probably inspired this last option.[21]

Success required self-discipline. "Because your people, the land, and the enemy are watching you, you must look good, act right and move with the precision of a clock," lectured Sánchez.[22] This required unquestioning obedience to superiors in the group, the more so because they are the "best qualified to handle any situation" and fully aware of Anglo "trickery."[23] Success also demanded high standards of personal conduct. Avoid scandal because it will only "reflect upon the organization in a bad way" and alienate it from the community. Avoid as well "theory and ideology" because "intellectuals aren't able to communicate with the dude on the street." In addition, when out of uniform Berets should wear "simple dress" since "if you dress like the greater part of the community, you will usually be accepted. If you dress different," Sánchez cautioned, "and are sloppy or dirty, you usually aren't accepted and your channel of communication is broken."[24]

Also suffusing Sánchez's "Birth of a New Symbol" and the organizational structure were gendered notions of nation. All Beret officers were male. Sánchez served as "prime minister," Carlos Montes was "minister of information," Cruz Olmeda held the post of "chairman," and Ralph Ramírez that of "minister of discipline." These titles, similar to those adopted earlier by the Black Panthers, reflected the militaristic, masculine, and hierarchical nature of the group.[25] Permeating all subsequent Beret statements and documents were these emphases on strict discipline, clean and unostentatious living, Anglos as the enemy, the leadership role of Berets, and Chicano identity and solidarity.[26]

The Brown Berets first gained wide notoriety in March 1968 when they became involved in student boycotts, known as "blowouts," of five East Los Angeles high schools. Prompting the protest was the high percentage (over 50 percent) of Chicano high-school students forced to drop out of school either through expulsion and transfers to other schools or because they had not been taught to read and thus failed their classes. Overcrowding and dilapidated buildings were endemic at Chicano schools, where teachers, a majority of whom were Anglo, often discriminated against their Mexican-Americans students, calling them "dirty Mexicans" and encouraging them to join the workforce rather than attend college.[27] Angered by the treatment, students demanded more Chicano teachers and administrators and better schools.[28]

The Berets did not directly participate in the planning of the demonstrations, but they did "back up, advise, and assist" those who did. This initially took the form of allowing students to meet at La Piranya and then involved defending them when the police used violence to crush the boycott.[29] "The Chicano students were the main action group," stated Sánchez later. "The Brown Berets were at the walkouts to protect our younger people [the students ranged in ages from 14 to 18, while the Berets were 18 to 24 years old]."[30] Such action won wide approval among the students. "Who Are the Brown Berets?" asked the *Chicano Student News* . They are people, who "served, observed and protected the Chicano community."

When the cops moved in, it was the Berets that were dragged behind bars. THE BROWN BERETS became a target for the PLACA [the police], and anyone wearing one [a brown beret] was suspect to be picked up. It is the BROWN BERETS who are presently behind bars or have warrants out for their arrests. You know, *ese,* when you lay it on the line, there are people who mouth about taking care of business, and there are people who TAKE CARE OF BUSINESS. The BROWN BERETS take care of business and leave the "politicking" and mouthing to others. The BROWN BERETS are strictly a defense organization but reserve the right and duty to defend themselves, Chicanos and La Raza wherever and by whatever means necessary. Already many community organizations have found this out and are in full support behind these young Chicanos who stand ready. Their numbers are growing, growing, GROWING. BUENO YA. . . . NO SE DEJAN.[31]

Support for the Berets increased when five of them (along with several other participants in the Blow Outs) were indicted by the Los Angeles County Grand Jury for engaging in conspiracies to disrupt the public schools, a felony punishable by up to forty-five years in the state penitentiary.[32] Following the arrests, *Inside Eastside* (a student newspaper) protested that "We will not tolerate the felony charges which . . . will prevent the Brown Berets from being effective because its leaders . . . will most likely be jailed."[33] The Berets quickly secured release on bail, but it took two years of litigation before the charges against the "conspirators" were dropped.[34] *La Raza* (a paper published by young Chicanos affiliated with the Church of the Epiphany) rallied to the defense of the Berets, arguing that Anglo injustices were the reason for their creation.

Because these injustices have existed and the Anglo Establishment shows no sign of changing them, because the cries of individuals have gone unheard and fallen upon deaf ears, a group of young Chicanos have come together under the name of the Brown Berets to demand an immediate end to the injustices committed against the Mexican-American. . . . The Brown Berets are not a gang, car club, or private social group; it is an organization of young Chicanos dedicated to serving the Mexican American community.[35]

The growing publicity about the Berets prompted the group to reex-amine its mission and in June 1968, in emulation of the Black Panthers,[36] whom they admired, to circulate a "Ten Point Program":

1. Unity of all of our people, regardless of age, income, or political philos-ophy.

2. The right to bilingual education as guaranteed under the treaty of Guadalupe-Hidalgo.

3. We demand a Civilian Police Review Board, made up of people who live in our community, to screen all police officers, before they are assigned to our communities.

4. We demand that the true history of the Mexican American be taught in all schools in the five Southwestern States.

5. We demand that all officers in Mexican-American communities must live in the community and speak Spanish.

6. We want an end to "Urban Renewal Programs" that replace our barrios with high rent homes for middle-class people.

7. We demand a guaranteed annual income of $8,000 for all Mexican-American families.

8. We demand that the right to vote be extended to all of our people regard-less of the ability to speak the English language.

9. We demand that all Mexican Americans be tried by juries consisting of only Mexican Americans.

10. We demand the right to keep and bear arms to defend our communities against racist police, as guaranteed under the Second Amendment of the United States Constitution.[37]

The ten points were reformist, not revolutionary. The Berets did not call for the overthrow of the U.S. government, but, rather, grounded many of their demands on the U.S. Constitution, the Bill of Rights, and the Treaty of Guadalupe Hidalgo. They also saw themselves as safekeepers of the Chicano community, a responsibility that found expression in their new three-part motto: "to serve, to observe, and to protect." "To serve" meant giving "vocal as well as physical support to those people and causes which will help the people of the Mexican-American communities," while "to observe" required keeping "a watchful eye on all federal, state, city and private agencies which deal with the Mexican American, espe-cially law enforcement agencies." As for the words "to protect," they meant working to "guarantee . . . and secure the rights of the Mexican American by all means necessary." The "means necessary" (reminiscent of

Sánchez's "any and all means necessary"), explained the Berets, depended upon the actions of those in power. If the Anglo establishment accommodated their demands "in a peaceful and orderly process, then we will be only too happy to accept this way. Otherwise, we will be forced to other alternatives."[38]

Like the Black Panthers, the Berets expressed a fondness for Marxism, with some of them also seeking guidance in the writings of Mao Zedong and arguing for the need to be "one with the masses of the people."[39] This caused tension within the organization, especially when Cruz Olmeda and several others took Mao's words to heart and insisted that the Berets be transformed into a militia in the service of the community. Sánchez, on the other hand, believed that the Berets should only *appear* to be a military group, projecting the image rather than the reality of a revolutionary cadre. His Cold War upbringing had produced in him a deep fear of Communism that became so intense that he burned Marxist literature. He also knew firsthand about violent police repression and believed the police would destroy the Berets if they moved in a Marxist direction.[40]

At first, Beret leaders also disagreed among themselves about the group's recruitment policies. The approximately thirty members who had joined the Berets by mid-1968 were mostly recruited from local high schools and now ranged in ages from 14 to 18.[41] Sánchez wanted to continue the emphasis on enlisting high-school students but Olmeda disagreed, arguing that such a policy would prevent the group from reaching a revolutionary takeoff point and relegate it to being just another pacifist organization. These differences were exacerbated by each man's personal desire to control the organization. The conflicts ended only when Olmeda and seven of his followers left the Brown Berets in July 1968 and founded a group called "La Junta," which recruited former gang members and aligned itself with adult leftists, reputed members of the Communist Party.[42]

The bickering among the Berets was accompanied by some criticism of the group from Mexican Americans. Not everyone shared the Berets' alienation from American society. In a letter in *La Raza,* a Lincoln High School student proclaimed his opposition to the group. "This is our country — the greatest country in the world and this is our school — the best there is!!! We love our country and our school so let's tell it like it is." The Berets, declared the student, were "outsiders" who had done nothing for "our country" or for "our community. . . . WE, THE REAL STUDENTS OF LINCOLN HIGH, demand that all you BROWN BERETS and outsiders leave our school alone. WE don't need you or want you. GET OUT!!!" [43]

Most residents, however, were either silent or vigorously defended the Berets. The student letter, for example, sparked a hostile response accusing the writer of doing the work of "The Man" and going "along with the white man's disinterest." The Berets, declared the rejoinder, were helping the community and fighting discrimination, as evidenced by their participation in "the Poor People's Campaign" organized in Washington, D.C., by the Southern Christian Leadership Conference. Moreover, they supported the United Farm Workers' struggle and, locally, were promoting educational reform and the introduction of classes in Mexican history, "not Anglo history that excludes the contributions of your forefathers."[44]

Although other periodicals reported on the Berets' activities, the organization initiated its own newspaper, *La Causa,* on May 23, 1969. Describing the monthly as "a Chicano newspaper dedicated to serve the Chicano barrio with local and national news," the Berets promised to reveal "the many injustices against the Chicano by the Anglo establishment," to inform "the Raza of current and coming events," and to seek "to better relations and communications between barrios throughout the country."[45] Sánchez, the editor, exhorted the Berets to redouble their efforts on behalf of the community and kept coming back to what he called the "8 Points of Attention": "(1) Speak politely to the people; (2) Pay fairly for what you buy from the people; (3) Return everything you borrow; (4) Pay for anything you damage; (5) Do not hit or swear at the people; (6) Do not damage property or possessions of people; (7) Do not take liberties with women; and (8) When working with the people do not get loaded."[46]

Though Sánchez exercised a powerful influence over the organization, he was not present at an incident that first dramatically brought the Brown Berets to the attention of those outside the Chicano community. This took place at Los Angeles's Biltmore Hotel during the third annual "Nuevas Vistas" Conference in April 1969. Arranged by State Superintendent of Public Instruction Max Rafferty, the convocation was a gathering of Mexican-American educators charged with exploring ways to improve relations between the schools and the Mexican-American community. Also participating were students from chapters of the United Mexican American Students (UMAS) at UCLA and the California State College campuses at Los Angeles, Long Beach, Fullerton, and Northridge. The keynote speaker for the Friday night banquet was Governor

Ronald Reagan, whose election in 1966 had weakened the power base of Mexican Americans in Sacramento. As a preeminent symbol of the "Anglo establishment," his presence almost guaranteed a disruption.[47]

Reagan had hardly begun his speech before shouts from some in the audience tried to drown him out. The protesters loudly denounced the condescending attitudes of educators and cuts in affirmative action programs. Firecrackers dropped from the mezzanine to the Biltmore Bowl floor, as fourteen demonstrators began doing the "famous Chicano clap." The governor shouted over the din that "these are the few that are wrecking what we are attempting to build," but the protesters succeeded in breaking up the proceedings and taking over the dance floor, until approximately fifty police and Biltmore security officers arrested them for disrupting a public assembly.[48]

In the meantime, authorities outside the banquet hall had barred other ticket-holding Mexican Americans from entering. When they heard the claps coming from inside, those waiting at the door joined in and began shouting "Viva la Raza!" The chants and claps subsided when the Chicanos realized that those emerging from the room were mostly non-Mexicans.[49] By that time, fires had broken out on the mezzanine and the second, fourth, ninth, and tenth floors. The blazes remained small and confined to linen closets, where they had been started with highway-type flares. Some guests had to be removed from their rooms, but no one was evacuated from the hotel. The damage was later estimated at $15,000.[50]

On June 9 the Los Angeles County Grand Jury indicted ten Chicanos for starting the fires.[51] The indictments were based on testimony provided by Fernando Sumaya, an undercover Los Angeles police officer who had infiltrated the Berets. The charges carried a possible maximum sentence of life in prison for each of those involved.[52] The first trial of two of those who were indicted (Ramírez and Cebada) ended in a mistrial in August 1971. Their second trial ended in May 1972 with acquittal verdicts on the grounds of insufficient evidence. Seven of the eight others indicted were never tried. Montes, who out of fear for his life went into hiding in 1970, was not brought to trial until 1979, when he was acquitted for lack of evidence.

The Berets believed that law enforcement agencies were the principal threat to Mexican Americans in the United States. They became even more convinced with the disappearance of Montes following his indictment for the Biltmore fire. *La Causa* attributed his disappearance to his being kidnapped by the CIA: "Sergeant Abel Armas (LAPD) of the Special Operation Conspiracy (SOC) has conspired to destroy Carlos Montes and

Brown Beret leaders by taking the law into their own hands which is typical of CIA policy." Montes was "truely [*sic*] a Chicano Revolutionist that has put his life on the line more than once for his Raza."[53] *La Causa* featured a likeness of him on its masthead for six months, effectively raising Montes's heroic status to mythical proportions.[54]

In the meantime, Montes had fled with his wife to El Paso, Texas, where he changed his name to Manuel Gómez and worked for seven years as a carpenter and a maintenance mechanic in the garment industry. In 1979 he returned to Los Angeles, where he voluntarily surrendered to authorities, was tried for conspiracy to commit a felony (arson), and acquitted.[55]

Sumaya's testimony during Montes's trial revealed that the Los Angeles Police Department had been systematically monitoring the Berets for four months. Going by the LAPD code name of S-257, Sumaya had joined the Berets in December 1968, grown a beard, and posed as a dedicated rebel. He alleged that on the day of the Biltmore Hotel incident he had met with Ralph Ramírez and Carlos Montes at the Brown Beret headquarters at 11 A.M. that morning. The three then went to the Biltmore and picked up Esmeralda Bernal, who was a San Jose State College student attending the conference. They drove to East Los Angeles College for a meeting of "La Vida Nueva," the campus's Mexican-American group. There, Willie Mendoza, an East Los Angeles College student, conducted a workshop on guerilla warfare tactics and civil disobedience. At the workshop Montes interrupted Mendoza, telling him that those present should not just talk about such acts but should actually perform them. The time to begin, he announced, was that night at the Biltmore Hotel, where they should disrupt Reagan's speech by breaking windows, turning off electrical power, and setting off fire alarms. Those present agreed. Montes added that he would purchase flares to ignite in the hotel. He also suggested that everyone choose a partner. That night about twenty people (including Ramírez, Montes, James Vigil, Ernesto Eichwald Cebeda, Moctesuma Esparza, and Rene Nuñez) gathered in Bernal's room (number 7341 of the Biltmore) to plan the evening's activity.[56]

Most of those present advocated walking out as soon as Reagan commenced his speech, while others proposed cutting the wires to the microphone. With a course of action unresolved, Ramírez, Montes, Cebeda, and Sumaya decided to take matters into their own hands. They left the room and went downstairs to look for an electrical power switch. When they failed to locate one, they went to the hotel's roof, where Montes spotted a metal cabinet labeled "Danger High Voltage." He stated that he would return to the roof after dark. The four then went back to room 7341 where they learned that in their absence the others had decided on a course of action. Two people would stand up in the middle of Reagan's speech. That would be a signal to the others to rise and begin shouting in order to silence the governor. Someone would then cut the wires to the microphone. In the meantime, two people stationed at the doors would let in those waiting outside so they could participate in disrupting the meeting.[57]

At Montes's trial, Sumaya testified that Montes had set the fires. According to his account, at approximately 7 P.M. he and Ramírez picked up Juan Ortiz, a "La Vida Nueva" member, in East Los Angeles and then returned to the Biltmore a half hour later. As they entered the lobby, they encountered Montes who announced, "Well that's one fire." Then, at approximately 8:15 P.M. Montes and Sumaya went to a mezzanine-level men's room near the Grand Avenue entrance of the hotel, where Montes told Sumaya, "Wait outside and call me if someone comes." Sumaya waited for about thirty minutes and then left. As he did so, he saw Montes igniting papers piled against the men's room door.[58]

At his trial, Montes accused Sumaya of starting the fire in the men's room. Sumaya had a history of violence, he claimed, citing in particular Sumaya's later involvement in the firebombing of a Safeway supermarket on May 10, 1969. According to Montes, on that occasion, Sumaya drove the car, provided the Molotov cocktails, and threw one of them into the store. He was accompanied by two youths to whom he promised membership in the Berets for helping him; the two were later arrested for the Safeway fire. Montes also accused Sumaya of openly using and advocating the use of such drugs as marijuana, "reds," and Seconal. In addition, he claimed that the undercover agent had advocated violence against the police and more militant actions on the part of the Brown Berets. Sumaya, stated Montes, was "a typical agent provocateur, advocating and committing illegal acts with the whole idea to get other members of the organization or their leaders busted, with the whole idea of trying to disrupt or destroy the movement of the Brown Berets."[59]

La Causa leveled similar charges against Sumaya. In an article entitled, "Is There a Frito Bandito in Your House?" the newspaper also criticized his personal life.

Brown Beret Intelligence reveals that the SUPER-HERO of the Dudley do-rights of the Protect and Serve Nazi Troops . . . was not so much in "the line of duty," but a married man who committed adultery, and a seducer of innocent young girls, and known by many males in this organization to be continuously looking for a girl. Casanova Sumaya had a tendency to have no self-control in the hand department, among other things. He was always trying to pick up young Chicanas from our barrios, and was a common sight on Whittier Blvd., trying to do his thing. There is no telling how many unwed mothers he left behind.[60]

Despite police infiltration and setbacks caused by trials, the Brown Berets persisted in their work on behalf of the Chicano community. A notable achievement was the creation of a free medical clinic in East Los Angeles, which opened in 1969.[61] The Berets established the clinic because they saw the need for free medical services for the East Los Angeles ethnic Mexican community. Modeled after the Fairfax Free Clinic in Hollywood, the facility opened on May 31, 1969, at 5016 East Whittier Boulevard and offered free social, psychological, and medical services as well as draft counseling. The only requirement for gaining entry was the "need to see a doctor." Open four days a week, the facility operated from 10 A.M. to 10 P.M. and maintained itself through donations from merchants, doctors, and other private benefactors, including the Ford Foundation, which provided funds for an endowment. Managing the facility was a board of directors composed of representatives from the community as well as medical professionals.[62]

Another project that attracted Beret participation was the Chicano antiwar effort. Despite their disparaging attitude toward college students, the Brown Berets joined with them to mount a major campaign against the Vietnam War. Among students, the initiative came from a group of Chicanos at UCLA who were particularly upset about the disproportionate number of Chicanos dying in the war, at a 3-to-1 ratio to whites.[63] In December 1969 the Berets and a group of college students formalized their alliance against the war by creating the Chicano Moratorium Committee, with David Sánchez of the Brown Berets and Rosalio Muñoz, a UCLA student, serving as co-chairs. Almost immediately, on December 20, they staged a demonstration against the war that attracted three thousand protesters. They had obviously touched an issue of widespread concern, one that also aroused hundreds of thousands of people of every ethnicity across the nation. But for Chicanos, as *La Causa* declared, the war was seen as "a matter of survival" and "freedom." The newspaper believed that the "the Vietnam War is the ultimate weapon of genocide of non-white peoples by a sick decadent *puto* western culture." It viewed the war as "a turning point in the history of mankind" because the "Vietnamese have shown that man's spirit and will to survive can overcome the most brutal punishment ever netted [*sic*] out to any nation." The newspaper went on to suggest parallels between the Vietnamese peoples' struggle for liberation and that of Chicanos. It called for Chicanos to learn from the Vietnamese "that to resist is to survive a free man and to submit is to be a *puto* and thus a slave. Dare to Struggle, Dare to Win — Hasta La Victoria Siempre!"[64]

During the next three years the Brown Berets proclaimed their message in other demonstrations and through symbolic acts. In an effort to "reconquer [Chicanos'] rights to be treated like people, and not like second-class citizens," the Berets initiated "La Caravana de la Reconquista" and drove through five southwestern states (California, Arizona, Colorado, New Mexico, and Texas) between October 1971 and August 1972.[65] Led by David Sánchez, the Berets participating in the "Caravan" issued their goals for the "National Policies of 1972," proclaiming "absolute militarism . . . [as] the fastest and strongest way to Chicano power."[66] They also underscored their intense sense of cultural nationalism and their view of themselves as a conquered people in their own land.

> We the Chicano people of the Southwest hereby declare ourselves a nation, and as a nation that has been the subject of a profit-making invasion. We are a nation with a land that has been temporarily occupied. And we are a nation with the ability to survive. We are a nation with great natural culturability. We are a nation, we who come from different ways, combining ourselves in one nation.[67]

The Berets called for reclaiming the Southwest and dramatically, though only symbolically, demonstrated their resolve on August 30, 1972, by "invading" Santa Catalina Island off the southern California coast and remaining there for nearly a month until September 22. The pretext for the invasion was their contention that the isle, along with the other Channel Islands off the California shore, had not been included in the lands ceded to the United States by the Treaty of Guadalupe Hidalgo following the U.S.–Mexico War.[68] The invasion was undoubtedly inspired by a similar action, the American Indian Movement's (AIM) takeover of Alcatraz Island in San Francisco Bay, from November 1969 to June 1971.[69] When, on August 30, 1972, in "Project Tecolote" (Project Owl) twenty-six Berets marched off the Catalina ferry and set up camp on land owned by the Santa Catalina Island Company, they attracted considerable public attention.[70] They left when asked to go by Judge William B. Osborne who, accompanied by Los Angeles County sheriffs, told them that they were in violation of an Avalon ordinance prohibiting camping in an area zoned for single-family dwellings. Following the warning, they unceremoniously abandoned "Campo Tecolote."[71]

The Catalina Island incident marked the last of the Berets' attention-grabbing exploits. Shortly thereafter, quarreling among the leaders robbed the organization of its effectiveness and it gradually disappeared. The bickering seems to have begun because of the ever-larger role being played by David Sánchez. He had always been prominent, first because of his inspiring jailhouse writings that galvanized the Berets during their earliest months, and later because of his role as editor of *La Causa*. Now, however, he was seen as exceeding his authority, writing about Beret policy without first getting permission of the Brown Beret National Headquarters Central Committee. He was also accused of having violated basic Beret tenets by killing a fellow member and committing rape. The final insult came when the Central Committee charged him with stealing money from the Berets. The committee fired him on October 21, 1972.[72]

Sánchez responded by calling a press conference and announcing that he was resigning and disbanding the organization. The Berets, he claimed, had a membership of five thousand in ninety chapters, but he was dissolving the group because others were using it "as a vehicle for their own purposes" and he feared there would be bloodshed. He also attributed his action to "police harassment and infiltration, internal squabbles and 'hippie-ism' among members, which ruined discipline."[73] Perhaps one reason for the Brown Berets' demise was Sánchez's narrow vision of a male-dominated Chicano community.[74] The Brown Berets disseminated a highly masculine view of what it meant to be a Chicano and they practiced this concept in symbolic ways: the organization's paramilitary structure, the exclusion of women from leadership positions, and the emphasis on recruiting young men as members.[75] Almost every issue of *La Causa* featured a recruitment appeal that urged readers to "Join Today" (listing meeting dates and times) and primarily targeted lower-income males who had little formal education and were gang members, the so-called "*vatos locos*." Illustrations depicted potential recruits as wearing *cholo* garb and carrying a bottle of beer underneath a banner proclaiming "Bato Loco Yesterday." That picture was followed by another showing the same man in a Beret uniform, with his right arm outstretched and his fist clenched in the power symbol. A banner above proclaimed "Revolutionist Today, Be Brown, Be Proud, Join the Brown Berets" (see figures 2 and 3).[76] Like the Boy Scouts of nineteenth-century England, the Berets sought to create a healthy nation of clean-living young men.

The Berets disparaged college students, however, even those belonging to UCLA's Movimiento Estudiantil Chicano de Aztlán (MEChA), as "bureaucrats" and out of touch with the community.

FIGURES 2 and 3. "Bato Loco Yesterday" and "Brown Beret Today" illustrations in the Brown Beret Newspaper *La Causa* depicted the organization's targeted audience (or represtative subject).

They have never related to the off-campus Chicano community in Venice or the Eastside and have alienated a substantial number of the current Hi-Potential students [a special admissions program at UCLA]. This group used to be on an ultra cultural nationalist kick, affecting the speaking of the Cholo dialect which sounded ridiculous because its pronunciation had a heavy English accent. Most of these people never toked a joint until they came to college — a white hippy undoubtedly taught them how, however they were and are extolling the virtues of the Cholo.[77]

As for women, the Berets patronized them and saw their contributions as of a lesser order of importance. Women were welcomed into the organization, but their roles were subordinate to those of men. They met at different times and in different buildings, where they focused on serving the male leadership's needs: bailing them out of jail, organizing a fundraiser for their activities, or typing the newspaper that carried information about men's actions. The men, on the other hand, busied themselves with the more weighty questions: planning demonstrations and discussing Beret policies and strategies. Women played a significant role, stressed *La Causa,* yet the newspaper's description of their activities indicated otherwise.[78] In an article entitled "Beautiful Bronze Women All Over Aztlán," Gloria Arellanes wrote that women "are beginning to realize how valuable they are in beauty and the movement."

Your role will be whatever you have to offer your people, whether it be leadership, a good rap, cooking or just to become involved, aware and educated, but find out. Every person has something to offer, every person is valuable. Get your head together, be aware — teach your awareness to those that are lost — teach your awareness to all those around you.[79]

That "awareness" took the form of an anonymously written love poem, "Mi Amor," in a subsequent issue. "To my eyes/A Chicana is an exotic queen,/She radiates a glow of exquisite sheen." Certainly, these saccharine lines only heightened the objectification of women. They were, as George Mosse has said of women within other national discourses, "sedate rather than dynamic," providing the "backdrop against which men determined the fate of nations."[80] In another *La Causa* article, "Chicanas de Aztlán," the author claimed that "women in the Brown Beret organization have left behind the traditional role that the Chicana has held for the past hundreds of years," but his description of their new "duties and assignments" were supportive roles: "anything from getting a brother out of jail to planning a fund raiser." Frequently, women acknowledged their traditional status. "We're not talking about women's liberation," announced one woman, "because, like that's not ours — we're talking about our Raza's liberation and in order to get our Raza liberated we all have to work together within our Raza."[81] By denying women full and meaningful participation in the struggle for liberation, the Brown Berets not only had a restricted concept of community but also lessened the attractiveness of their organization to women's participation.[82]

Yet gender bias and internal bickering were not the only reasons for the Berets decline. From the beginning they were plagued by harassment from law-enforcement authorities and weakened by infiltrators. Besides Sumaya, there were at least two other local infiltrators. Police officer Abel Armas began working within the Berets in 1967 while a member of the LAPD's Criminal Conspiracy Section. A year later, he was joined by Los Angeles County Deputy Sheriff Robert Acosta, who remained undercover from May 1968 through April 1969. Their assignments resulted from a law enforcement belief that the Berets were a subversive organization involved in bombings, fires, and the killing of deputy sheriffs and policemen. Acosta later testified that he attended many Beret functions, but never saw anyone commit a criminal act.[83] Documents obtained through the Freedom of Information Act reveal that beginning in March 1968 the Federal Bureau of Investigation also began investigated the organization.[84] The reason for doing so was the FBI's belief (shared by other law enforcement agencies) that the Berets were controlled by "rabble rousing" Mexican Americans who were apt to incite "racial violence" and therefore posed a threat to national security. The FBI continued their surveillance for more than five years, until the group's dissolution in November 1973, focusing not only on activities in Los Angeles but also on ethnic Mexican communities outside of California.[85] Eventually, the FBI came to the conclusion that the Berets were not acting in a subversive manner.[86]

The Brown Berets' short-lived, yet celebrated, existence, as "a new symbol" for challenging the "Anglo Establishment" mirrored the Black Panthers' experience. Like the Panthers, they pushed a paramilitaristic form of cultural nationalism that captured the imagination of the young, particularly young men, beginning with the "Blow Outs." Later, they caught the attention of a larger audience in their support of health projects and especially in their protests against the Vietnam War. Though the Brown Berets did little to change the status quo, they were not without significance, for their example inspired others equally dedicated to reform and the creation of Aztlán.

"Chale No, We Won't Go!"

The Chicano Moratorium Committee

The Vietnam War had a profound effect on Chicano youth of the 1960s and '70s. The high proportion of Mexican Americans fighting and dying in Southeast Asia, coupled with these young people's heightened awareness of social issues, led to a vigorous protest against the war. In this maelstrom of discontent, Rosalio Muñoz, a former UCLA student-body president and in 1968 a minority recruiter for the Claremont Colleges, received his induction orders in December of that year for the following September. "I was concerned and wanted to do something," he later recalled, "but when I was drafted, and it happened to be for September 16, it catalyzed for me as . . . an opportunity to strike a blow against the war and the draft."[1]

Though Muñoz's initial motives were inherently selfish, he quickly became convinced that he had "to do something for all Chicanos."[2] There was, first of all, the symbolic importance of the day on which he was to report for induction: September 16 was Mexican Independence day. He had also already become disenchanted with the draft because of his experiences at the Claremont Colleges. The Chicano students whom he visited told him how draft boards tried to discourage them from considering college by telling them that student deferments were not available. These incidents only served to crystallize Muñoz's sense of the war as an act of discrimination against Mexican Americans. As he saw it, "There were so few of us even qualified [to go to college] and those that were qualified they would try to discourage to get a deferment." For him, "the horribleness of the war and discrimination against people and then the upsurge of peoples' forces and of the Chicano Movement" created the climate necessary for a Chicano struggle against the conflict in Vietnam.[3]

Initially, Muñoz set out to organize protests against the draft, not the war. Shortly after receiving his induction orders, he discussed his plan with his friend and former fellow student Ramsés Noriega. Muñoz turned to him because of the latter's experience as an organizer with the United Farm Workers and as the manager of Muñoz's earlier campaign for student-body president. The two had also worked closely in founding the United Mexican American Students. Noriega warned Muñoz that what he proposed was dangerous. "Do you want to die?" he asked his friend. "Because what you're asking is to take on the United States government on this. It's a very large issue, very dangerous — many people will die." "I'm ready to die," replied Muñoz. "If you're ready," responded Noriega, "let me think about it and start putting [together] a program of a movement." Several days later, the two embarked on a tour of the state to survey Mexican-American attitudes toward the war and the feasibility of their plan.[4] In August 1969, following the tour, they created Chale con el Draft (To Hell with the Draft) to aid individual Chicanos in their deliberations about whether to seek a deferment or to resist being drafted.[5]

Muñoz's own decision was to resist, and he chose September 16, 1969, the day that he had been ordered to report for induction, as the occasion for his announcement. His intention was to go through pre-induction processing and then to refuse induction.[6] On September 16, he went with more than a hundred supporters to the Armed Forces Induction and Examination Center on Broadway Street in Los Angeles. In an apparent effort to appease the crowd, officials postponed his induction until the October draft call.[7] This news caused Muñoz to pull from his pocket a prepared statement that he read to the press:

Today the sixteenth of September, the day of independence for all Mexican peoples, I declare my independence of the Selective Service System. I accuse the government of the United States of America of genocide against the Mexican people.

Specifically, I accuse the draft, the entire social, political, and economic system of the United States of America, of creating a funnel which shoots Mexican youth into Vietnam to be killed and to kill innocent men, women and children. I accuse the law enforcement agencies of the United States of instilling greater fear and insecurity in the Mexican youth than the Viet Cong ever could, which is genocide.

I accuse the American welfare system of taking the self respect from our Mexican families, forcing our youth to the Army as a better alternative to living in our community with their own families, which is genocide. I accuse the education system of the United States of breaking down the family structure of the Mexican people. Robbing us of our language and culture has torn the youth away from our fathers, mothers and grandparents. Thus it is that I accuse the educational system of undereducating Chicano youth.[8]

Muñoz's action brought him and his new organization instant recognition. It also caused him to realize that opposition to the draft was not enough. "Very quickly we began to see that [going against the draft] . . . was not actually going to change the problems of the war — the disproportionate number of Chicanos dying in the war."[9] Hard statistics on these deaths had only recently been brought to Muñoz's attention. They were the work of Ralph C. Guzmán, a founder of the CSO and MAPA, and, at the time, the sole Mexican American on the staff of the UCLA Mexican-American Study Project.[10] Guzmán, a recent Ph.D. in political science, revealed that between January 1961 and February 1967, a period when Chicanos constituted 10 to 12 percent of the population of the Southwest, they comprised 19.4 percent of those killed in Vietnam.[11]

Guzmán offered three reasons for the disproportionately high casualties. Mexican Americans joined the military in larger numbers than others in order to gain social status and to provide financial assistance to their families. They were also driven by a strong desire to prove their "Americaness." Finally, the number of Mexican Americans who could circumvent obligatory military service by going to college was quite small. At the University of California, for example, only 1 percent of the 97,000 students enrolled in 1969 were Chicanos.[12]

The economic factors pushing Chicanos into the military were strikingly evident in East Los Angeles, where the greatest concentration of Mexicans in the United States lived. The median income of a Mexican-American family was $7,622, as compared to the median income for all California families of $10,729, a difference of 29 percent. Of 23,752 families in East Los Angeles, some 3,974, or 17 percent, lived below the poverty line (as defined by the Social Security Administration).[13] Housing conditions were deplorable, with 75 percent of the 23,381 housing units having been built before 1949. In 1968 the Los Angeles County Department of Urban Affairs reported that only 28.67 percent of the houses in East Los Angeles were in livable condition.[14]

As they had been in previous decades, East Los Angeles residents were also subject to harassment from county sheriffs and city police. Law enforcement officials regularly stopped and questioned Mexican-American youths in the evenings, often using abusive language and sometimes beating them. Sheriff's deputies heavily patrolled the streets where youths congregated in East Los Angeles, issuing citations and stopping cars for no apparent reason.[15] If the streets were troublesome, the jails were deadly. In a two-year period, from 1968 to 1970, six Chicanos allegedly hanged themselves in the East Los Angeles sheriff's station. To many in the community, the deaths were acts of murder by the Sheriff's Department.[16] Residents felt besieged in their own community. "We not only face genocide when they shove us into the battlefields . . . but [also] when the police repress us on the streets of our own barrio," declared a resident. "Some cops inspire more fear and hatred than the Viet-Cong."[17]

To engage in a war abroad while these conditions existed at home became anathema to many Chicanos, especially the youth who were expected to fight the war. The combination of the social inequalities and the war's impact prompted young Chicanos to react angrily. Muñoz shared these sentiments and broadened his goal to ending not only the draft but also the entire war effort.[18] In November 1969 he quit his job with the Claremont Colleges and began a fast to protest the war. He chose his alma mater, UCLA, as the locale for his announcement. "I am beginning a fast which will continue until the people of this country realize that the genocide in Vietnam is, besides the Vietnamese, directed towards the Chicanos." He committed himself as well to combating "the most powerful and oppressive system the world has ever known."[19]

In the meantime, another Chicano effort against the war emerged in Denver under the leadership of Rodolfo "Corky" Gonzales. His Crusade for Justice had been criticizing the Vietnam involvement since August 1966. Gonzales knew of Muñoz's actions, but the two did not meet until November 15, 1969, at a symposium on "Chicano Liberation" held at California State College at Hayward. Muñoz suggested that they organize a nationwide demonstration by Chicanos against the war modeled after the moratoriums against the conflict that had been sponsored by the Student Mobilizing Committee (the MOBE) in October and November 1969. Gonzales liked the idea, and so did the three hundred people attending the symposium. The protest was to be a Chicano-run event. Other antiwar activists could attend, but Chicanos would be in charge.[20] As Noriega explained, "The reason why they [whites] were against the war was very different from why we were against the war."[21]

A planning meeting was held in Denver in early December 1969. Those present agreed that their national protest should take place in the summer of 1970 in Los Angeles. That gathering would be preceded by a smaller demonstration in Los Angeles in December to build enthusiasm for the main summer protest. Responsibility for the demonstrations would fall to the newly formed Chicano Moratorium Committee, created when the Brown Berets and student groups joined in their efforts to end the war. Also helping to generate support for the summer meeting would be a Youth Liberation Conference, already scheduled for March in Denver.[22]

On December 20, 1969, the Chicano Moratorium Committee, with David Sánchez and Rosalio Muñoz as co-chairs, staged a rousing protest that attracted two thousand people. Advertised as a "March Against Death" to "Bring All Our *Carnales* Home . . . ALIVE!," it began at twelve noon at the Memorial Monument (a memorial to Mexican Americans killed in the Second World War), located at Brooklyn and Indiana Streets in East Los Angeles.[23] Its success led to another demonstration on February 28, 1970, which attracted five thousand people despite a driving rain. Participants came from all over California, as well as from Colorado, New Mexico, and Texas. "It's time we got rid of this political system," declared local attorney Oscar Acosta. "It's time we did more than march; your whole life has to be for the Chicano. . . . So far as the Vietnam war is concerned, I have nothing to say about it; it doesn't exist; our fight is here." Woodrow "Niño" Díaz, speaking for the Puerto Rican Young Lords of New York, added: "This social system is killing our brothers in Vietnam. We have one enemy, the capitalist system and their agents in the Democratic and Republican parties. We must organize independent political parties along with Puerto Ricans and including poor whites in a political coalition."[24]

Not everyone warmed to the idea of joining with others, especially whites, in combating the war. Muñoz was among them, and he stressed the need for a *Chicano* antiwar movement.

Historically, Chicanos have only been offered the dirtiest work of American society. Chicanos pick the crops, man the factories, sew the clothes, wash the dishes and clean the mess of white America. . . . This demonstration aims to expose the fact that second to Vietnamese, the heaviest burdens of the war have fallen on the Chicano community. . . . The Chicano people, through its moratorium, is now saying that the front line for Chicano youths is not in Vietnam but is the struggle for social justice here in the United States.[25]

Though the rain soaked the demonstrators, it failed to dampen their ardor. They left the gathering chanting "Che, Che, Che Guevara" and waving red "Che" flags in the air.[26]

The three thousand people who convened in Denver on March 25–29,

1970, for the Chicano Youth Liberation Conference were just as outraged about the war and eagerly looked forward to the summer protest in Los Angeles, now set for August 29 (see figure 4). Indeed, by this time, demonstrations against the war were widespread, with eighteen taking place during the months before August in such cities as Fresno, Riverside, San Francisco, San Diego, Santa Barbara, San Antonio, Austin, Houston, and Chicago.[27]

The principal organizer of the protest scheduled for Los Angeles was Ramsés Noriega. He worked behind the scenes offering guidance and advice to Muñoz, who served as the co-chair and main spokesperson for the Moratorium Committee. Sánchez, the other co-chair, was responsible for garnering support from the Brown Berets, but enthusiastic help also came from many people in the community who were unaffiliated with a specific protest group. "Everybody [did] everything from stuffing envelopes to public speaking," explained a member of the committee.[28] A "semiofficial," volunteer central committee of ten to fifteen people planned the demonstrations. Central committee membership was acquired as a result of longtime commitment to the moratorium effort. Members ages ranged from 18 to 35, with most being in their twenties. Their plans were then presented to the community in open meetings where, usually after brief discussions and minor revisions, the recommendations won approval. Membership in the Moratorium Committee was open to all Chicanos who were willing to participate and who agreed with the Moratorium's nonviolent goals and tactics.[29]

Despite attempts to maintain consensus among those in the Moratorium Committee, disputes broke out. The most serious involved the Brown Berets, who became angry when the committee denied their request to have a speaker at the forthcoming summer moratorium. The hostility between the committee and the Brown Berets stemmed from the former's perception that the latter were only engaging in attention-grabbing efforts while having done little to protest the war.[30] Nonetheless, denial of a Beret speaker incensed David Sánchez and his followers, who convinced themselves that they had been responsible for the success of the protests of December 20 and February 28. The Berets' *La Causa* singled out Muñoz, Noriega, and Moratorium Committee member Robert Elias for special criticism, accusing them of being "ego trippers and opportunists." They also denounced the Moratorium Committee for funding the travel expenses of a "rumor and scandal team of which we have received reports from Fresno, Frisco, Oakland and Denver, in their purpose to sabatage [sic] and cut off Brown Beret National resources." These differences were eventually papered over, but not before the Berets

FIGURE 4. "National Chicano Moratorium" poster, August 29, 1970. Artist unknown.

threatened to disassociate themselves from the committee. When the Berets sensed that the demonstration would succeed without them, they reconsidered their stance and participated in the August 29 event.[31]

Such disagreements did not sidetrack effective publicity for the upcoming demonstration that emphasized a measure of ethnocentrism and cultural nationalist ideals.[32] The organizers' principle vehicle for reaching the public was Los Angeles's Spanish-language television station KMEX, Channel 34. Radio was also used, as Noriega said, "to make Los Angeles a classroom." Daily broadcasts on news radio station KFWB kept the community abreast of the plan for the moratorium.[33]

Security was considered as important as publicity in ensuring success for the August event. Organizers obtained the necessary parade permit and met regularly with officials of the sheriff's department (the law enforcement agency for unincorporated East Los Angeles, where the demonstration would take place), informing them of their plans and seeking advice. Two to three monitors were assigned to each block along the parade route in order to guarantee order. As another precaution, moratorium leaders created a special corps of attorneys and law students to observe the procession and provide legal advice.[34] To house the large number of people expected to come from out of town, California State College at Los Angeles offered its dormitory facilities. To the chagrin of everyone, however, the college rescinded its offer with no explanation on the day before the event. The out-of-towners were left to find their own lodging.[35]

On August 29, 1970, at 10 A.M. the demonstrators met at Belvedere Park on Third and Fetterly Streets. Eventually, an estimated twenty thousand people made their way to Whittier Boulevard, a mile from Belvedere Park, and occupied six lanes of the street. The atmosphere was festive. Marchers carried brightly colored banners and flags bearing the names of the groups represented: the Brown Berets, El Movimiento Estudiantil Chicano de Aztlán (MEChA), and the Emma Lazarus Jewish Woman's League, among others. Also much in evidence were placards carrying such slogans as "CHALE CON LA DRAFT," "BRING THE 'CARNALES' HOME," "OUR WAR IS HERE," and "DEAR MOM AND DAD, YOUR SILENCE IS KILLING ME." Chanting "Chale No, We Won't Go!" and "Chicano Power!" the paraders proceeded peacefully down Whittier Boulevard. County sheriffs dressed in full riot gear lined the route.[36] They remained in position because the moratorium monitors took swift action at any sign of a potential outburst, as when a demonstrator threw a rock. At approximately 1:00 P.M. the procession reached Laguna Park and the rally began.[37]

The program proceeded peacefully. Thirteen speakers from a variety of organizations, among them Rodolfo "Corky" Gonzales of Denver's Crusade for Justice, attorney Oscar Acosta, and Rosalío Muñoz, addressed the crowd. The program opened with three entertainment groups that reinforced the peaceful, festive atmosphere. Muñoz then spoke, calling for social change and pointing out that a war had now broken out in East Los Angeles — a war for social justice. He asked for support of Chicano leaders, specifically naming Ricardo Romo, the Peace and Freedom Party candidate for California governor.[38] When he suggested that Laguna Park be renamed Benito Juárez Park in memory of the nineteenth-century Mexican president, the crowd roared its approval, prompting Muñoz to proclaim that the park's name had been changed.[39]

In the meantime, a dispute had begun across the street at the Green Mill Liquor Store. Because of the hot weather, many paraders had gone to the liquor store, the only establishment open in the area, to buy soft drinks and beer. When about fifty customers had filled the building, the owner, Morris Moroko, locked the door. Moroko then refused to unlock the door so individual customers could depart, intending to open it once all the customers inside had completed their transactions. After a half-hour with the doors still locked, many customers became restive, as the cold drinks they purchased got warm. Moroko panicked and called the sheriffs. At 2:34 P.M. three officers arrived, two carrying clubs while the other held a riot gun. Immediately, the door was unlocked and the deputy sheriffs inquired about the "looting." Meanwhile, outside the store, someone tossed an empty can at the sheriff's car parked in front. Within minutes, approximately twenty-five officers were on the scene.[40]

The deputies formed a skirmish line at the store, which was only several hundred yards from the speakers' platform. Most of the people at the rally, however, had their backs turned to the fracas and were unaware of the sheriffs.[41] By 3:10 P.M. deputies with riot guns had stationed themselves at hastily set up street-corner barricades. They then declared the situation to be critical and told those assembled outside the store to disperse.[42] Instead of moving people away from the site, however, the officers pushed and followed them to nearby Laguna Park, where Muñoz was speaking. When he saw the deputies charge the crowd, he shouted at them, "Police, hold your line!"[43] The Moratorium monitors then formed a line of their own between the people and deputies and asked the officers to leave. The deputies responded by calling for reinforcements, including the LAPD. As squad cars arrived and plainclothes policemen went into the throng trying to arrest the protesters, some in the multitude began pelting the police with rocks and bottles, which, in turn, gave the deputies the excuse to move further into the masses.[44]

Many people now began to exit the park and seek safety in adjacent homes. Police shot tear-gas canisters onto the front porches of those homes, causing even more paraders to seek refuge in other houses. Officers also began boarding buses and beating passengers who had sought shelter there. Angered by the police actions, many in the crowd returned to Whittier Boulevard and began breaking the windows of white-owned businesses, sparing only those stores they believed were owned by Mexicans and other minorities. Two hours later, at around 6 P.M., with 1,500 officers occupying Laguna Park and the nearby streets, the violence came to an end.[45]

The melee resulted in 158 damaged buildings and 4 that were completely destroyed. Some four hundred people were arrested, an uncertain number hurt, and three killed. Angel Gilberto Díaz died when he tried to leave the area and rammed his car into a telephone pole. Lynn Ward, a fifteen-year-old Brown Beret, received fatal wounds from an explosion that hurled him through a plate-glass window. Witnesses testified that a tear-gas canister exploded in front of Ward, but the police claimed that a bomb planted by demonstrators killed him.[46]

The death attracting most attention was that of Ruben Salazar, a *Los Angeles Times* reporter who was well known and highly respected in the ethnic Mexican community. Salazar's weekly column in the *Times* sought to explain the Chicano community and its concerns to a larger public. His topics ranged from racism aimed at Mexicans to exploring ways to bridge the gap between Chicanos and the older "traditionalists" who were not always sympathetic with the aims of their youth.[47] He was in no sense a political activist, but his untimely death made him a martyr in the ethnic Mexican community, every bit as esteemed as John and Robert Kennedy, and Martin Luther King Jr. Salazar's death also dramatically affected the future of the Moratorium Committee.[48] Originally, he was thought to have been shot, but a subsequent investigation revealed he had been hit in the head by a tear-gas projectile as he sat inside the Silver Dollar Cafe on Whittier Boulevard, where he had gone in hopes of escaping the commotion.[49]

In the days that followed, the sheriff's department sought to discredit the Chicano Moratorium Committee. Peter Pitchess, who headed the department, accused the committee of never having intended a peaceful protest and cited leftist propaganda found at the demonstration site as evidence. Moratorium organizers vehemently disagreed, claiming that the event had begun as a peaceful demonstration against the war and the socioeconomic conditions of Mexicans and only became violent when the police overreacted and began brutalizing the crowd.[50]

The FBI had also been present in Laguna Park on August 29 and offered no support for Pitchess's claims. The views of the FBI agents present were sought by U.S. Attorney General John Mitchell, who wanted to brief President Richard Nixon on the matter in anticipation of his meeting in San Diego in September 1970 with Mexican President Gustavo Díaz Ordaz. Mitchell specifically wanted to know "whether there was substance in the allegations some persons may have traveled interstate for the purpose of inciting a riot." Here, he had in mind Gonzales, who had come from Denver. The FBI told him there was no evidence to support such charges.[51]

Perhaps the best example of the Los Angeles authorities' aims to discredit the Chicano Moratorium Committee and the August 29 march was the inquest into the death of Ruben Salazar.[52] This public drama — described by the *Los Angeles Times* as a "quasi-judicial proceeding that looks, acts and sounds a little bit like a trial, but isn't" — lasted from September 10 to October 5, 1970, and was televised live on local stations.[53] Conducted by the Los Angeles County coroner's office, with seven jurors, the inquest was actually an investigation into the August 29 violence, the Mexican-American character, sheriff's department procedures, and the credibility of Chicanos and law enforcement officials. The questions asked by the county attorneys probed all aspects of the march and were thinly disguised attempts to brand the Chicano activists as radical leftists. Mexican Americans responded with hostility to the questions and spoke passionately about the innocence of the marchers and parade organizers and especially about the injustice of Salazar's death.[54]

Police set the tone of the investigation on the first day when Captain Thomas W. Pinkston unhesitatingly blamed the violence on Chicanos. Immediately challenging him was Loyola University Law School student Robert Fernández, whose loud protests resulted in deputies quickly escorting him out of the room. That action brought a sharp reaction from Jorge "Cokie" Rodríguez, a former MEChA leader at Roosevelt High School. "You're being biased in this whole . . . thing," he yelled.[55] Such emotional outbursts punctuated the entire proceedings.[56] At 18, Rodríguez was the youngest member of the "blue-ribbon" committee composed of twelve community activists appointed by the coroner's office to quell any potential disruptions at the proceedings. Among the other blue-ribbon committee members were Father John Luce of Lincoln

Heights's Church of the Epiphany; Alicia Escalante and Robert Gándara, welfare rights activists; attorney Oscar Zeta Acosta; *La Raza* editor Raúl Ruiz; and Católicos Por La Raza member Gloria Chávez.[57]

By the time the inquest ended, sixty-one witnesses had testified, 204 exhibits had been offered in evidence, and 2,025 pages of repetitive testimony gathered. Though many residents of the Chicano community testified during the inquest, Moratorium Committee members refused to do so because, as Noriega explained, the proceedings were "a kangaroo court . . . a show." The coroner's jury had two verdicts: Salazar's death was at the hands of Deputy Sheriff Thomas Wilson, and it was accidental. Two weeks later, Los Angeles County District Attorney Evelle Younger affirmed that "no criminal charge [was] justified, and that [the] . . . case was considered closed."[58]

The investigation into the death of Ruben Salazar, along with the violence that occurred at the annual September 16th celebrations a few weeks later, led the Moratorium Committee to rethink its strategy.[59] In October 1970, during a well-attended demonstration against police abuse at the East Los Angeles sheriff's substation, the committee announced its intention to broaden its concerns to include police brutality.[60] The war in Southeast Asia would remain a major issue, but, as *La Causa* noted several months later, the committee was soon acting as if its "mission on that subject [had] . . . been accomplished. Anyone who participated on that day [August 29] is now clear on the fact that our war is here — that we really live in the belly of the monster."[61] The shift in focus had the potential of attracting wider support since it affected more people than those directly impacted by the draft and the war. On the other hand, by emphasizing a local issue, the committee weakened and then lost its coalitions with the Crusade for Justice and other antiwar groups.

The shift did not lessen the LAPD's and the sheriff department's harassment of the organization. On November 11, 1970, more than a dozen LAPD squad cars parked in front of the committee's office at 3053 Whittier Boulevard. There was no raid, probably because there were several Chicano law students and newspaper reporters present, but the police presence proved intimidating nonetheless. Two days later, on November 13, six officers of the Special Operations Conspiracy (SOC) squad entered the Moratorium headquarters without knocking. When asked for a search warrant, the officers pulled their revolvers. "This is all the search warrant we need," declared one of them. They then ransacked the office.[62]

The next night, November 14, approximately thirty officers of the LAPD Hollenbeck Division entered the building. A fight resulted, in which three teenage boys were injured and required medical attention. The young men were subsequently arrested and charged with "felonious assault on a police officer." In addition, three other men, Ralph Ramírez, Sergio Robledo, and Frank Martínez (who, it was later discovered, was an informant for the LAPD and the U.S. Treasury Department's Alcohol, Tobacco and Firearms Division) were also apprehended and charged with "interfering with an arrest."[63] The LAPD told Sue Marshall of the *Los Angeles Free Press* that the raid occurred after officers in a patrol car saw five young men sitting outside the Moratorium office with a shotgun. Moratorium Committee members, who were at the office during the confrontation, denied the accusation.[64]

A week later, there was another incident. On November 21, 1970, Los Angeles police officers followed eight Berets and one student from California State College at Los Angeles from the Moratorium office to the city of Downey (a suburb of Los Angeles). There, the young men were stopped and, according to *La Causa,* were charged with armed robbery on the flimsy grounds that a carbine (legally registered and containing no clip) was found in their car. No money or evidence of stolen goods was in the vehicle.[65]

These incidents led the committee to set up a weekly picket line on Saturday mornings at the Hollenbeck Division station of the LAPD on First Street in Boyle Heights.[66] Committee members followed this with a demonstration against police brutality in early January 1971. The protest consisted of a march from East Los Angeles to Parker Center, the Los Angeles Police Department's downtown headquarters. A flyer called for a large turnout:

The National Chicano Moratorium Committee, along with other community groups, has been attacked, harassed and beaten day after day since the August 29th Moratorium by flunkies of the LAPD. The Metro Squad and Hollenbeck Division of the L.A.P.D. have conspired with each other to annihilate the Movement in East Los Angeles. We are calling for a mass rally and demonstration on January 9, 1971, here in our community we have dared to speak out against the police brutality, and are now being attacked by a racist police department.

The flyer also noted other provocations: "Fifty-two members of the National Chicano Moratorium Committee have been arrested on false charges within a month. The L.A.P.D. along with the Sheriffs and FBI have shown us a good example of what kind of governmental conspiracy is going on by their ruthless murder of Ruben Salazar." The attacks were the result of a "conspiracy!"[67]

The leaflet attracted over a thousand people to Hollenbeck Park, from where they set out for Parker Center at 1 P.M. on January 9. As they reached the First Street Bridge, which crosses the Los Angeles River and links East Los Angeles to downtown, they encountered a large number of police who aroused anger by asking jaywalkers for identification and sometimes issuing them a citation. Upon arriving at Parker Center, some marchers congregated at a construction site across the street. After about an hour, a policeman announced through a loudspeaker that everyone at the building site had to clear the street or face immediate apprehension. As the participants began dispersing, a large formation of helmeted policemen emerged from the station while an equally large group of motorcycle officers confronted the demonstrators on the street. In the resulting melee, windows were broken and marchers were chased, beaten, and arrested.[68] By the end of the day, there had been thirty-six arrests and numerous, but no serious, injuries.[69]

In the aftermath of the violence, both the Moratorium Committee and the Los Angeles Police Department issued conflicting explanations. "We have a half-dozen people trying to sift the rumors and find out what really happened," declared Gonzolo Javier of the Moratorium Committee. "We don't want to guess now at the connection between the rally and the window-smashing. We hear too many rumors. It's too early to be sure of anything." Rosalio Muñoz, however, did not hedge his words, blaming the police for the violence and claiming that the protesters at Parker Center had been ready to disperse when the police tried to speed up their departure. The LAPD had another story: Inspector Peter F. Hagan stated that there had been no order to disperse until the crowd began throwing bricks and bottles at the officers, interfering with police employees attempting to enter a parking lot, and breaking the window of a passing car. LAPD Chief Edward Davis described the violence as the work of "Communist agitators working within the Mexican-American community." "By God," he declared, "we're going to have peace in this city. A revolution isn't going to start here."[70]

The events of January 9 led to a larger demonstration on January 31, which the Moratorium Committee publicized as the "Marcha por Justicia" (March for Justice). The committee, announced Muñoz, is "planning a non-violent demonstration, but if the officers attack there will probably be civil disobedience."[71] Police behavior, not the war, was the sole issue. "We must not forget the lesson of August 29th that the major social and political issue we face is police brutality," declared a leaflet calling for public support. "Since the 29th police attacks have been worse. Either the people control the police or we are living in a police state."[72]

Participants came to the protest site at Belvedere Park from all over Southern California, many of them walking from such areas as the San Fernando Valley, Long Beach, San Pedro, Santa Ana, and La Puente.[73] The rally ended peacefully with Muñoz telling the crowd, estimated by the *Los Angeles Free Press* at four thousand, to avoid provocative behavior. "Disperse peacefully — the most important part of the rally is the way we disperse. I hope you're going to respect those who came a long way. Don't go to the police station unless you want to get involved in a suicide." Unfortunately, not everyone heeded his advice. About a hundred young people gathered around the East Los Angeles sheriff's substation on Third Street, adjacent to Belvedere Park. They began chanting for the release of the prisoners inside: "Let them go! Let them go!"[74]

What followed next was a riot that resulted in the destruction of twelve sheriff's cars, one highway patrol vehicle, two floodlights, and a sign at the substation. In addition, more than eighty stores were burned or had their windows broken. Also destroyed were a bail-bond office and a car dealership, including six of the agency's cars. The riot produced ninety arrests, many injuries, and one death. Among those arrested were sixty-three men, eight women, and nineteen male juveniles. Seventeen adults and two juveniles sustained gunshot wounds, while two juveniles and sixteen adults suffered other injuries (included in this number were ten sheriff's deputies and one woman reserve officer). The one fatality of the day was Gustav Montag Jr., a twenty-four-year-old East Los Angeles College student who was killed when a ricocheting buckshot pellet pierced his heart. A resident of East Los Angeles, he went to the demonstration because, as his sister-in-law recalled, "he was just curious. . . . People were predicting a riot and he wanted to find out what one was like."[75]

In the days that followed, the Chicano Moratorium Committee blamed the police for the devastation. Muñoz, at a meeting of other Chicano leaders held on February 1 at the East Los Angeles Community Union (TELACU), charged that "the police opened fire with guns against people with sticks and stones. There was no order to disperse, no tear gas fired. They used Russian tactics [a probable reference to the force used by Russian troops against the citizens of Prague in August 1968]. They let the people come in and then they opened fire on them. They drew them in and then opened fire with guns."[76]

Muñoz weakened his explanation by also acknowledging that the crowd had ignored the warnings of both Moratorium Committee members and law enforcement officers. Monitors had used bullhorns in an attempt to disperse the crowd toward the north, away from the sheriff's substation and heavily traveled Whittier Boulevard. Nonetheless, one group had headed south. "I was making efforts to get bullhorns from the sheriff to get to the front of the crowd and disperse it," he said, "but they said they couldn't get them. We didn't get any kind of cooperation. The monitors tried to get to the front of the crowd but before they could force their way to the front the police had opened fire." KMEX reporter Roberto Cruz confirmed the presence of an angry and unruly crowd. "They were . . . screaming and waving rocks and what looked like sticks. I tried to talk to some of them to ask them to go home, and one wanted to fight me." He continued, "It looked like a thousand of them were streaming down the street. Then one sheriff's car arrived with three officers in it. The mob kept on coming. The officers stepped back a few paces, firing in the air. I ducked, and when there were more shots I looked up and saw men falling."[77]

Richard Martínez of the Congress of Mexican American Unity testified to much the same. He told the *Times* that he had joined Muñoz at the sheriff's substation and tried to "keep things calm." "The crowd went on," he said. "I tried to get up in front of it, but it had gone on. There didn't seem to be a leader; it was more a spontaneous thing."[78]

The sheriff's department blamed the Moratorium Committee for the violence. Two days after the disruption, Sheriff Peter Pitchess informed a press conference that, while the committee professed to serve the best interests of the Mexican-American people, it had "accomplished nothing but destruction." Later, Pitchess told the Los Angeles County Board of Supervisors that the five events staged by the committee in the last six months had reaped "a rather grim harvest — vandalism, arson, burglary, assault and death." The rally and the rioting that followed, he declared, were "typical of the pathetic pattern [of the Moratorium Committee] — a grave disservice to the Mexican-American people." Pitchess also accused Muñoz of engaging in deception. Muñoz, he stated, told him prior to the event that the police brutality issue was just an "attention getter," and that the demonstration was actually to protest inadequate housing and education. "Muñoz said law enforcement people were simply the visible symbol of the establishment against whom they were revolting. The only hope for stopping this," declared Pitchess, using words reminiscent of Richard Nixon's, is for "the silent majority in the Mexican-American community to stand up on their feet and say we don't want this," by which he meant the "hoodlum element of the Moratorium group." Muñoz denied he had told Pitchess that the brutality issue was only an attention-getter. "I told him we have to overcome the fear placed upon us by his and other agencies before we can deal with the issues of life, such as better housing and education."[79]

The recriminations ended but not the bitterness between the Moratorium Committee and the law enforcement agencies. The district attorney's office heightened that bitterness when it filed formal charges against those arrested. Eight persons were indicted for felonies and forty-one for misdemeanors. In addition, charges were filed against twenty juveniles.[80]

Several sheriff's deputies were also charged with mistreatment of prisoners following the January 31 demonstration. On February 4 the Sheriff's department dismissed deputies Roy C. Bell, Michael W. Crowley, and George Guinn for hitting two prisoners who had shouted obscene remarks at them and for firing type of gas aerosol spray, called a "federal streamer," through the bars of a holding tank. The department also suspended Sergeant Robert T. Decker for five days for failing to stop the above incident, and charged Sergeant John Love with improper behavior and then later reassigned him.[81]

Following the January 31 demonstration the Moratorium Committee kept a low profile, reassessing its tactics and finally deciding to take its message to other parts of the state. In May it held a "Marcha de la Reconquista," which began on May 5 in Calexico, in southeastern California near the Mexican border, and proceeded to Sacramento, covering approximately eight hundred miles before ending on August 7. Implicit in the march's name was the notion that the land — the Chicano nation — rightfully belonged to Chicanos and needed to be taken back from the Anglo invaders. This protest revealed that the Moratorium had abandoned its single-issue focus on police brutality in favor of a wide range of vague goals. "The events of the last few months," announced a leaflet, "have clearly shown us that it is useless to place any trust in the present political system." Now the issues, besides police brutality, included Immigration and Naturalization Service deportations of undocumented Mexican workers; the Vietnam War; attempts by California State College at Los Angeles officials to remove Chicano student groups from the campus and to reduce funding for Educational Opportunity Programs (EOPs); and Governor Ronald Reagan's proposed reform of the state welfare program.[82]

The march proceeded peacefully until August 7, when it reached Sacramento. There, the participants, now numbering about two thousand, gathered at South Side Park, approximately two miles from the State Capitol, where they rested and ate a lunch provided by a local Chicano organization before going on to the Capitol building. For that march, they arranged themselves in double columns, with the Brown Berets as monitors and the Mescaleros (a Chicano bike club) leading the way and securing the traffic ahead. As they approached the Capitol, the protestors noticed other Chicanos on the building's steps and joined with them in shouting "Chicano Power," "Que Viva La Raza," and other slogans. A large Mexican flag was placed in the center of the steps and then surrounded by banners from other organizations. A sense of elation ran through the crowd and, according to a participant, "tears ran from the marchers eyes."[83]

The joy was short-lived. As Beret leader David Sánchez began speaking to the crowd, someone lowered the American flag from the pole in the Capitol plaza and set it on fire while others hoisted the Mexican flag to the same pole. Two dozen masked police in riot gear proceeded to haul down the Mexican flag and return it to the marchers. That action aroused the demonstrators' anger and caused the Brown Berets to lock arms and form a buffer between the authorities and the Chicanos. Both sides remained calm and the police left the area.[84]

Not long thereafter, as another speaker addressed the rally and the California state flag was lowered from its pole, the police returned and charged the demonstrators. Again the Berets locked arms and formed a buffer. Once more, both sides avoided violence and the police retreated. Alarmed at what could occur, however, march organizers ended the rally and the demonstrators left the capital peacefully.[85]

This rally was the last for the Moratorium Committee, since shortly thereafter the group disbanded. The immediate cause was an incident at nearby Deganawidah–Quezalcoatl University (D.Q.U.), a Native American–Chicano university located seven miles north of Davis, California.[86] Many of the marchers were staying at D.Q.U. before returning home. On August 7 forty-three young men from Oxnard arrived at the university seeking to kill Brown Berets. It seems that a group posing as Berets had beaten up one of the members of the Oxnard group in San Francisco and they wanted to retaliate. Ramsés Noriega believed that the people who did the actual beating were undercover law enforcement officers who hoped the Berets and the Oxnard group would engage in a fight, thereby giving the National Guard, which had a base in Sacramento, an excuse to violently end the conflict. He took aside David Sánchez and the leader of the Oxnard group and explained to them his suspicions, eventually persuading them and their followers to leave the area and go home.[87]

Not long after the incident, Noriega called a meeting of the Moratorium leadership and urged them to disband the organization. "The Moratorium is over. The reason why is that there is too many killings, too many attacks, everybody's confused, there's too many problems. . . . It's over with, go home, go underground and surface in ten years and maybe in ten years you'll know what has happened. But I am not going to be responsible for one death, because from now on the killings are going to escalate." Because those present respected Noriega, they went along with his request and disbanded the organization.[88] That the action was final became clear when the planned rallies scheduled for the weekend of August 28–29, 1971, did not occur.[89]

Though never a group with a national following, the Chicano Moratorium Committee had a large coterie in Southern California, where it brought greater awareness of the Vietnam War's effect on the Mexican-American community through mass demonstrations against the Anglo establishment. Chicanos, like other American youth of the 1960s and the 1970s, opposed the Vietnam War. Unlike their white counterparts, however, they viewed the disproportionate number of Spanish-surnamed casualties as evidence that the conflict was a genocidal war against Mexican-American males.

While the war served to unify a large number of Chicanos around a single issue, the effort gave way when the committee shifted its emphasis to local issues not shared with the Mexican-American communities elsewhere. Although police brutality occurred in other Chicano communities, the Moratorium Committee framed the issue as affecting only East Los Angeles. Thus, as broad concerns gave way to local issues, the committee fractured and lost its vitality and sense of larger purpose. Yet the Moratorium Committee had organized twenty thousand Chicanos — the largest gathering of that group in the nation — around a single issue, the Vietnam War. Even if that unity may have been for only one day, it was nonetheless significant, though to this day it has not been repeated.

4

"The Voice of the Chicano People"

La Raza Unida Party

Alarmed by the violence of the Chicano Moratorium and other demonstrations, many local activists returned to the formula pioneered by the Mexican American Political Association (MAPA): to work for reform peacefully and within the political system. They chose, however, a party of their own, since neither the Republicans nor the Democrats had effectively responded to their needs. The vehicle they found most attractive was La Raza Unida Party (LRUP), created in Texas in the early 1960s. "I . . . began to look at La Raza Unida Party," recalled Richard Martínez, a former member of the Congress of Mexican American Unity, "and the idea [of La Raza Unida Party] struck me because of the need to build as opposed to just have these 'golpes' [actions]" and "because I had seen people killed."[1]

La Raza Unida Party did not call for a unified plan of action by Chicanos in those states (primarily Texas, Colorado, and California) where it emerged. Rather, its agenda varied from place to place, with the only common feature among party chapters being a commitment to vote Chicanos into office. Specific programs and goals reflected the experience of local communities. In Los Angeles, the party mirrored a fragmented Chicano community held together by a desire to gain greater political power.

The roots of La Raza Unida can be found in Crystal City, Texas. In

1963 five Mexican Americans ("Los Cinco") were elected to the city council of the tiny South Texas town. Success was short-lived, however, when those elected failed to maintain the confidence of their constituents, who soon repudiated them. Nothing much happened thereafter until June 1969, when José Angel Gutiérrez arrived in Crystal City with his wife Luz and their first child.[2] Three months earlier, Gutiérrez had been released from the army reserve after serving six months of active duty. While in the service, he had come to the conclusion that the key to Chicano empowerment was partisan politics. After leaving the military, he attended a Mexican American Youth Organization (MAYO) meeting in San Antonio where he argued for creation of a third political party.[3] The conference seemed like the logical place to present his appeal, since MAYO had just participated in its first political campaign, endorsing three candidates for the San Antonio city council. Under the name of the Committee for Barrio Betterment, MAYO had challenged the conservative Good Government League, which had dominated San Antonio politics for more than two decades. One of the candidates, Mario Compeán, coined the expression La Raza Unida — "a united people" — and publicized the slogan in his campaign literature. He called for "Chicano self-determination" and a political alternative to the Republicans and Democrats. Though limiting his campaign to the westside barrios, he still came within a few hundred votes of attaining a runoff with the incumbent mayor. This experience prompted him to respond favorably to Gutiérrez's idea of a third party, but at first the community considered the notion premature.[4]

Most MAYO activists, while impressed with Compeán's showing, did not believe that a third party was feasible. They were more inclined to support a plan that would, it was hoped, lead to control of a particular area of Texas. Moreover, they sought to capture existing institutions rather than use confrontational tactics to gain power.[5] At the 1969 conference where Gutiérrez spoke in favor of a third party, the MAYO delegates shifted the discussion from such a party to how they could capture four possible target areas that had a large number of Mexican Americans. They had selected those regions based on four criteria: degree of poverty; Anglo political control, which made the identification of racism easier; the extent of successful MAYO activities, taken as a sign of probable future success; and the size of the Mexican-American population. The four targets were the so-called "Winter Garden" area, a seven-county tract that included Crystal City; Plainview and Lubbock in West Texas, with their significant number of former migrant workers and field hands; the

Kingsville area; and the Rio Grande Valley, which was the area closest to the Mexican border, had the largest number of migrant workers in the state, and was noted for being among the poorest parts of the country.[6] Eventually, the delegates decided on three of Winter Garden's seven counties: Zavala (where Crystal City was located), Dimmit, and La Salle. Residents there were familiar with the organizers: Gutiérrez hailed from Zavala, MAYO member Juan Patlán was from Dimmit, and the organization had a strong chapter in La Salle. Since Gutiérrez was especially anxious to organize his home area, Compeón appointed him head of the project.[7]

At the outset, Gutiérrez changed some of MAYO's tactics. Realizing that a rebellious approach would alienate rather than attract poor and tradition-oriented Mexican Americans, as had occurred when "Los Cinco" took over the city council of Crystal City in 1963, he called for a low-keyed, pragmatic strategy that avoided confrontation and inflexible ideological views.[8] His counsel proved attractive, and at MAYO's national conference at Mission City, Texas, in December 1969, he finally brought delegates around to building a third party as a means for achieving empowerment and reform. Delegates also agreed on the need to adapt readily to shifting political winds and to concentrate on achieving immediate results.[9] The conference's most important outcome was the adoption of a resolution calling for the formation of a third party.[10]

In January 1970 Ciudadanos Unidos (United Citizens), a core group of leaders, who had emerged from a MAYO meeting at Mission, Texas, settled upon the name La Raza Unida for the new party. They filed applications with the county registrars of Zavala, Dimmit, La Salle, and Hidalgo to form chapters in those counties. La Raza Unida then launched a campaign to register voters in the respective counties. In April 1970 La Raza Unida Party's slate swept the school-board elections in Crystal City and two LRUP candidates were elected to the five-member city council, while in two other Texas towns, Carrizo Springs and Cotulla, the party won the mayor's office.[11]

Just as in Texas, Mexican Americans in California were considering independent political action. The first significant push for a Chicano political party there came in November 1969 at a student conference on the campus of California State College at Hayward. The gathering also showed that there was little agreement on the party's goals and tactics. Attended by five hundred people, mostly Chicanos, the conference featured Colorado's Rodolfo "Corky" Gonzales, who stressed the need for ethnic political unity. The idea received a warm endorsement by those present, including activist Armando Valdez of Oakland. "We need a sep-arate, independent party," declared Valdez, director of La Causa in Oakland, "that will be the voice of the Chicano people, without the sup-posed Chicanos like those who are [Governor Ronald] Reagan aides, or the type of guys that are just *tio-tacoing* [Uncle Tom-ing] all around and claiming to represent us."[12] Antonio Camejo of the Socialist Worker's Party agreed for special reasons of his own. A La Raza Unida Party, he believed, would "probably . . . develop a socialist program as the revo-lution" approached. Camejo envisioned a party that would not confine itself to electoral politics but would also agitate for Chicano Studies departments at universities and protest against the Vietnam War.[13]

Though activists in southern California were aware of efforts on behalf of a La Raza Unida Party in Texas and the Bay Area, there was no meaningful cooperation among the groups. Bert Corona, a political activist and professor at California State College at Los Angeles, assumed responsibility for organizing the party in Southern California. Corona, a former president of MAPA, was especially outspoken in justifying the need for the party to those outside the Chicano community. "Both par-ties have been guilty of using the Spanish-speaking and the Chicano vote for their imperative of control of the legislature," he told the California Advisory Committee to the U.S. Commission on Civil Rights in January 1971. The legislators "are cynical in their dealings with our needs and aspi-rations. . . . Both parties ultimately have shown that they represent the big money interests."[14]

As a professor, Corona had easy access to students. He encouraged them to become politically active, even taking more than a hundred of them to Sacramento when the critical issue of reapportionment came before the legislature. "Bert took a whole contingent of people to Sacramento because of the reapportionment [of California legislative dis-tricts] here [in Los Angeles]," recalled Richard Santillán, a student at the university and later a leader in La Raza Unida. "They were having hear-ings. Bert put us on a bus, a bunch of us."[15]

Besides students, Corona also brought the support of major Chicano organizations to La Raza Unida because of his close ties to them, espe-cially MAPA and the Centro de Accion Social Autónomo (CASA). "MAPA," he announced confidently, "must and will join with our youth, students, militants and 'pueblo in general' to establish our own political party — La Raza Unida."[16] "Through its candidates and its platform," he added, La Raza Unida Party could gain more power for Mexican Americans than had MAPA or MEChA, the Brown Berets, the National

Chicano Moratorium Committee, the United Farm Workers, the Crusade for Justice, and Chicano trade unionists. Those groups, he argued, would "not go out of business in order to establish La Raza Unida Party, but rather, by using the strength and experience of their organizations, [they would] guarantee the establishment of the strongest possible Raza Unida Party in the U.S.A."[17]

Several of Corona's students at Cal State Los Angeles — Reggie Ruiz, Gilbert Blanco, and John Olivares — organized the first La Raza Unida conference in Southern California as part of a class project. At the gathering on their campus in February 1971, Corona lambasted the Democratic Party. "Our job is to unmask the Democratic Party," he told the two hundred people in attendance. "We must clear this [party] out of our mind. Democrats have always put nails in our coffin." Among those present who cheered this message were Christopher Cebeda, editor of the Brown Beret's *La Causa;* Roger López, representing the advocates of La Raza Unida Party in San Bernardino; and Robert Elias, formerly of the Chicano Moratorium Committee and now a Raza Unida Party organizer.[18] The participants broke into eight workshops that reflected their concerns: education, welfare, immigration, penal reform, administration of justice (police and courts), public health and drug abuse, political representation, and control of the land. The reports that emerged called for Chicano control of their own education, open admissions to college with full financial aid, and "non support of any [political] candidate that exploits La Raza."[19]

Many in the activist community saw the conference as a watershed. La Raza Unida Party, declared *La Causa,* represented a major departure from the constant "endorsing [of] Democrats, candidates of the ruling class who don't have our peoples' interests at heart." The monthly praised the party's efforts to raise "issues that our people feel are relevant" and concentrate "on winning control over local institutions that effect the people's everyday lives. . . . The R.U.P [Raza Unida Party] will be a political party with a difference in that it will be controlled by the people and not by a handful of rich party contributors."[20]

Following the conference, party chapters sprang up throughout the Los Angeles area. Though activists agreed on the necessity of Chicano political empowerment, there was no agreement on to how to achieve that goal. Thus, the party chapters emerged in various communities throughout the Los Angeles area in a haphazard manner and sometimes in close proximity to each other. A group of Cal State Los Angeles students, including Ruiz and Blanco along with Richard Santillán and

Gloria Ramírez, formed the East Los Angeles chapter in March 1971. In the City Terrace neighborhood of East Los Angeles, Pedro Arias, Richard Martínez, Gilbert López, and Raúl Ruiz organized a chapter about the same time. By November 1971, Rosemary Pimental and Fred Aguilar had formed a chapter in La Puente, while Armando Navarro was key in the creation of a San Bernardino chapter. These leaders were both students and longtime community activists.

The first task of LRUP organizers was to get the party on the ballot. The state had two methods for doing so: signatures gathered from 10 percent of the total number of voters in the previous governor's election; or from 1 percent of the total population of registered voters. The numbers amounted to 660,344 for the first option and 66,344 for the second. LRUP advocates naturally opted for the latter.[21]

In the spring of 1971 supporters launched a massive voter-registration drive throughout California. Spanish-speaking deputy registrars targeted churches, shopping centers, and Chicano neighborhoods in East Los Angeles and the San Fernando Valley. Distributing party literature, volunteers steered potential voters toward a convenient registrar's table. In August 1971 an East Los Angeles La Raza Unida committee of twelve volunteers and approximately a hundred registrars moved door-to-door through neighborhoods, going from middle-class districts to housing projects, such as Ramona Gardens, and enlisting additional volunteers in the effort to win over voters. The East Los Angeles group established a cadre of registrars in Ramona Gardens who held classes on registration with the local residents and distributed bumper stickers, leaflets, and posters that could be used for, in one organizer's view, "further grass-roots registering."[22]

In the San Fernando Valley a group of mostly students limited their efforts to shopping centers in Chicano barrios in San Fernando and Pacoima, where they later claimed to have registered a thousand voters. As in Texas, this low-key traditional approach to register voters and attract non-activist Mexican Americans was adopted because, as San Fernando volunteer Richard Loa observed, "We've learned that demonstrations [such as those sponsored by the Chicano Moratorium Committee] are dramatic and get attention, but they don't change the *politicos*. They only understand power."[23] Registrations increased, but not as dramatically as many hoped. Each chapter then devised its own solution to the problem. In the City Terrace chapter, Richard Martínez, who wielded substantial power there, decided that the party's chance for success would improve if it ran a candidate in an election even before the party had gained official recognition (and thus the person would have to run as an independent). Such action would send out the message that the party was a viable possibility.[24] An opportunity to field a candidate presented itself when David Roberti, who represented the 48th Assembly District, won election to the California State Senate and vacated his Assembly seat.[25] To Martínez, the 48th district, which encompassed the northern tip of unincorporated East Los Angeles, was "our turf." He decided on his own (the party at this time had adopted no mechanism to choose candidates) that the best candidate for Roberti's seat would be Raúl Ruiz, the *La Raza* editor who had gained fame during the inquest into Ruben Salazar's death.[26] Though reluctant to do so, Ruiz agreed to run.[27]

Martínez's decision alienated other chapters of the party in Los Angeles, which saw it as an example of boss rule. "We said that La Raza Unida was a different party from the Republicans and the Democrats, that we were democratic and that it would be the people who would choose the leadership," declared Richard Santillán of the East Los Angeles chapter. "The next thing we know Raúl [Ruiz] announced that he was going to run. It was never brought to us. It was never brought to anybody. He just decided that he was going to run." Such internal strains did not augur well for the party's future.[28]

The 48th district election was also the first time that the party had to contend with outside forces trying to "help" — in this case, the Republican Party, which offered to underwrite LRUP's campaign costs. A meeting allegedly took place at the Euclid Community Center between several La Raza Unida supporters from East Los Angeles and City Terrace and two white males, who refused to give their names but identified themselves as representatives of the G.O.P. The Republicans offered not only money but also help in LRUP's quest to qualify for the ballot. Santillán later claimed that he told the men to "go to hell and to get out of there" and threw them out, but silence from the other LRUP representatives resulted in the discussion continuing. It ended with LRUP members agreeing not to accept Republican funds or help on behalf of the party, but the decision did not prevent individuals who claimed no affiliation with the party from accepting aid. On the basis of later interviews with members of the Ruiz campaign in the City Terrace chapter, Santillán concluded that Republicans funded the campaign in order to take votes away from the Democrats, a charge Ruiz subsequently denied.[29]

Regardless of whether Ruiz received Republican help, he obtained only 1,378 votes, less than 4 percent of the total, a tally that placed him fourth in a competition that included two Democratic Mexican

Americans, a Republican, and a Peace and Freedom Party candidate. This poor showing nonetheless qualified him for a runoff election, scheduled for November 16, against the Democratic front-runner Richard Alatorre, who had garnered 7,685 votes; Republican William Brophy, who had received 12,236 votes; and John Blaine, the Peace and Freedom Party candidate, who had obtained only 638 votes. The total number of ballots cast revealed an unusual amount of interest in a special contest, with nearly 44 percent of the district's eligible voters going to the polls. Doubtless this showing was helped by the extension of the franchise earlier that year to eighteen-year-olds, an action that helped Ruiz win the votes of the many young people who supported him.[30]

The young LRUP volunteers involved in the runoff election employed confrontational tactics, which reached their nadir on November 7, 1971, when U.S. Senator Edmund Muskie visited Los Angeles to campaign for Alatorre. The mostly young Mexican-American demonstrators denounced Muskie's visit as an attempt by the Democrats to undermine the fledging party in Los Angeles. Placards proclaimed, "Muskie is a carpetbagger," "Democrats No, Raza Unida Si!," "Alatorre is a Vendido [a Sellout]," "Chale con Muskie [To Hell with Muskie]," and "Gringo Go Home." A leaflet explained:

El Partido de La Raza Unida has frightened the Democratic Party and is posing a threat to Richard Alatorre's campaign in the 48th Assembly District to the point where he is about to receive outside help. This Sunday, Alatorre, a so-called Chicano who claims to be Italian, will be paraded through the barrio by one of his multimillionaire *patrones*, Senator Muskie.

Muskie refused to comment on the protest, but the LRUP's tactics evidently succeeded because the Democrats cancelled the last of their three scheduled engagements.[31]

Despite all the energy that LRUP spent on the campaign, Brophy defeated Ruiz and Alatorre. The media attributed the Republican victory primarily to the split within the Democratic Party between those supporting Ruiz and those backing Alatorre. They also cited as benefiting Brophy the publicity he gained when shots were fired at his house just before the election.[32] Ruiz, on the other hand, attributed Alatorre's defeat to LRUP. As he told the *Los Angeles Times,* "Brophy did not get more votes than expected. His vote was not surprising. The surprise is that Alatorre did not get the votes the Democrats expected him to. We are responsible for that. We pulled the traditional Democratic Chicano voters away from him. We stopped their machine. Brophy didn't win this. We did."[33]

The election returns suggest that LRUP did indeed prevent Alatorre from gaining victory. Brophy received 16,346 votes (46.70 percent), while Alatorre gained 14,759 votes (42.17 percent), Ruiz 2,778 votes (7.93 percent), and Blaine 1,108 votes (3.16 percent). The significant dent that LRUP made in the Democratic tally was confirmed by Democratic Assemblyman Henry A. Waxman of Los Angeles, but he attributed it to an alliance between La Raza Unida and the Republican Party: "The reason we lost was the cynical alliance of neo-segregationist[s] in the Chicano community with the Republicans." The Socialist Workers' Party's newspaper, *The Militant,* labeled Waxman's accusations "vicious slander."[34]

La Raza Unida leaders described the election results as LRUP's "first major step in California." The City Terrace–based Chicano magazine *La Raza,* edited by Raúl Ruiz, proclaimed: "We Did It" — by overcoming the "frenzied efforts [of the Democrats to] . . . beat La Raza Unida Party." In the struggle, "We saw new faces, heard new opinions and felt new energy." It was a "campaign [that] brought together a variety of people," who were "able to function as a team, not as a conglomeration of *jefes* [bosses] with no *trabajadores* [workers]." This was "our first attempt, but it is by no means our last."[35]

Such outward self-congratulation masked uncertainty and even pessimism on the part of some LRUP leaders. Richard Martínez, the campaign manager, labeled those who worked on behalf of Ruiz "a bunch of novices" — "students" and a broad array of other "activists" — who had "never really participated in a political campaign." Their "method of campaigning was all wrong," relying as it did on "a few stormtroopers' type of approach." They also failed to identify the most promising precincts and then go door-to-door, arranging house meetings and distributing effective literature. The newsletter "was a waste of time [and] . . . money." Martínez spared no one, including himself. We had "great ambition, lousy tactics, a lousy campaign manager [and] a candidate who wanted to dominate every aspect of the campaign." In effect, he later recalled, "we had two campaign managers: myself and the candidate. And since the candidate was the leader of the faction, we had the candidate running the campaign manager and everyone else." There was a positive side, however. He and his co-workers learned the hard way about the "demographics of the community — who can vote, who can't vote." They also learned of the need to do a more effective job in distinguishing themselves from the Democratic and Republican parties. "Neither party addresses our needs. We are a great people . . . [and yet] we face [conditions] every day that deny us the ability to live our greatness and be part of this country. And neither party is addressing that. We need to bring that to the public, to the politicians. To force them to begin to address that. We need a voice."[36]

Others believed that the campaign had been a failure because it pitted Mexican Americans against one another. "Chicano activists who have been involved in the Los Angeles area aren't sharing Raúl Ruiz's glee over the recent defeat of Democrat Richard Alatorre," declared Vincente Cárdenas in a letter to the *Los Angeles Times.* "Those of us with any memory and experience know that both Republicans and Democrats have effectively used 'ringer candidates' to beat our legitimate and qualified candidates." To Cárdenas, the idea of a La Raza Unida Party was outdated: it "may have been appropriate in 1960, 1965, or even 1970 to convince Democratic party officials of the need to support Chicano candidates, but instead it was used in 1971 to defeat a man who finally had a definite chance to win."[37]

The 48th Assembly race made clear the divisions within the ethnic Mexican community in Los Angeles, as well as the party in general. In an effort to bring about more unity among the chapters, LRUP organizers in Los Angeles held a conference in November 1971. According to a resolution passed at that gathering, a chapter's sole responsibility was to "inform its community on voting procedures by any means necessary."[38] This mandate to avoid meaningful cooperation and activism ensured that there would be no agreement on forging the party. Chapters throughout the city now turned even more inward and organized their constituents as they deemed appropriate. The resolution served only to accelerate the local political autonomy that had been evident at the outset.

The increased fragmentation led the Southern California chapters to call for creation of a central committee that would bring uniformity in strategy among the party's cells. At a meeting of ten chapters on January 15, 1972, those present established themselves as a central committee and then discussed the party's activities for the coming year, how better to coordinate communication among themselves, and criteria for creating chapters. Another impetus for the gathering was an attempt to present the semblance of a unified party at the approaching national LRUP conference scheduled for September 1972 in El Paso, Texas. The central committee agreed that a chapter required a minimum of ten members, five of whom had to be deputy registrars. It also decreed that chapters had to define the specific geographical area which each served, maintain communication with that community and other chapters in the state, and register fifteen new voters a week. One issue that caused tension at the conference, and foreshadowed future problems in the party, was a discussion of the relationship between local chapters and the central committee. Some organizers believed that LRUP should have decentralized power and that chapters should have sole jurisdiction over their organizing area. Others believed that without a central mechanism the party would fall apart. This point was never resolved and would lead to greater problems in the future. Yet the party continued to plan for victory at the polls.[39]

At the same time that the Southern California chapters were struggling with organizational issues, so, too, were their Northern counterparts. In anticipation of the September 1972 conference, they called a statewide conference for April 1972 to revitalize registration efforts and to increase the party's appeal.[40] The several hundred attendees agreed that the party should not "organize solely for political elections" but "also emphasize the economic and social endeavors reflecting the needs of each specific barrio, area, and state." They called for local chapters to play up the party's commitment to providing legal assistance, free breakfast programs, income-tax services, and to improving police–community relations. To better coordinate these efforts, they authorized the creation of organizing committees in Northern and Southern California that would oversee the efforts for establishing the party in those areas. Working with the organizing committees would be central committees in six cities (San Diego, Santa Barbara, San Jose, Sacramento, Los Angeles, and San Bernardino), charged with overseeing campaigns and registration drives, screening potential candidates, and approving new chapters. To achieve greater unity and coordination, the party throughout the state undercut those efforts with its ballooning bureaucracy.

At another conference three months later in July in Los Angeles (attended by some five hundred people), there was palpable tension over LRUP's purpose and tactics.[41] What should be the party's relationship to the Democrats and Republicans? Should the party run candidates in its own name? Some of those present also questioned the notion of Chicano nationalism and asked whether the party's membership should be multi-ethnic, with appeals to non-Chicanos, or exclusively Mexican American.[42] Such uncertainties made it even clearer that building a party was much more difficult than was originally thought.

Rather than helping the situation in Los Angeles, the September 1972 La Raza Unida Party national conference in El Paso led to the party's further splintering. The convention split over who would emerge as the national party's chairman — Denver's Rodolfo "Corky" Gonzales or Crystal City's José Angel Gutiérrez. This jockeying for power by the two candidates led to the further fragmentation of the California party. A majority of the Golden State's LRUP members present supported Gonzales, and decided to cast their votes as a bloc, which caused the delegation's Gutiérrez supporters to walk out of the convention. In the end, Gutiérrez emerged the victor and Gonzales joined him on the podium, embraced him, and together they raised their hands in a sign of unity. However, it was clear that the party was fragmented along state lines and would not be able to serve as the vehicle to bring unity to the diverse ethnic Mexican community in the United States.[43]

The growing dissidence on the national and state level prompted some local groups to devise their own agendas. The Southern California Organizing Committee and Los Angeles's City Terrace chapter, the most active and unified in the state, had thought through more carefully the implications of the 48th district election and concluded that a third party controlled by Chicanos and dedicated to improving life in the barrios was mandatory. The Southern California Organizing Committee had also become fed up with the delays in achieving organizational unity. In a "position paper," it announced:

We must face the facts. We are still at the starting gate or at the position ZERO with all do [sic] respect to those *carnales* who have already engaged in electoral politics. To date there is no true or legitimate statewide leadership. It is our position that we do not yet have a Party, either in legal terms (since we have yet to get the required 67,000 registrations) nor do we have a party in the structural sense. "Political Education" campaigns alone do not make a Party. They are important, but without a viable local organization they are meaningless in [the] long run. At worst, without viable organization both our oppressor and our people will interpret the Partido as a paper Tiger.[44]

The Southern California Organizing Committee called for building the party from the bottom up, an objective that it believed could be accomplished only by drawing "battle lines" at the local level and creating the region's own "Crystal Cities." It also sought an "ideology [that] must be culturally based and aimed at raising the consciousness of [the] people." This lodestar could not be a "dogmatic 'cultural nationalism,'" but, rather, a "humanistic nationalism that can make possible a political party that can meet the human needs of our barrios." Time should not be spent on state conventions and resolutions, but on developing "methods, tactics, and strategy."[45] Though criticizing some aspects of cultural nationalism, the committee still held on to the concept and offered no alternative to it.

For the City Terrace chapter in Los Angeles, this meant continuing with its strategy of registering voters and backing a candidate. In April 1972, it again launched a campaign to elect Raúl Ruiz, this time as representative of the 40th Assembly District. "If engineered correctly," declared campaign manager Gilbert López, the race "can provide an avenue to giving the party a high degree of exposure to the people."[46] As before, Ruiz had to run as an independent since LRUP had still not qualified for the ballot.

Chicanos constituted about 30 percent of the 40th district's population, and this time LRUP organizers set out systematically to identify the voters among them and to win them over. Party leaders appointed precinct captains for the 54 precincts (out of a total of 138 in the district) where Chicanos were predominant, and they worked with teams of registrars and volunteers, going house to house, attending community meetings, distributing leaflets, making telephone calls, putting up signs, issuing press releases, and going on radio and television. Volunteers visited assigned neighborhoods at least three times a week until the November 7 election. Over 2,000 mailers went out in mid-August, with second and third mailings of 17,000 each in October. The daily maintenance of this machine required several fundraisers, speaking engagements, and small donations from community members.[47]

Despite all the energy, Ruiz lost to Alex García, the Democratic Party candidate, by a vote of 21,000 to 5,000. The loss caused Ruiz to reflect on the campaign, publishing his observations in *La Raza:* "What we . . . fail[ed] to do was to evaluate properly the relationship of the Democratic party to our people. We assumed that we had the truth and that the Democratic party was just a totally useless and irrelevant political institution. Perhaps we are correct in our analysis but that isn't necessarily what the majority of our people think." Ruiz then lambasted LRUP campaigners for failing to "politicize the people to any meaningful depth, at least the Chicanos in our district anyway. We failed to realize that Chicanos, whether young or old, do not necessarily create a dependable block of potential voters. . . . The *partido* needs to establish a stronger base in the community; campaigns are good but campaigns in and of themselves are not enough to politicize the community."[48]

Campaign manager Gilbert López had a more positive view of the election. La Raza Unida's greatest accomplishment, López believed, was netting 13 percent of the votes in a district where Spanish-surnamed registered voters comprised only 18 percent of those eligible to go to the polls. Moreover, this race and the earlier one in the 48th Assembly District had helped push the number of Spanish-surnamed registered voters to 10,000. Such a gain could be used to advantage in the newly reapportioned Los Angeles 14th Councilmanic District.[49]

Such optimism was shared by few. The City Terrace chapter was the most active and unified in the state, and yet it had failed to gain a victory in two attempts. Disappointment was all the more bitter in the second race because so many had worked so hard. Also discouraging was the fact that the party had not yet been qualified for the ballot, perhaps because the Mexican-American voting base was wedded to the Democratic Party. City Terrace members became disillusioned, losing their sense of direction and unity. Many concluded that emphasizing class would be more effective in winning gains than in stressing race or ethnicity. They now joined with others of a like mind — Rodolfo Quiñones, James Franco, Daniel Estrada, and Cruz Olmeda Becerra — all of whom had earlier successfully petitioned LRUP's Los Angeles Central Committee for membership as a Labor Committee chapter dedicated to organizing workers rather than representing a geographical area. They were not really interested in registering voters, preferring instead to focus on raising the consciousness of laborers and supporting strikes and boycotts, but they agreed to accommodate registration in order to gain LRUP recognition.[50]

Armed with a newspaper of its own, *El Obrero (The Worker)*, the Labor Committee chapter achieved some significant victories by launching wildcat strikes and boycotts that led to the improvement of wages and working conditions for ethnic Mexicans in factories and service industries in the Los Angeles area. But those victories stood in sharp contrast to LRUP's failures to gain political recognition and served to undermine further attempts to do so.[51] The City Terrace chapter's *La Raza* lamented the lack of a "clearly defined direction" to the Chicano insurgency, while acknowledging that, "as the mobilization and rebellion of the workers intensifies, the movement naturally and correctly takes on a more clearly defined class character."[52]

As opposed to the campaigns and labor activity engaged in by the City Terrace and the Labor Committee chapters, the East Los Angeles chapter focused on service to the community, in the form of free income-tax services, free-lunch programs, and links to government agencies that could help people with their problems. Though the chapter believed that voting Chicanos into office was important, it felt that the only way to gain the trust of the community was to provide help with a neighborhood's needs, and then, after about two to three years, it could generate support for a candidate whom they would choose democratically. Thus, the East Los Angeles chapter's work entailed building a base, rather than striving for electoral victories or agitation in the work place.[53] Such service-oriented activities, however, did not translate into what the LRUP needed most, registered voters and electoral victory.

LRUP made one last attempt to achieve political success and reassert its commitment to Chicano cultural nationalism in 1974 when it supported efforts to incorporate East Los Angeles as a separate municipality. Again, City Terrace was the most prominent of the LRUP chapters in the campaign. "The struggle for self-determination in the Chicano community," stated *La Raza,* "has taken on a new dimension in the present attempts to incorporate East Los Angeles, . . . [for it is] the only alternative to preserving our culture, gaining political power and improving the living conditions of the people of the barrio." East Los Angeles had a population of over 106,000, with 82 percent of the residents possessing Spanish surnames. If incorporated, it would become the largest ethnic Mexican city in the United States, considerably larger than Crystal City, Texas, whose Chicano residents had taken over its municipal government.[54]

The attempt to incorporate East Los Angeles did not originate with La Raza Unida. There had been earlier attempts in 1925, 1926, 1931, 1933, 1961, and 1965. All had failed for a variety of reasons, but especially because homeowners feared higher taxes. This latest effort began in 1970 with an Ad Hoc Committee to Incorporate East Los Angeles (ACTIELA) that consisted primarily of Democrats with no connection to La Raza Unida Party. Community activists created ACTIELA following the violence that erupted at the National Chicano Moratorium on August 29 and at the Mexican Independence Day parade on September 16. It emerged as a result of concerned community leaders, but the catalyst that galvanized them into action was the city of Monterey Park's move to annex that portion of unincorporated East Los Angeles that included East Los Angeles College and its adjacent residential neighborhood.[55]

The Ad Hoc Committee effectively thwarted Monterey Park in 1974, when it achieved the go-ahead for its plan to incorporate East Los Angeles from the Local Agency Formation Commission of Los Angeles. ACTIELA then found support in a major change in California's incorporation law, which modified the criteria for the initiation of cityhood efforts. No longer would the signatures of 25 percent of property owners be required. Instead, incorporation initiators need gather the support of only 25 percent of the registered voters in the proposed city. Under the new procedure, incorporation proponents had to obtain 5,000 signatures from a pool of 25,000 registered voters in unincorporated East Los

Angeles.[56] This had to be accomplished within a 120-day period from the filing date in order to put the issue before the voters in a general election.[57] In June 1974 the Los Angeles County Board of Supervisors approved the incorporation initiative as Proposition X and placed it on the November ballot.[58]

La Raza Unida Party saw the election as an opportunity to create Aztlán through the ballot box. Although the election was supposed to be nonpartisan, LRUP pressed for incorporation and proposed a five-person slate of its own members for the new city council.[59] The candidates were the already twice-defeated Ruiz, George García, Celia Rodríguez, Arturo Sánchez, and Daniel Zapata. The LRUP cadre competed against thirty-four other nominees for the council, including four ACTIELA members calling themselves United Democrats for Incorporation and two members of the Socialist Workers' Party.[60]

The LRUP candidates ran modestly funded campaigns against their thirty-four competitors. No one on the five-person slate received a contribution exceeding $500. The party spent a total of $515.44, which included $179.44 for campaign posters, $154 raised by selling souvenir posters, and $182 for bumper stickers. In comparison, independent candidate Vernon (Benito) Juárez funded his campaign chest with $5,000 from his savings and spent at least $2,804 on billboards and other printed materials.[61]

Not everyone supported incorporation, with the strongest opposition coming from the Committee Opposing Incorporation Now (COIN) and the Maravilla–Belvedere Park Property Owners Association. COIN concentrated its opposition in the Bella Vista and Montebello Park areas of East Los Angeles, while the other group focused on the proposed municipality's east side. They appealed to property owners' fears by projecting heavy taxes to support the new government. Incorporation proponents, with ACTIELA the most outspoken among them, denied that taxes would rise, claiming that the city could support itself solely with state tax subventions and revenue-sharing grants from the federal government.[62]

The opponents carried the day, defeating incorporation by a vote of 7,197 to 5,256. Of the thirty-nine candidates for the proposed municipality's city council, LRUP candidate Ruiz received the most votes, 2,440; since the top vote getter would in all probability have become East Los Angeles's chief executive, Ruiz had lost not only his bid for a city but also a job.[63]

The incorporation campaign proved to be La Raza Unida's last major venture into politics. The San Fernando chapter later backed a candidate

(Andrés Torres) for a California Assembly seat and then for the San Fernando city council, but in both instances he lost, though by only fifty-four votes in the latter attempt.[64]

A major reason for LRUP's demise was its failure to qualify for appearance on the ballot. That was clearly a reflection of its inability to sell itself to the registered Chicano voters of California. Though voting records showing who supported and voted for La Raza Unida Party are not available, information regarding Mexican-American voting behavior is. Data collected for 1965–66 by the UCLA Mexican American Study Project show that of 945 Mexican-American registered voters surveyed in Los Angeles County, only 225 were under twenty-nine years old, while 720 were thirty years old or older.[65] This small sample points to an older voting bloc. That this constituency was overwhelmingly registered Democrat is evident in data collected by the Urban Coalition of Greater Los Angeles in 1970. That survey of 133 voting precincts in East Los Angeles revealed that 87.3 percent, or 15,790, of the 18,088 Spanish-surnamed registered voters (a majority of whom were probably of Mexican descent) were registered Democrats.[66]

These numbers suggest that La Raza Unida's failure to gather a constituency was a result of most voters' being older and apparently wedded to traditional electoral vehicles like the Democratic and Republican parties.[67] Such allegiance to traditional parties, especially the Democrats, guaranteed that the LRUP would never gather the signatures necessary to qualify it as an official political party in California. La Raza Unida's candidates also faced the disadvantage of having to appear on the ballot as independents, who were further handicapped by the lack of unity among LRUP's chapters. There was no clear agreement as to how to build the party and what tactics to use. Should the party concentrate solely on registering voters or should it bring greater awareness to Chicano communities through the use of marches and protests. In Los Angeles, this split was clearly evident in the differences between the City Terrace chapter's push to register voters and run candidates in elections; the Labor Committee chapter's attempt to build Chicano solidarity with workers by using demonstrations and supporting strikes and boycotts; and the East Los Angeles chapter's emphasis on serving the community with income-tax preparation, free-lunch programs, and other services. There was no effective plan for cooperation. This factionalism makes clear the multi-faceted nature of the so-called Chicano community.

Yet another problem hindered LRUP's attempt to empower Chicanos in Los Angeles. This was its contradictory nature. In advocating a third party that would be guided by Chicano nationalism, it challenged the notions of assimilation and consensus at the foundation of American electoral politics. However, as a political party dependent for its existence on registered voters, and, therefore, U.S. citizens, LRUP inherently supported the nation-state, though it never consciously acknowledged that allegiance. Its narrow focus cost it the support of the majority of Mexican-American voters, who were older and owed their ambiguous allegiance to the United States rather than to a Chicano nationalist movement. LRUP's failure left the door open for another group to attempt to empower Mexican Americans in Los Angeles, the Centro de Acción Social Autónomo.[68]

5

"Un Pueblo Sin Fronteras"

The Centro de Acción Social Autónomo (CASA)

La Raza Unida Party's failure saw the mantle of Chicano champion in Los Angeles fall upon a workers' group, the Centro de Acción Social Autónomo–Hermandad General de Trabajadores (Center for Autonomous Social Action–General Brotherhood of Workers), commonly known as CASA. Originally founded in 1969 as a mutual-aid group, CASA soon broadened its mandate to include supporting workers' efforts to improve their wages and working conditions, as well as defending those whom it believed had been unjustly accused of crimes and imprisoned.[1] The latter efforts led to CASA's involvement with the Committee to Free Los Tres (CTFLT), a defense organization that sought to free three men accused of federal crimes but who were looked upon as community crusaders. Eventually, this association with the CTFLT would insure CASA's transformation into a radical voice for revolutionary change in America.[2]

To CASA, the plight of Mexican Americans (and Mexican immigrants) as underpaid, powerless laborers living in blighted barrios was the result of oppressive U.S. capitalism. Improvements could come only through organizing and empowering workers. Though CASA members subscribed to a Marxist–Leninist philosophy and publicly disparaged Chicano nationalism, which they believed divided Mexican immigrants and Mexican Americans, CASA, like other Chicano movement groups, also acknowledged ethnic Mexicans' unique historical circumstances in the United States. Consequently (and somewhat contradictorily), CASA sought to blend Marxism–Leninism and Chicano nationalism. In doing so, however, it fatally undercut its efforts by imagining the complex and multifaceted ethnic Mexican working class as a monolithic and undifferentiated mass of people.

CASA's transformation into an organization espousing such ideas originated with Los Tres — Alberto Ortiz, Juan Fernández, and Rodolfo Sánchez. They were members of the Casa de Carnalismo (House of Brotherhood), a community group established in 1969 to provide legal and educational services and cultural programs for the residents in the Pico Gardens Housing Project of Los Angeles.[3] They were former gang members firmly against drugs and committed to the principle that "the people have the human right to destroy the forces threatening their survival." They sought out drug dealers, ordering them to stop their sales and threatening them with force if they failed to do so. The tactic worked, and drug traffic declined significantly in Pico Gardens.[4]

Success led to no letup in their efforts. On July 22, 1971, Ortiz, Fernández, and Sánchez attempted to remove suspected drug dealer Bobby Parker from their neighborhood. Parker had earlier contacted Sánchez, a former drug addict who had served a prison sentence, in hopes, he told Sánchez, of being introduced to people interested in buying large quantities of narcotics. In an effort to stop this "pusher," Sánchez agreed to meet him the next day with some "buyers." At the designated hour, Fernández and Ortiz confronted Parker, ordering him to turn over his wallet because it contained proceeds from his sales that belonged to the residents of the housing project. Pretending to cooperate, Parker took out his wallet and then dropped it to the ground, distracting the others long enough to draw a gun from his waistband and fire at the two men, missing them. Fernández and Ortiz then pulled out guns of their own and shot Parker, leaving him partially paralyzed. What they did not know was that they had shot an undercover agent of the U.S. Bureau of Narcotics and Dangerous Drugs.[5]

While the confrontation was occurring, Sánchez waited in his car nearby. Hearing the shots, he drove to the spot where he had left Fernández and Ortiz, picked them up, and took them to his house, where they remained for about an hour. Meanwhile, law enforcement authorities blocked off the Pico Gardens Housing Project while federal and local police swept the area. As soon as the three noticed two suspicious cars driving past Sánchez's house, they fled unnoticed to the adjacent city of

Montebello. There, they sought shelter from an acquaintance, who, fearing for her safety, called the police. When the authorities arrived, the three surrendered and were taken to the city jail.[6]

The arrest of Los Tres set in motion a lengthy legal process, during which the men emerged as symbols of U.S. oppression of community activists. On July 26, 1971, federal authorities charged Los Tres with "robbery of . . . property of the United States," assault on a custodian of federal monies, and conspiracy to commit crimes against the federal government. The U.S. Attorney's office set bail at $50,000 for each, an action that prompted the creation of a defense committee to raise funds to set the men free.[7]

At the trial that began on October 19, 1971, the defense tried to show that the men had not known Parker's identity and, hence, could not be charged with conspiracy to rob and assault him. They also hoped to show that the shooting was a result of entrapment by a federal officer and that they had fired their guns in self-defense. Judge Lawrence Lydick refused to allow the jury to consider the evidence that Parker's identity was unknown to Los Tres or that, since he shot first, the three had fired back only to defend themselves. After a trial of nearly a month, the jury, on November 15, found the three men guilty of conspiracy to assault and rob a federal agent. In January 1972 Los Tres were sentenced, with Sánchez receiving the stiffest penalty of forty years in prison because of his prior conviction on drug-related charges and Parker's allegation that he masterminded the plot to attack him. Fernández's earlier criminal record resulted in a twenty-five-year sentence for him, while Ortiz, a first-time offender and a UCLA student, received ten years in prison.[8]

In February of the following year, the attorneys for the three men appealed the conviction on the grounds that the judge had erred in disallowing evidence crucial to the defense's case and that Parker had entrapped the defendants. Pending appeal, bail was set in May 1973 for each of them at $50,000. Because of the high amount, it took the defense committee until October 1973 to post the funds, but the judge refused to accept the deposit, questioning the value of the stock and real estate offered as collateral.[9] Law enforcement officials then sought to raise the bail to $150,000 for each defendant, arguing that "Mexicans out on bail tend to flee to their haven in Mexico."[10] That move failed, and eventually, on November 9, 1973, supporters of Los Tres persuaded the U.S. Supreme Court that their deposit should be accepted. The three men were released pending a review of their case.[11] The following May, the U.S. Ninth Circuit Court of Appeal dismissed one of the three counts against Los

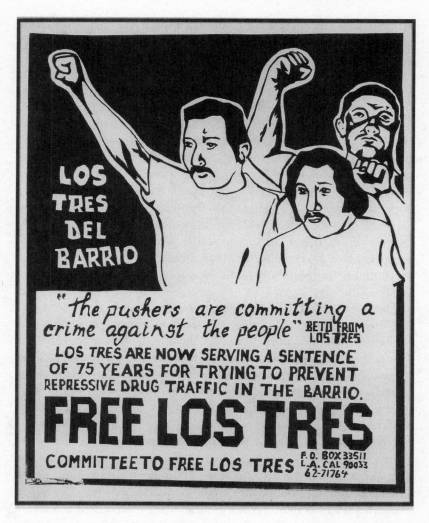

FIGURE 5. "Committee to Free Los Tres" poster, ca. 1973. Propaganda poster courtesy of the artist, Carlos Callejo.

Tres, the charge of "robbery of mail, matter, money, or other property of the U.S." It also reduced two of the men's sentences: Sánchez's from 40 to 15 years, and Fenández's from 25 to 10 years. The court, however, refused to rule favorably on the defense's argument that the three men had no prior knowledge of Parker's identity as a federal agent.[12] The defense appealed to the U.S. Supreme Court.

The arrest, trial, and subsequent sentencing of Los Tres angered a group of young people with Marxist leanings, who broke away from the larger defense committee and, in April 1974, created the Committee to Free Los Tres (see figure 5). The Comité, as it was known, consisted of a five-person central committee governed by Communist Party rules. Others soon joined this "collective," most of them students from universities and colleges in the Los Angeles area, especially East Los Angeles College, California State University at Los Angeles, and UCLA.[13] Most knew one another through their school activities, but to prevent the kind of police infiltration that occurred with the Brown Berets and the Chicano Moratorium Committee and to purge police informants on the committee, applicants had to fill out a five-page questionnaire on their reasons for wanting to join, their backgrounds, and family histories. They also had to go through a screening process administered by three senior members of the group. These formidable procedures produced thirty-six people committed to Marxism and the liberation of not only Los Tres but also the Chicano people.[14]

The Comité's emphasis on Marxism derived from its members' belief that the drug trade and the U.S. government were intertwined. U.S. authorities, they contended, promoted the drug trade as a way to extend U.S. power internationally and to control minority neighborhoods at home. Drawing on the views expressed in their neighborhoods by Marxists visiting from Mexico and argued in Alfred McCoy's *The Politics of Heroin in Southeast Asia,* they denounced drugs as the ultimate act of imperialism. "The cultivation of opium, its refinement into heroin, and its transportation to the United States have been proven to have the active involvement and assistance of the Federal Government through the Central Intelligence Agency," declared the Comité. "Heroin Traffic . . . is a vital part of the foreign policy of the U.S. in Southeast Asia" and also a major element of domestic policy as illustrated by the case of Los Tres.[15] The three men were trying to stop the drug traffic, yet they had been arrested, tried, and sentenced by the U.S. government. "When . . . [the U.S. court] sentenced Los Tres," it was "protect[ing] the promoters of the insidious crime of drug addiction upon the people" and, in the process, "kill[ing] any kind of social consciousness" in the Chicano community and subjecting its residents to "colonialism, degradation and exploitation." To combat such oppression, "we . . . no longer can rely on the self-effacement of a cultural nationalism which only romantizes [*sic*] the past," but must instead invoke "dialectical and historical materialism" against "the mechanations [*sic*] of capitalism and the workings of imperialism."[16]

In typical Marxist fashion, the Comité emphasized the need for discipline and self-control by circulating a seven-page document, called the "Principles," containing the regulations necessary for maintaining a "revolutionary organization" and achieving "victory upon victory in the class struggle."[17] Found there were the usual nostrums: "criticism and self-criticism," "centralized direction," and "democratic centralism" — all harnessed "toward a common end, giving unity to the disperse actions of individuals and groups." The result was a Marxist veneer on the Chicano struggle against discrimination and for self-determination.[18] Eliminating that veneer revealed the Comité as struggling for what most other Chicano activists sought: "a society free of exploitation of human beings by other human beings, a society . . . [free of] racism, where equal education is a human right for all, where all people are guaranteed food, shelter, clothing, medical care and employment."[19]

What set the Comité apart from others at this time was not only its Marxist nostrums but also its desire to establish links to students, women, undocumented workers, and, especially, the campaign to free Los Tres, which it made its own campaign. The first issue of its newsletter, *Sin Cadenas* (*Without Shackles*) proclaimed in August 1974:

The National Committee to Free Los Tres has developed very progressively in the past years and has been, with the support of the people, victorious in fighting the case of Los Tres. But the complete victory for the freedom of Los Tres is yet to be seen. Through this bulletin we ask all people of consciousness to give support politically and financially, in the interest of unity, in the struggle against repressive drug traffic and political repression in all its forms.[20]

To win support among students, the Comité two months earlier had created the Comité Estudiantil del Pueblo (Student Committee of the People), known as CEP, which worked with existing student organizations, such as the Movimiento Estudiantil Chicano de Aztlán, on behalf of educational reform — specifically, more financial support for Chicano students and more courses in Chicano Studies. The Comité also sought "anti-imperialist solidarity with student struggles within the United States and throughout the world, particularly with Latin America."[21] The organization, in addition, appealed for women's support by establishing the Los Angeles Committee to Stop Forced Sterilizations. This was a hot-button issue in the community that involved the alleged forced sterilizations of Asian, black, and Latina women at the Los Angeles County–University of Southern California Medical Center located in the Boyle Heights neighborhood of East Los Angeles. According to the Comité,

Coordinator Antonio Rodríguez's family had received special privileges denied to others. There was also a growing split over tactics, with one faction arguing for continuing the campaigns focused on such issues as Bakke and Medina and another group insisting that CASA should now turn its attention to producing a cadre of intellectuals to work within the ethnic Mexican community.[69]

The recriminations culminated in April 1978 with the creation of an Evaluation Task Force, which reported four months later that CASA had never been a "revolutionary organization" but had only adopted the outward forms of Marxism–Leninism. The disintegration of CASA now accelerated, with increased charges and countercharges. The July 1978 issue of *Sin Fronteras* was the last, and by year's end CASA had ceased to exist except in name only. Even that formality ended following its last meeting in August 1979.[70]

The roots of CASA's demise could be found in its beginnings. Its death stemmed in large part from its contradictory philosophy — the merger of nationalism with Marxist–Leninism — and its hierarchical and overly bureaucratic structure. CASA's ideology appealed to only a small sector of the ethnic Mexican community in the United States. Moreover, its goal of organizing both ethnic Mexicans in the U.S. and those in Mexico, as well as other Latin Americans, dissipated its funds and energy. This emphasis on organizing domestic and foreign laborers, which for CASA constituted "Un Pueblo Sin Fronteras" (one people without borders) ensured that little time and effort would be placed in providing services for its members. Its failure to be of real use to its constituency made dwindling membership no surprise. Additionally, CASA's leaders — young professionals and students with no immediate identification with the working class — left them out of touch with their targeted community group, inward looking, and soon convinced that they knew what was best for ethnic Mexicans throughout the nation. That attitude led to fractures within the organization as well as sharp attacks from ethnic Mexicans outside the group. Put another way, CASA's collapse testified to the multifaceted views of ethnic Mexicans. They did not constitute a single monolithic community, but, rather, reflected a variety of communities and interests incapable of bowing to the dictates of a centralized body.

CASA failed in its even narrower goal directed at workers and reflected in its slogan, "Obreros Unidos, Jamás Serán Vencidos" (Workers United, Shall Never Be Defeated). Still, its outspokenness prompted at least some Chicanos to think more deeply about the intertwined issues of immigration, labor, and citizenship that continued to shape their lives.

"Why Are We Not Marching Like in the '70s?"

Performance artist Luis Alfaro's video "Chicanismo" portrays a Chicano Studies professor, Salvador Rodríguez, as his people's self-professed savior. "If we're so retro," laments Rodríguez, "why are we not marching like in the '70s?"[1] This is a question that has been on the minds of many Mexican Americans since the demise of the Chicano movement in Los Angeles. The end of that dramatic era did not mean the death of ethnic Mexican reform efforts. Rather, the emphasis shifted, as it had on earlier occasions, to electoral politics. The present, in other words, is in harmony with the past's preeminent goal — Mexican-American empowerment — while acknowledging a variety of strategies to achieve that goal. As this study has demonstrated, the Chicano movement embraced a multiplicity of protest groups that differed sharply in their tactics and emphases during that eventful decade from the early 1960s into the 1970s.

Setting the pace in the 1950s and 1960s was MAPA (the Mexican American Political Association), which emphasized, like the present generation, working within the existing political system while also stressing ethnic solidarity and cultural nationalism in its pursuit of reform through electing Mexican Americans to public office. Dramatic success came in 1962, when Edward Roybal, who had earlier beaten the odds and won a seat on the Los Angeles City Council, became the first Mexican American elected to the U.S. Congress. That victory was unique, however, for other ethnic Mexican candidates encountered only defeat at the polls as a result

Angeles, CASA had chapters in Oakland, San Jose, San Diego, San Antonio, Chicago, and Greeley, Colorado, where the Comité could establish branch offices of its own.[26]

CASA had been created in 1969 as a mutual-aid society for Mexican artisans and laborers. The founders included Bert Corona, a longtime local politician, and labor organizers Soledad Alatorre, Francisco Amaro, María Cedillos, Juan Mariscal, and Rafael Zacarías.[27] Mexican immigrants joined in large numbers to take advantage of the social services and cultural activities. To defray costs, the association required annual dues of fifteen dollars, for which members could receive help with their residency applications and take classes in English, self-defense, and first-aid. In addition, cultural reinforcement came through courses offered on Mexican history, ballet folklorico, and guitar.[28] Because of CASA's services and visibility, it grew quickly in size, claiming a membership of four thousand by 1973. Most members, however, seldom took the time to vote for the organization's leaders or on policy issues since their primary interest was in the services provided to them.[29]

Unification did not mean that Los Tres would be forgotten, but neither would their plight receive the same degree of attention from CASA as it had from the Comité.[30] In the future, individual members — those who were friends of Los Tres — would continue to agitate on their behalf and correspond with them, as would, under orders from the CASA leadership, the staff of the organization's newspaper, *Sin Fronteras*.[31]

Some Comité leaders questioned the wisdom of merging with CASA on the grounds that its members had not been "really engaged in making revolutionary activity their profession" or in opposing the "Indochina war . . . , police brutality, forced sterilization and other . . . [forms] of repression."[32] Such doubts began to melt away in November 1974 when CASA's old leadership was voted out of office. This action resulted from the Comité ordering its members to join CASA prior to the merger. When the election took place, they voted, whereas most of CASA's longtime members did not. Bert Corona was asked to stay on as Secretary-General in order to ease the transition and because the new leaders needed his expertise in managing the organization, especially its social service programs. He declined, preferring to go back to his first concern and work with trade unions. With Corona gone, the new members voted to merge CASA with the Committee to Free Los Tres.

The merger exacerbated rather than eliminating the cleavages within CASA, cleavages that reflected the fractured nature of the ethnic Mexican community. The Comité men and women in the vanguard of the CASA takeover were young activists — college students, young professionals (primarily attorneys and teachers), and union organizers who had either been born in the U.S. or had emigrated from Mexico at a young age. Their revolutionary style contrasted with the less-radical demands of the older Mexican immigrants who had made up CASA's basic constituency. For a time the two groups worked together, but with Corona's absence, the inevitable decline in the organization's social services, particularly the lack of informed advice on obtaining legal residency, led to the older members' dropping out. As they did so, the Comité newcomers super-imposed their organizational structure on CASA.[33]

Along with the merger came a change in the editorial policy of *Sin Fronteras*. Instead of focusing solely on immigration issues, the new edi-tor, Isabel Rodríguez Chávez, promised to keep readers informed about the "general struggle of the people" and to work on behalf of "national and class consciousness."[34] Typical issues of the twenty-page, bilingual monthly contained columns on labor activities; economic, political, and social conditions in Mexico; the struggles of women; and commentaries on economic and political developments in the U.S.[35] These writings reflected CASA's new emphasis, which received official approval at a con-ference in Los Angeles in July 1975. CASA described itself as a Marxist–Leninist organization, but its policies reflected the preeminence of eth-nicity and cultural nationalism. Our "main task," declared the resolution endorsed by the delegates (most of them from the Los Angeles area), "is to unite the Mexican people born in the U.S. with those born in Mexico. To do this we must build a mass organization along national [ethnic] lines which will raise our class and national consciousness while bringing our people [Chicanos and Mexican nationals] to an understanding and acceptance of the need for proletarian revolution in this country."[36] The delegates then approved several "principles," later sent for endorsement to chapters in San Antonio, Oakland, Chicago, and Greeley: Marxism–Leninism as the ideology of CASA, national unity among the ethnic Mexican people, the participation of Mexican-American workers in the trade-union movement and in the struggle of Mexican people everywhere for full equality and democratic rights, and the ethnic identity of CASA members as solely Mexican.

Not all CASA chapters agreed with these sentiments, and the members in San Jose and San Diego not only rejected them but also resigned in protest. Such resistance notwithstanding, CASA produced a twenty-four-page, bilingual "Reglamento," or rule book, which described the new organizational structure and served as a kind of constitution. Much of it

uted the poor showing to its "uneven development nationally and the lack of follow-up [that] insured a poor organizational impact among the Mexican working class in this country."[50]

CASA now launched a major campaign on behalf of affirmative action in order to enhance its visibility and gain more members. It targeted the Bakke decision, which it believed clearly defined "the ideology of the imperialists, their tactics, and politics and the role of its ideology in education and in maintaining the national oppression and exploitation of oppressed nationalities."[51] In 1975, Allan Bakke, a thirty-four-year-old aerospace engineer, sued the University of California for denying him admission to the UC Davis Medical School. He was the victim of race discrimination, he contended, because of the university's affirmative action program which, while denying him admission, guaranteed admission to disadvantaged non-white students (blacks, Asians, Chicanos, and Native Americans), some of them less qualified than he. On September 16, 1976, the California Supreme Court ruled in Bakke's favor, finding that the university had violated the equal protection clause of the Fourteenth Amendment.[52]

CASA joined with other minority and civil rights groups in calling for an appeal to the U.S. Supreme Court. Instead of actively engaging the legal system, however, CASA used speeches, press releases, and demonstrations to argue that the Supreme Court should not only reject Bakke's "racist claims," but also expand special admissions programs. To CASA, the "inequality of formal education is directly related to inequality in the labor market and super-exploitation." [53] Hence, for ethnic Mexicans and other exploited minorities "to demand educational equality is not to demand special privileges."[54] Educational opportunity was the means for the oppressed working class to share in the wealth created by working people's labor.[55] Moreover, insisted CASA, that opportunity belonged to all U.S. residents — citizens, non-citizens, workers. (On June 28, 1978, two months before CASA's demise, the U.S. Supreme Court ruled that special admissions quotas were unconstitutional but held that race could be among the criteria considered in determining admissions.)[56]

The Bakke decision was followed by another major CASA effort to drum up membership and enhance its visibility. This time the issue involved a person whose problem was reminiscent of Los Tres. José Jacques Medina, a Mexican national and member of CASA, became the target of a U.S. government attempt to deport him. On March 26, 1976, he was arrested and charged by the Immigration and Naturalization Service with illegal entry into the country. A month later, CASA launched a campaign to gain political asylum for Medina on the grounds that he had participated in the 1968 Mexico City student demonstrations and would surely face prosecution, if not death, in his mother country were he to be sent there. As in the Bakke case, CASA did not exist long enough to finish this battle, but, like the earlier Los Tres incident, the fight provided CASA with opportunities to keep its name before the public and, it was hoped, arouse and win the working class to its cause.[57] (In the mid-1980s, after CASA's demise, Medina gained asylum as a political refugee in the U.S.)

Another CASA effort to increase its international as well its national visibility involved establishing ties with kindred groups abroad — "horizontal groups subject to and subject of the state."[58] Its first visit abroad was in November 1975 to the Congress of the Puerto Rican Socialist Party. There, and in later talks throughout the island, CASA political commission members (Antonio Rodríguez, Felipe Aguirre, and Carlos Vásquez) called for solidarity between the Mexican-American struggle and the Puerto Rican Independence movement. A year and a half later, in March 1977, CASA sent Carlos Vásquez to the World Federation of Trade Unions Conference on Youth, in Nicosia, Cyprus, where he affirmed common cause with national liberation struggles being waged in the eastern hemisphere. Two months later, at the Partido Communista Mexicano's Eighteenth Congress in Mexico City, CASA representatives announced their support of the Mexican left, including the Communist struggles in Mexico. Such forays, CASA's leaders believed, would not be complete without a visit to Fidel Castro's Cuba. That came in December 1977, following an invitation from the Cuban government. The CASA delegation publicized its solidarity with all working-class people, especially Latinos, through visits to newspaper offices, factories, schools, and meetings with political leaders.[59]

How much of this international barnstorming came to the attention of the Mexican workers in the U.S. is unclear, but the Federal Bureau of Investigation was fully aware of such activity and much more as well. Some 660 pages of documents obtained through the Freedom of Information Act reveal that the FBI had infiltrated CASA and gathered information for more than four years, from April 1972 to August 1976. The FBI justified its action on the grounds "that the organizations [CASA and the Committee to Free Los Tres] are involved in activities that could constitute violations of Title 18, U.S. Code, Sections 2383 (Rebellion or Insurrection), 2384 (Seditious conspiracy), 2385 (Advocating Overthrow of the Government) as well as possible violation of the Neutrality Laws statutes."[60]

to violent conflict. The two groups first clashed when they shared office space at the Los Angeles Black Congress, an umbrella organization that served as a clearinghouse for war on poverty programs and funds.[44] However, their most violent confrontation would occur when members of both organizations were students in UCLA's High Potential Program (a special admissions program that sought to bring minority students into the university's fold). On January 17, 1969, following a meeting to discuss the direction of the university's newly formed Black Studies program, an US member insulted Panther member Elaine Brown, which resulted in a scuffle between the US member and Bunchy Carter, the Los Angeles Black Panther Party's founder, which resulted in Carter and John Huggins, the Los Angeles chapter's chairman, being shot to death by a high-ranking US member (which some suspected was acting on Karenga's and the FBI's orders).[45] Though their differences were similar to black ideological debates, Chicano activists never took to killing each other. That is not to say that one ethnic group was more violent than the other. Instead, the conflict between the Black Panthers and US points to the specificity of activism within a given community.

Instead of resorting to violence, CASA faced the challenges of the ATM by reassessing its strategy and becoming more willing to work with other groups, even those of non-Marxist persuasion, so long as they agreed to fight for the rights of ethnic Mexicans and against what they perceived as an imperialist United States.[46] This led to broad and loose cooperation with individuals and organizations. In May 1975, for example, in its opposition to the Rodino bill (calling for fines on employers who knowingly hired undocumented workers), CASA worked with congressmen (Herman Badillo, D–New York; Edward Roybal, D–California), governors (Raúl Castro, D–Arizona; Jerry Apodaca, D–New Mexico), civil rights organizations (the Mexican American Political Association and the Association of Immigration and Nationality Lawyers), and labor unions (the United Farm Workers, the United Auto Workers, the International Longshoremen and Warehouses).[47] In response to Peter Rodino's insistence that his bill would produce more jobs for U.S. citizens, CASA called for a "united front of trade unions, progressive organizations, and all democratic individuals."[48] CASA also waged cultural war against the legislation through its theatre group, "Teatro Movimiento Primavera." In a play entitled *Cochino Rodino,* the highlight was a raid by immigration agents on a factory employing undocumented workers. The agents made no distinction between Mexicans born in Mexico and those native to the United States, an action

FIGURE 7. "¡Resistencia!" poster, August 29, 1977. Protest announcement courtesy of the artist, Elsa Flores.

that vividly underscored CASA's contention about the unity of ethnic Mexicans above and below the border.[49]

Such efforts helped to defeat the Rodino bill in December 1975 and encouraged CASA in its coalition-building venture. Still, CASA was disappointed in failing to win the cooperation of as many ethnic Mexican groups, especially laborers, as anticipated. An internal evaluation attrib-

repeated the Comité's prescriptions about discipline, criticism/self-criticism, and democratic centralism. Most of the remainder dealt with structure, especially the new three levels of membership, of which the highest was that of "militant." Those in this category had to be at least eighteen years old, not belong to any other group or organization, and were eligible for election to positions of higher authority and as delegates to the National Congress. The next level of membership was "affiliate," which was similar to militant except in two respects: affiliates could belong to other organizations that did not contravene CASA's principles, but they were ineligible to vote or hold office. The *simpatizantes,* or sympathizers, contributed money to the organization but did not have to adhere to its regulations, and, like affiliates, were ineligible to vote or hold office.[37]

CASA described its organizational philosophy as "Democratic centralism," a notion also reflected in its highest body, the National Congress, which met annually, with delegates elected in the proportion of one representative for every three militants. The Congress's duties included approving (and modifying when deemed necessary) the Reglamento, ensuring that the membership complied with its regulations, and formulating the organization's position on political issues. The body also elected, by majority vote, a five-person Central Committee whose primary function was to implement the decisions of the National Congress. The Central Committee, in turn, appointed members to four secretariats: Organization, in charge of studying the political, economic, demographic, and ideological conditions of the local chapters; Information and Propaganda, which oversaw *Sin Fronteras* as well as coordinating and implementing political study plans and compiling a propaganda manual; Finances, in charge of raising money; and Labor and Workers' Affairs, whose task was to maintain communication with labor unions and to conduct a census of CASA membership. From its ranks the Central Committee elected the Political Commission, which had responsibility for preserving the political and ideological purity of CASA's members and expelling those suspected of deviations.[38] As with La Raza Unida Party, a smothering bureaucracy had been put in place.

CASA's structure was predicated on the unity of an imagined ethnic Mexican community, but the release of its organizational Reglamento, just like the resolutions approved at the Los Angeles conference, underscored the reality of a multifaceted ethnic Mexican community. The Greeley chapter greeted the Reglamento by breaking with the national organization. "Democratic Centralism," declared the Greeley protesters, will produce "opportunism, vacillation, and confusion" because the leadership, not the member, will be determining CASA's direction. "Priority," they insisted, should go "to build[ing a] revolutionary cadre who will not blindly tail the mass movement but will in fact lead and guide the mass movement to proletarian revolution." Proclaiming that "conditions are objectively different in the areas" served by CASA's various chapters, the Greeley protesters insisted that each chapter should go its own way in "the process of cadre building" and advancing "the struggle against imperialism and the ending of the exploitation of man by man."[39]

Resistance to CASA came from without as well as within. Perhaps the sharpest outside criticism was that of the August Twenty-Ninth Movement (ATM), which challenged CASA's contention that Chicanos and Mexicans constituted a single Mexican nation. Such an idea was "preposterous," ATM stated, for Chicanos were a distinct people with a history of their own in the United States.[40] U.S. imperialists had suppressed the Chicano people by annexing their land and oppressing them through gerrymandering political districts, suppressing the Spanish language and culture, and encouraging "police terrorism, [and] job and educational discrimination." Chicanos, declared ATM, drawing on writings by Joseph Stalin, must wage their own struggle for self-determination, elimination of imperialism, and creation of a socialist state.[41]

CASA's immediate response to ATM — it was Maoist "in the most sectarian and dogmatic sense of the term" — only seemed to exacerbate divisions among Chicano radicals. These differences over what was best for the ethnic Mexican community were similar to the cleavages that existed among black activists in Los Angeles. The prime example in that fault line were the disagreements between the Black Panther Party and United Slaves (US). Fundamentally, this conflict stemmed from the unique vision that each group had for Los Angeles's African-American community. The Panthers subscribed to black revolutionary nationalism, which derived from Marxist thought, and believed that the foremost problem facing black and other Third World peoples was American-led, capitalist control of the international economy.[42] US, on the other hand, operated within the tenets of black cultural nationalism, an ideology that sought to affirm a black cultural renaissance. A distinctive black national culture was US's ultimate goal. As a step in that direction, in December 1966 US founder Maulana Ron Karenga instituted Kwanzaa — a six-day holiday that celebrated the first fruits and was based on African harvest-time festivals — as an alternative to Christmas.[43]

The divisions among the Black Panthers and US would eventually lead

Numerous FBI agents, with the help of at least twenty-one informants, investigated CASA's activities in Los Angeles, Greeley, San Diego,
and San Jose. They produced detailed reports on such matters as the
teaching of Marxist classes at CASA headquarters, the drafting of the
Comité's "Principles," the merger of the Comité and CASA, and such
everyday events as telephone calls between members and even trips to
the bank.[61]

In January 1975, FBI agents in Washington, D.C., concluded that the
voluminous reports revealed nothing dangerous about CASA and
instructed its Los Angeles office to discontinue the investigation: CASA's
"activities fail to indicate possible violation of Federal Statutes."[62] The
agents in Los Angeles disagreed, pointing out that CASA had claimed solidarity with Mexican Communists and was "presently involved in indoc-
trination of members in revolutionary theory."[63] FBI superiors backed
down and allowed the investigation to continue, but a year and a half
later, in July 1976, they again told the Los Angeles agents to cease. This,
as before, prompted a protest.

The Federal Bureau of Investigation (FBI) has conducted a full investigation of
Centro de Acción Social Autónomo (CASA) and has obtained information giving reason to believe that CASA may be involved in activities which involve or will
involve the violation of Federal law for the purpose of overthrowing the
Government of the United States. . . . The harm threatened by CASA is believed
to be of considerable magnitude in view of its objectives, affiliation with the PSP
[Partido Socialista Puertorriqueño] and the involvement of Mexican Nationals
known to have been agitators in a riotous situation [perhaps a reference to some
CASA members being present at the 1968 Mexico City student uprising]. The like-
lihood of the threat materializing into acts of violence and immediacy of the threat
are uncertain. However, . . . the threat and the immediacy of that threat cannot
be minimized.[64]

The memo identified four actions believed to be in violation of federal
law: the burning of the U.S. flag at a demonstration by CASA members
in March 1974; the purchase in June 1974 of two M-1 carbines by a CASA
member who used them to arm revolutionaries in Mexico; the purchase
in October 1975 of weapons by CASA member Mario Cantú, who
allegedly shipped them to Mexican guerillas; and CASA's affiliation with
the Partido Socialista Puertoriqeño and possible alliance with the Armed
Forces for Puerto Rican National Liberation.[65]

Following a reexamination by the FBI's Investigative Review Unit,
U.S. Attorney General Edward Levi, on November 16, 1976, ordered the
Los Angeles office to call off its investigation.[66]

The facts presented by the FBI's investigative summary portray a group of approximately 50 persons whose stated goals are reform of United States Immigration laws and a movement toward a Marxist form of government both in the United States and elsewhere. . . . The facts here presented do not establish the use of force or violence and violation of the federal law for the purpose of overthrowing the government of the United States. Demonstrations organized to protest United States immigration laws do not meet this burden. Nor does the teaching of Marxist thought to the membership. . . . For the reasons stated above I have concluded that the domestic security investigation of Centro de Accion Social Autonomo should be closed. This decision does not preclude domestic security investigations of individuals who are members of CASA; however, such investigations must be predicated on something other than CASA membership alone.[67]

As the FBI was drawing its investigation to a close, CASA was entering its death throes. Despite the expenditure of much energy, there had been few dramatic victories and none that CASA could claim as its own. The working class remained no more unified than before, and CASA had not emerged as the leader of that class or of ethnic Mexicans, whether citizens or not. Indeed, CASA's switch from a service-oriented, mutual-aid society to a mass revolutionary organization had caused membership to fall dramatically from the pre-merger high of four thousand to three hundred registered members. Only fifty of them were actively involved in CASA activities for "reasons other than immigration aid," as the FBI investigation revealed.

Such bitter disappointments prompted members to look to themselves for the causes of their failure. "Self-criticism" soon became wholesale criticism, name-calling, and bitter conflicts between those claiming to be the real revolutionaries living up to the letter of the Reglamento and those viewed as backsliders. The first public sign of discord was the resignation of Carlos Vásquez, director of *Sin Fronteras* and a member of the Political Commission. He was leaving, he announced, because of "fundamental weaknesses for [a] revolutionary organization among our people to fall into at this time, and more seriously not correct when these errors are pointed out."[68]

Vásquez's resignation served only to intensify the internal bickering and search for scapegoats. Hours were spent in discussions of the fine points of CASA orthodoxy in order to determine who might have "fallen" into "spontaneous methods of work," or was guilty of "ideological putchism," "lack of development and lack of growth," "intimidation," "corruption," "double standards, exceptionalism, and nepotism." Further exacerbating these tensions was the widespread belief that CASA National

hospital authorities asked women to consent to the sterilization while they were in labor or in the delivery room and obviously unable to make an informed and conscious decision. Since the U.S. Department of Health, Education and Welfare subsidized the sterilizations performed there and at other hospitals, the Comité viewed these actions as another example of the violation of the rights of Latinos and working-class people by an imperialist nation.[22]

Another sensitive issue that the Comité sought to make its own was the plight of undocumented Mexican workers. Through conferences and demonstrations, CEP highlighted its solidarity with the workers and vigorously denounced deportation efforts. At a conference called "¡Despierta Chicano/Defiende Tu Hermano!" (Wake Up Chicano/Defend Your Brother) in February 1975 at California State University at Los Angeles, Arturo Chávez, a CEP member, sharply criticized "dragnet raids within the Latino communities and the anti-immigrant sentiment advocated by government officials and legislators." Such actions, he declared, "raise the possibility of Mexicanos undergoing mass deportation campaigns comparable to the ones of the '30s and '50s. We must take a lesson from history and realize that citizenship papers don't really matter when it comes to a terrorist campaign where an entire group of people are being blamed for the crisis in a country."[23] To the Comité, there were no fundamental differences between Chicanos and the residents of Mexico — all comprised a single ethnic Mexican community. Capitalism had made both Mexicans and Chicanos into workers, and they should organize along class and ethnic lines.[24]

Merging class with ethnicity reflected a larger evolution that the Comité was undergoing. It now sought to go beyond concentrating only on political propaganda and to move into serving and organizing working-class people. As a result of these changing goals, the Comité sought an organizational structure better suited to achieve them. Another motive for reorganization was that by late 1974 the only remaining step in the defense of Los Tres was review by the U.S. Supreme Court. Given this situation, the Comité leadership examined the prospect of joining both the Communist Party (CP) and former Southern California CP leader Dorothy Healey's New American Movement, because these groups had more-comprehensive agendas. Though the Comité claimed to have moved beyond Mexican protonationalism, a strong nationalist current still remained among its members that made impossible the group's joining of a non–ethnic Mexican group. Comité leaders then proposed a merger with CASA as a better way to serve the ethnic Mexican working

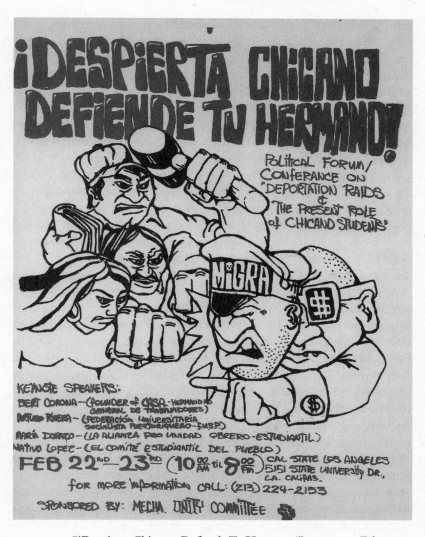

FIGURE 6. "¡Despierta Chicano, Defiende Tu Hermano!" poster, ca. February 1974. Conference poster courtesy of the artist, John Alvarez.

class and also to assure its continued existence once the U.S. Supreme Court had ruled on the Los Tres appeal.[25] Another consideration for favoring such a union was the rather close agreement on policy issues of the two groups. Still another inducement was the opportunity for the Comité to spread its message elsewhere in the Southwest. Besides Los

of gerrymandered districts and inadequate campaign funds. Such disappointments saw MAPA slip into obscurity and change tactics as other more radical organizations, driven by anger over persistent poverty, an inadequate educational system, police brutality, and the unequal effects on Chicano youth of the Vietnam War, sprang onto the scene voicing an even more strident ethnic nationalism and engaging in militant confrontation to bring about change. Their tactics and emphases varied, perhaps most dramatically with the Brown Berets, a male-centered paramilitary group that captured the imagination of young people and the media by encouraging the East Los Angeles "blow outs," creating a free clinic, and calling for an end to the Vietnam War before that demand became widespread. Internal bickering, equivocal grandstanding, as in their "invasion" of Santa Catalina Island, and capture of the popular anti-Vietnam issue by the Chicano Moratorium Committee propelled the Berets into oblivion.

The Moratorium Committee, with its vigorous opposition to the "genocidal war" in Vietnam, galvanized the Chicano community, especially draft-age youth, more than any other organization or issue throughout the 1960s and '70s. The committee's greatest triumph — the antiwar protest attended by thousands in Los Angeles on August 29, 1970 — also became its undoing. The violence, property damage, and deaths that followed later that day created a backlash. As supporters fell away, the Moratorium Committee changed its emphasis from ending the war to combating police brutality, and vitality ebbed to the point where the committee disbanded.

As the Moratorium Committee lost momentum, Chicano activists began turning to the example of Texas's La Raza Unida Party (LRUP) and attempted to use the ballot box to empower Mexican Americans. Instead of uniting behind the effort, the party's chapters bickered among themselves over tactics and priorities, failing not only to elect their candidates but also to collect the signatures needed to obtain ballot status for the party. This debacle brought to the forefront the Centro de Acción Social Autónomo (CASA), which emphasized tight central control in place of LRUP's dispersed, almost anarchical, behavior; Marxist–Leninist ideology instead of LRUP's appeal to the ballot box; and a focus on fomenting revolution while neglecting the needs of the ethnic Mexican working class. Such a sharp swing to the left proved no more successful than LRUP's effort or those of earlier activists who failed to adopt programs attractive to the larger ethnic Mexican community. They appeared to be splinter groups appealing to narrow constituencies and gaining media attention but little else.

By the late 1970s the Chicano movement was a phenomenon of the past, as ethnic Mexicans returned to smaller efforts like those of the 1950s that emphasized electoral politics. With CASA's demise, the mass demonstrations of the previous decade gave way in the 1980s to smaller efforts focused on electoral politics.[2] Viewed in relation to MAPA's work in the 1960s, the turn toward electoral politics is part of a continuum rather than a new beginning. Thus, the Chicano movement, in the words of David G. Gutiérrez, emerges as a moment of radical potential that never engendered a revolution and ultimately brought complacency.[3] The turn toward mainstream electoral politics is perhaps the best evidence that the Chicano movement was indeed a moment of potential radicalism.

The movement's ability to change the course of Mexican-American electoral politics is evident in Los Angeles, which has a Mexican-American county supervisor and three ethnic Mexican councilmen in 2001.[4] This impact is also visible in the California Assembly, where three members are Mexican Americans representing the Los Angeles area.[5] In addition, there are four Mexican-American members of Congress representing greater Los Angeles. Included in this august group is Lucille Roybal-Allard, Edward Roybal's daughter. Another member of Congress from Southern California is Loretta Sánchez, who in 1996 defeated Robert K. Dornan, the Republican incumbent, in a bitter campaign later contested by the former Congressman. This was quite a remarkable feat, given the traditionally conservative constituency of her Orange County District.[6] Her victory was aided by citizenship efforts and registration drives spearheaded by Hermandad Mexicana, a civil rights organization whose leadership includes former members of CASA. Thus, the Chicano movement's lasting legacy has been to ensure that Los Angeles's — if not Southern California's — ethnic Mexican population is represented in government. Yet, in being transformed into purely electoral efforts, the grassroots elements and the ability to truly redefine the American political landscape — to bring about days of revolution — has disappeared.

Given the current state of affairs in California, and the nation in general, vis-à-vis ethnic Mexicans and other people of color, it seems pertinent to forge a politics that goes beyond upholding the status quo. Though there is more Latino representation in government, there are also more flagrant attacks against minority groups than ever before. Perhaps the anti-Latino bias is a result of the perceptions of reactionary politicians that such groups, and people of color in general, are taking over the state. Indeed, in the year 2000, U.S. Census data revealed that California's "minority" population had become its majority.[7] Yet this demographic shift has not necessarily been transferred into political power. A step towards re-imagining empowerment may lie in Chicana feminist critic

27. Dolores Delgado Bernal, "Grassroots Leadership Reconceptualized: Chicana Oral Histories and the 1968 East Los Angeles School Blowouts," *Frontiers* 19, no. 2 (1998): 120.

28. Rodolfo Acuña, *Occupied America: A History of Chicanos,* 3d ed. (New York: Harper and Row, 1988), 336.

29. David Sánchez, *Expedition Through Aztlán* (La Puente, Calif.: Perspectiva Press, 1978), 2.

30. Ruben Salazar, "Brown Berets Hail 'La Raza' and Scorn the Establishment," *Los Angeles Times,* June 16, 1969, sec. 1, p. 24.

31. "Who Are the Brown Berets?" *Chicano Student News,* March 15, 1968, p. 5.

32. Oscar Zeta Acosta, "The East L.A. 13 vs. the L.A. Superior Court," *El Grito* 3, no. 2 (winter 1970): 12.

33. Victor Franco, "E.L.A. Raided," *Inside Eastside,* June 10–13, 1968, p. 3.

34. Becerra, interview.

35. "For the Black Panthers' "Ten Points", see "October 1966 Black Panther Party Platform and Program: What We Want and What We Believe," in Foner, *The Black Panthers Speak,* 2–4.

36. "Brown Berets: Serve, Observe, and Protect," *La Raza* (newspaper), June 7, 1968, p. 13.

37. Ibid.

38. Ibid.

39. Becerra, interview.

40. Ibid.

41. In May 1969 the Beret newspaper *La Causa* reported that the organization had twenty-eight chapters in cities including San Antonio, Texas; Eugene, Oregon; Denver, Colorado; Detroit, Michigan; Seattle, Washington; Albuquerque, New Mexico; and most major California cities (see *La Causa,* May 23, 1969, p. 2).

42. Becerra, interview.

43. "The East Los Angeles 13 Are Ready," *La Raza* (newspaper), October 15, 1968, p. 13.

44. Ibid.; Della Rossa, "Poor People's Coalition," *La Raza* (newspaper), July 10, 1968, p. 7.

45. "News for a More Aware Community," *La Causa,* May 23, 1969, p. 8.

46. "Brown Berets: 8 Points of Attention," *La Causa,* December 1970, p. 19. The Brown Berets appear to be modeled after Mao Zedong's 1928 "Eight Rules" for the Red Guard; for more on this, see Zhong Wenxian, ed., *Mao Zedong: Biography, Assessment, Reminiscences* (Beijing: Foreign Language Press, 1986), 60–61. The Black Panthers also had a similar "Eight Points"; for these, see Foner, *The Black Panthers Speak,* 6. One such recruitment message was entitled "Becoming A Brown Beret: A Reason For Existing" (see *La Causa,* December 1970, p. 12).

47. "Third Annual Nuevas Vistas Conference" program, April 1969, Richard and Gloria Santillán Collection, University of California at Berkeley, Chicano Studies Library.

48. Those arrested were Chris Augustine, Luis Arroyo, Chris Cebada, Jaime Cervantes, Adelaida R. Del Castillo, Ernest Eichwald, Moctesuma Esparza, Reynaldo Macías, Francisco Martínez, Rene Núñez, Frank Sandoval, Victor Resendez, James Vigil, Thomas Varela, and Petra Valdez ("Ronnie's Show Flops as Biltmore Burns," *La Raza* [newspaper], April 30, 1969, p. 3).

49. "Ronnie's Show Flops as Biltmore Burns," *La Raza* (newspaper), April 30, 1969, p. 3; and Tom Newton, "Demonstration Disrupts Talk by Governor," *Los Angeles Times,* April 25, 1969, sec. 1, p. 1.

50. "14 Jailed in Biltmore Hotel Outburst," *Los Angeles Herald-Examiner,* April 25, 1969, sec. 1-A, p. 1.

51. The ten were Anthony Salamanca, Esmeralda Bernal, Carlos Montes, Ralph Ramírez, Thomas Varela, Rene Núñez, Ernest Eichwald Cebeda, Juan Robles, Moctesuma Esparza, and Willie Mendoza ("Nuevas Vistas 10," *La Raza* [newspaper], July 1969, p. 13).

52. "Nueva Vistas 10," *La Raza* (newspaper), July 1969, p. 10.

53. "Carlos Montes Disappears," *La Causa,* February 28, 1970, p. 9.

54. These issues were vol. 1, nos. 6–10, and vol. 2, nos. 1–2.

55. "Opening Statement Recorded on the Carlos Montes Trial," October 2, 1979; and "Superior Court of the State of California for the County of Los Angeles — The People vs. Carlos Michael Montes" (trial transcript), February–April 1979, p. 579; both in Oscar Zeta Acosta Papers, Department of Special Collections, University of California at Santa Barbara.

56. Ron Einstoss, "Undercover Officer Describes Role at Biltmore Fire Trial," *Los Angeles Times,* June 7, 1969, p. 2.

57. Los Angeles Police Department, Intelligence Report, file S-257.

58. Ibid.

59. "Opening Statement Recorded on the Carlos Montes Trial," October 2, 1979, pp. 3–4, Oscar Zeta Acosta Papers, Department of Special Collections, University of California at Santa Barbara.

60. "Is There a Frito Bandito in Your House?" *La Causa,* July 10, 1969, p. 3.

61. "Serving the People: The E.L.A. Free Clinic," *La Causa,* December 16, 1969, p. 2.; Ruben Salazar, "Brown Berets Hail 'La Raza' and Scorn the Establishment," *Los Angeles Times,* June 16, 1969, sec. 1, p. 24.

62. "Serving the People: The E.L.A. Free Clinic," *La Causa,* December 16, 1969, p. 2.; Ruben Salazar, "Brown Berets Hail 'La Raza' and Scorn the Establishment," *Los Angeles Times,* June 16, 1969, sec. 1, p. 24.

63. Though Sánchez claims, in *Expedition Through Aztlán* (p. 4), that he came up with the idea for the group, my research shows that Rosalio Muñoz, a UCLA student, was thinking along the same lines, and along with fellow Bruin, Ramsés Noriega, formed an organization, "Chale Con La Draft," to bring awareness on the draft to the Chicano community (see chapter 3).

64. "Chicano Moratorium: A Matter of Survival," *La Causa,* February 28, 1970, p. 1.

65. "La Caravan De La Reconquista is Coming," *La Causa,* ca. 1972, p. 1.

66. "Brown Berets National Policies" *La Causa,* ca. 1972.

8. Gutiérrez, *Walls and Mirrors*, 77.

9. For more on the Congress of Spanish-Speaking Peoples and the Asociación Nacional Mexico Americana, see Mario T. García, *Mexican Americans: Leadership, Ideology, and Identity, 1930–1960* (New Haven: Yale University Press, 1989).

10. For more on the G.I. Forum, see Henry A. J. Ramos, *The American G.I Forum: In Pursuit of the Dream* (Houston: Arte Público Press, 1998).

11. David G. Gutiérrez had argued this in "Significant for Whom?: Mexican Americans and the History of the American West," *Western Historical Quarterly* 24, no. 4 (November 1993): 527.

12. Rafael Pérez-Torres, "Reframing Aztlán," *Aztlán* 22, no. 2 (fall 1997): 37.

13. Eric J. Hobsbawm, "Popular Proto-Nationalism," in *Nations and Nationalism Since 1780: Programme, Myth, and Reality* (Cambridge: Cambridge University Press, 1990), 73.

14. David G. Gutiérrez discusses this tension in *Walls and Mirrors*.

15. Raymond Williams, "Base and Superstructure in Marxist Cultural Theory," in *Problems in Materialism and Culture*, 2d ed. (New York: Verso, 1997), 40.

16. Literary critic Mikhail Bakhtin argues that a dialogic contact occurs when "the text" comes "into contact with another text (with context). Only at the point of this contact between texts does a light flash, illuminating both the posterior and anterior, joining a given text into a dialogue" (see Bahktin, *Speech Genres and Other Late Essays* [Austin: University of Texas Press, 1986]), 22.

17. Williams, "Base and Superstructure," 40.

18. Elleke Boehmer, as quoted in Anne McClintock, *Imperial Leather: Race, Gender and Sexuality in the Colonial Contest* (New York: Routledge, 1995), 355.

19. Stuart Hall, "Ethnicity: Identity and Difference," *Radical America* 23, no. 4 (October–December 1989): 15.

20. Van Gosse, *Where the Boys Are: Cuba, Cold War America, and the Making of a New Left* (New York: Verso, 1993), 8.

21. Ernesto Laclau, *Emancipation(s)* (New York: Verso, 1996), 35.

22. Among the books that have examined the Chicano movement are Ignacio García, *Chicanismo: The Forging of a Militant Ethos Among Chicanos* (Tucson: University of Arizona Press, 1997); Juan Gómez-Quiñones, *Mexican Students por La Raza: The Chicano Student Movement in Southern California, 1967–1977* (Santa Barbara: Editorial La Causa, 1978); Carlos Muñoz, *Youth, Identity, Power: The Chicano Movement* (New York: Verso, 1989); Armando Navarro, *Mexican American Youth Organization: Avant Garde of the Chicano Movement in Texas* (Austin: University of Texas Press, 1995); Armando Navarro, *The Cristal Experiment: A Chicano Struggle for Community Control* (Madison: University of Wisconsin Press, 1999); and Ernesto Vigil, *The Crusade for Justice: Chicano Militancy and the Government's War on Dissent* (Madison: University of Wisconsin Press, 1999).

CHAPTER 1: "A MOVABLE OBJECT MEETING AN IRRESISTIBLE FORCE"

1. Raymond Williams, "Base and Superstructure in Marxist Material Culture," in *Problems in Materialism and Culture*, 2d ed. (New York: Verso, 1997), 40.

2. Bureau of the Census, *U.S. Census of Population, 1950. Special Reports. Persons of Spanish Surname* (Washington, D.C.: Government Printing Office, 1953), 3C-43; Bureau of the Census, *U.S. Census of Population, 1960. Subject Reports. Persons of Spanish Surname. Final Report PC (2)-1B* (Washington, D.C.: Government Printing Office, 1963), 132–33.

3. Leo Grebler, Joan Moore, and Ralph C. Guzmán, *The Mexican American People: The Nation's Second Largest Minority* (New York: Free Press, 1970), 15.

4. Ibid.

5. Although the census uses the category "Spanish surname," given California's large ethnic population, most of those counted were probably of Mexican descent (see Bureau of the Census, *U.S. Census of Population, 1960, PC(2)-1B*, table 5; and vol. 1, pts. 4, 6, 7, 33, and 45, tables 65 and 139, as found in Grebler, Moore, and Guzmán, *The Mexican American People*, 181).

6. Grebler, Moore, and Guzmán, *The Mexican American People*, 187.

7. Grebler, Moore, and Guzmán, *The Mexican American People*, 209. The U.S. Census and *The Mexican American People* only give information for men. This is not in any way to imply that women were not a vital part of the workforce and that they did not serve as the primary wage-earners in some families. It is doubtless that information for women would reveal that as a whole they were economically disadvantaged when compared to men. It would also probably show that Anglo women earned more than Spanish-surnamed women. The percentage of Anglo professional women would also probably be higher than that of Spanish-surnamed women.

8. Vicki L. Ruiz, *From Out of the Shadows: Mexican Women in Twentieth-Century America* (New York: Oxford University Press, 1998), 153.

9. Mario T. García, *Mexican Americans: Leadership, Ideology, and Identity, 1930–1960* (New Haven: Yale University Press, 1989), 4–5. García worked from a concept originally conceived by sociologist Rodolfo Alvarez. In his 1973 article, Alvarez used the term to refer to a biological generation rather than a political generation (see Alvarez, "The Psycho-Historical and Socioeconomic Development of the Chicano Community in the United States," *Social Science Quarterly* [March 1973]: 920–42).

10. García, *Mexican Americans*, 4–5.

11. Gary Gerstle, *Working-Class Americanism: The Politics of Labor in a Textile City, 1914–1960* (New York: Cambridge University Press, 1989), 8.

12. Ibid., 9–13.

13. William H. Chafe, *The Unfinished Journey: America Since World War II*, 2d ed. (New York: Oxford University Press, 1991), 109–10.

14. Jackson Lears, "A Matter of Taste: Corporate Cultural Hegemony in a Mass-Consumption Society," in *Recasting America: Culture and Politics in the Age of the Cold War*, ed. Lary May (Chicago: University of Chicago Press, 1989), 42.

15. Sanford D. Horwitt, *Let Them Call Me Rebel: Saul Alinsky — His Life and Legacy* (New York: Alfred A. Knopf, 1989), 228.

16. Ibid., 229.

17. Ibid., 228–29.

18. Ibid., 229.

119. Mexican American Political Association [hereafter MAPA], "State Constitution and By-Laws" (May 1961), Manuel Ruiz Papers, M295, box 6, folder 6, Stanford University Library, Department of Special Collections.

120. García, *Memories of Chicano History,* 200.

121. MAPA, "Mexican American Political Association" (September 18, 1964), Manuel Ruiz Papers, M295, Stanford University Library, Department of Special Collections.

122. MAPA, "State Constitution and By-Laws" (May 1961), Manuel Ruiz Papers, M295, box 6, folder 6, Stanford University Library, Department of Special Collections; Briegel, "History of Political Organizations Among Mexican-Americans," 51.

123. Briegel, "History of Political Organizations Among Mexican-Americans," 52.

124. Ibid., 52–53; MAPA, "Mexican American Political Association" (September 18, 1964), Manuel Ruiz Papers, M295, Stanford University Library, Department of Special Collections; Louis F. Weschler and John F. Gallagher, "Viva Kennedy," in *Cases in American National Government and Politics,* ed. Rocco J. Tresolini and Richard T. Frost (Englewood Cliffs, N.J.: Prentice Hall, Inc., 1965), 55–56.

125. Weschler and Gallagher, "Viva Kennedy," 56.

126. Ibid., 57.

127. Ibid., 58.

128. Ibid., 59.

129. Eventually, García served on the United States delegation to the United Nations and as a special ambassador to the West Indies.

130. García, *Memories of Chicano History,* 209.

131. García, *Mexican Americans,* 141.

132. García, *Memories of Chicano History,* 209.

133. MAPA, "Mexican American Appointees — Governor Edmund G. Brown," Eduardo Quevedo Papers, M349, box 4, folder 1, Stanford University Library, Department of Special Collections; García, *Memories of Chicano History,* 209.

134. Ralph Guzmán, "The Political Socialization of the Mexican American People" (Ph.D. diss., University of California at Los Angeles, 1970), 259.

135. Ibid., 259–60.

136. Reynaldo Macías et al., *A Study of Unincorporated East Los Angeles* (Los Angeles: Aztlán Publications, Chicano Studies Center, University of California at Los Angeles, 1973), 22.

137. Guzmán, "Political Socialization of the Mexican American People," 259–60.

138. Ibid., 262.

139. Acuña, *A Community Under Siege,* 353.

140. Guzmán, "Political Socialization of the Mexican American People," 263.

141. Ruben Salazar, "Negro May Win Roybal Seat in City Council," *Los Angeles Times,* December 12, 1962, in Ruben Salazar, *Border Correspondent: Selected*

Writings, 1955–1970, edited and with an introduction by Mario T. García (Berkeley: University of California Press, 1995), 80.

142. Ibid.

143. Briegel, "History of Political Organizations Among Mexican-Americans," 55.

144. *Carta Editorial,* vol. 1, no. 7 (July 3, 1963), p. 2.

145. Ibid.

146. MAPA, "By-Laws of the Mexican American Political Association, 1963," Manuel Ruiz Papers, M295, Stanford University Library, Department of Special Collections.

147. "Mexican Americans Face Defeat," *Carta Editorial,* vol. 2, no.2 (June 12, 1964), pp. 1–2.

148. "The Assault on the Fair Housing Act," *Frontier,* February 1964, pp. 4, 13.

149. Acuña, *A Community Under Siege,* 154.

150. "The Irony of the Mexican American Position," *Carta Editorial,* vol. 2, no. 7 (September 8, 1964), p. 1.

151. "The Fast Shuffle," *Carta Editorial,* vol. 2, no. 6 (August 20, 1964), pp. 1–2.

152. MAPA, "Minutes of the Executive Board of the Mexican American Political Association, held on April 24, 1965 at Felipe's Restaurant in Downey, California," Manuel Ruiz Papers, M295, box 7, folder 17, Stanford University Library, Department of Special Collections; and "MAPA Holds Statewide Meeting," *Carta Editorial,* vol. 2, no. 21(May 3, 1965), pp. 3–4.

153. MAPA, "Policy Resolution Adopted by State Executive Board of the Mexican American Political Association at Downey, California, April 25, 1965, Resolution on Farm Labor," Manuel Ruiz Papers, M295, box 7, folder 18, Stanford University Library, Department of Special Collections; and "MAPA holds statewide Meeting," *Carta Editorial,* vol. 2, no. 21 (May 3, 1965), pp. 3–4.

154. Letter, W. Willard Wirtz, U.S. Secretary of Labor, to Eduardo Quevedo, July 21, 1965, Eduardo Quevedo Papers, M349, box 3, folder 10, Stanford University Library, Department of Special Collections.

155. "MAPA Convention Report," *Carta Editorial,* vol. 3, no. 1 (August 10, 1965), pp. 1–3.

156. MAPA, "Resolution on State-Wide Unity of Mexican-American Organizations Number 4, Adopted by the Mexican American Political Association, April 24, 1965," Manuel Ruiz Papers, M295, box 6, folder 7, Stanford University Library, Department of Special Collections.

157. MAPA, "Open Resolution Directed to the President of the United States and Executive Departments and Agencies, By National Hispanic and Mexican American Organizations on Civil Disobedience and Riot Investigations" (September 1965), Manuel Ruiz Papers, M295, box 8, folder 8, Stanford University Library, Department of Special Collections.

158. "MAPA Chickens Out," *Carta Editorial,* vol. 3, no. 2 (August 30, 1965), p. 3.

159. "MAPA Endorsements," *Carta Editorial,* vol. 3, no. 16 (July 15, 1966), p. 2.

160. Ibid.

76. Dan Kohn, "Mass Rally Against Freeway December 10 at 2nd St. School," *Eastside Sun,* December 3, 1953, p. 1.

77. Dan Kohn, "Eastsiders Jam State Highway Freeway Hearings: To Check Alternatives," *Eastside Sun,* December 17, 1953, p. 1.

78. "Golden State Freeway Fight Lost," *Eastside Sun,* March 10, 1955, p. 1.

79. Joseph Eli Kavner, Editorial, *Eastside Sun,* January 3, 1957, p. 1.

80. "Pomona Freeway Planners Don't Tread on Us!" *Eastside Sun,* October 17, 1957, p. 1. For Mexican-American literary production in response to the building of the freeways, see Raúl H. Villa, *Barrio-Logos: Space and Place in Urban Chicano Literature and Culture* (Austin: University of Texas Press, 2000), especially chapter 3.

81. Don Parson, "'This Modern Marvel': Bunker Hill, Chavez Ravine, and the Politics of Modernism in Los Angeles," *Southern California Quarterly* 75, nos. 3–4 (fall/winter 1993): 335–37.

82. Ibid., 337.

83. Flyer, "Resist the Rape of Our Downtown Community" (1954), reprinted in Parson, "This Modern Marvel," 338.

84. Parson, "This Modern Marvel," 339–40.

85. Joseph Eli Kovner, "Land Hungry Group Wants Piece of Boyle Heights," *Eastside Sun,* April 10, 1958, p. 1.

86. Joseph Eli Kovner, "Is There a Hospital Town in Boyle Heights Future?" *Eastside Sun,* June 5, 1958, p. 1.

87. Ibid.

88. Joseph Eli Kovner, "Proclamation of the Property Owners for the Preservation of Boyle Heights," *Eastside Sun,* June 12, 1958, p. 1.

89. "Petition Protesting Declaration of Boyle Heights An Urban Renewal District by the Los Angeles City Council," Edward R. Roybal Papers, box 47, University of California at Los Angeles, Department of Special Collections.

90. Acuña, *A Community Under Siege,* 68.

91. Ibid., 340.

92. Ibid.; "Chavez Ravine Fact Book" (April 2, 1962), pp. 6–7, Edward R. Roybal Papers, box 6, University of California at Los Angeles, Department of Special Collections.

93. Joseph Eli Kovner, Editorial, *Eastside Sun,* May 14, 1959, p. 1.

94. Ibid.

95. "Chavez Ravine Dispute," *Los Angeles Times,* May 14, 1959, p. 1. The story reports that John Arechiga (the elder Arechiga's son) owned a house at 2651 Benedict Street, "which is being condemned for the route of the Golden State Freeway."

96. "Arechigas Agree to Get Off Land," *Los Angeles Times,* May 15, 1959, p. 1.

97. I borrow this concept from Alexander Saxton. He uses this label to describe ethnic Chinese workers in the late nineteenth century (see Saxton, *The Indispensable Enemy: The Anti-Chinese Campaign in California* [Berkeley: University of California Press, 1966]).

98. As quoted in Patricia Nelson Limerick, "Has 'Minority' History Trans-

formed the Historical Discourse?" *Perspectives: American Historical Association Newsletter,* vol. 35, no. 8 (November 1997), p. 34.

99. Williams, "Base and Superstructure," 40.

100. "A-9 Graduation Program," Belvedere Junior High School (January 26, 1950), Roybal Scrapbook, Edward Roybal Papers, California State University at Los Angeles, Department of Special Collections.

101. Mexican-American literature would not be published until the end of the decade, with the publication of José Antonio Villareal's *Pocho* (Garden City, N.Y.: Doubleday, 1959). The journal that did regularly publish Mexican-American short stories was the *Arizona Quarterly.* For examples, see the summer 1947 issue, which includes stories by Mario Suarez. In his story "El Hoyo," the term *Chicano,* not in its political form, appears in print for the first time.

102. John Mendez, "The Significance of Cinco de Mayo to the Mexican-American Community of the Eastside," *Eastside Sun,* May 1, 1952, p. 1.

103. John Mendez, "Pan-American Panorama" (column), *Eastside Sun,* April 9, 1953.

104. John Mendez, "Pan-American Panorama" (column), *Eastside Sun,* July 2, 1953. In 1998, the restaurant still exists and still bears the name "El Cholo."

105. John Mendez, "Pan-American Panorama" (column), *Eastside Sun,* December 18, 1952, and January 29, 1953.

106. Mexican Independence Day had been sponsored by various groups in Los Angeles since the nineteenth century.

107. Eloy Duran, "Letter to the Editor," *Eastside Sun,* September 11, 1952, p. 7.

108. Kaye Lynn Briegel, "The History of Political Organizations Among Mexican-Americans in Los Angeles Since the Second World War" (master's thesis, University of Southern California, 1967), 45.

109. Julie Leininger Pycior, *LBJ and Mexican Americans: The Paradox of Power* (Austin: University of Texas Press, 1997), 121.

110. Mario T. García, *Memories of Chicano History: The Life and Narrative of Bert Corona* (Berkeley: University of California Press, 1994), 195.

111. Briegel, "History of Political Organizations Among Mexican-Americans," 45–46; García, *Memories of Chicano History,* 196. In his narrative, Bert Corona claims that López ran for state treasurer, while Briegel says that the office sought was secretary of state. Since Briegel's is the most contemporary source, I have chosen to go with her rendering. In addition, in *Occupied America: A History of Chicanos* (New York: Harper and Row, 1981), Rodolfo Acuña identifies the office as secretary of state (p. 341).

112. Pycior, *LBJ and Mexican Americans,* 121.

113. García, *Memories of Chicano History,* 196.

114. Ibid.

115. Ibid.

116. García, *Memories of Chicano History,* 197.

117. Briegel, "History of Political Organizations Among Mexican-Americans," 50.

118. García, *Memories of Chicano History,* 198.

19. Community Service Organization [hereafter CSO], "Across the River: The CSO Quarterly" (ca. 1950), 5–6, Ernesto Galarza Papers, M224, box 13, folder 7, Stanford University Library, Department of Special Collections.

20. Horwitt, *Let Them Call Me Rebel*, 234.

21. Katherine Underwood, "Pioneering Minority Representation: Edward Roybal and the Los Angeles City Council," *Pacific Historical Review* 66, no. 3 (August 1997): 412.

22. David G. Gutiérrez, *Walls and Mirrors: Mexican Americans, Mexican Immigrants, and the Politics of Ethnicity* (Berkeley: University of California Press, 1994), 273; CSO, "Here is Your Community Service Organization" (Los Angeles, ca. 1951), Ernesto Galarza Papers, M224, box 13, folder 7, Stanford University Library, Department of Special Collections.

23. Gutiérrez, *Walls and Mirrors*, 275.

24. Ibid., 276–77.

25. Ibid., 277–78.

26. García, *Mexican Americans*, 221.

27. Horwitt, *Let Them Call Me Rebel*, 228.

28. García, *Mexican Americans*, 200.

29. Ibid., 202.

30. Ibid., 202; Liliana Urrutia, "An Offspring of Discontent: The Asociación Nacional México-Americana, 1949–1954," *Aztlán* 15, no. 1 (spring 1984): 179.

31. García, *Mexican Americans*, 202–3.

32. Ibid., 204.

33. Ibid., 205.

34. Ibid., 206.

35. Ibid.

36. Ibid., 206–7.

37. Ibid., 208.

38. Ibid., 209–10.

39. Ibid., 210–11.

40. Ibid., 211–12.

41. Ibid., 218–19.

42. Ibid., 224–26.

43. Ibid., 225–27.

44. Martin Hall, "Roybal's Candidacy and What it Means," *Frontier,* June 1954, p. 7.

45. "Red Sign-up Ordered by City Council," *Los Angeles Times,* September 14, 1950, p. 1.

46. "Councilman Charges He Was Victim of Minorities Ban," *Los Angeles Daily News,* September 2, 1949, p. 4.

47. "Roybal Raps Bias in LA Realty Deals," *Los Angeles Daily News,* September 18, 1950, p. 9.

48. Ibid.

49. Ibid.

50. "Councilmen Irked at Being Called Scum in Housing Row," *Los Angeles Daily News,* April 5, 1952, p. 3.

51. "Revive War with Mexico in Council Riot," *Los Angeles Daily News,* September 5, 1952.

52. Ibid.

53. For example, see Ada Shuster's letter to the editor in the *Eastside Sun,* September 11, 1952.

54. "History Made in Council: Roybal Speaks to Local Youngsters in Native Language," *Eastside Journal,* January 11, 1950; "Roybal Announces Sidewalks to be Built on Marengo Street," *Eastside Sun,* February 17, 1955, p. 1.

55. Joseph Eli Kovner, "Groups Assail Language Used by Chief Parker in Speaking of the Wild Tribes of Mexico," *Eastside Sun,* February 4, 1960, p. 1.

56. Martin Hall, "Roybal's Candidacy and What it Means," *Frontier,* June 1954, p. 5.

57. Rodolfo Acuña, *Occupied America: A History of Chicanos,* 2d ed. (New York: Harper and Row, 1981), 341; Bill Boyarsky, "Lost Drama in Voting Rights Suit," *Los Angeles Times,* March 7, 1990, p. B2.

58. Manny Hellerman, "East of the River," *Eastside Sun,* September 11, 1952, p. 1.

59. CSO, "The CSO Story: Democracy is not a Fake," (Los Angeles: Community Service Organization), 4, Bert Corona Papers, M248, box 13, folder 7, Stanford University Library, Department of Special Collections.

60. "Probe Report 2 L.A. Cops Beat Citizens," *Los Angeles Daily News,* March 12, 1952.

61. Ibid.

62. Ibid.

63. CSO, "The CSO Story," 4.

64. "Judge in New Blast at Police," *Daily News,* March 26, 1952, p. 2.

65. "Witness Says that Lieutenant Told Her of Yule Mauling," *Daily News,* April 17, 1952.

66. "Beating Victim Tells of Wild Night of Carousing," *Daily News,* March 19, 1952, p. 2.

67. Ibid.

68. Charlie Erickson, "Police-Minority Relations Get Better," *Los Angeles Mirror,* December 22, 1954, p. 13.

69. "Police Brutality Charges," *Daily News,* February 26, 1952, p. 1.

70. "Assault, Battery Suits Brought By Community Service Group and CLU Against Sheriff," *Eastside Sun,* September 17, 1953, p. 1.

71. CSO, "The CSO Story," 5.

72. R. Cortez Guzmán, "'Law and Order' Through Brutality?" *Eastside Sun,* September 24, 1953, p. 1.

73. Rodolfo F. Acuña, *A Community Under Siege: A Chronicle of Chicanos East of the Los Angeles River, 1945–1975* (Los Angeles: UCLA Chicano Studies Research Center Publications, no. 11, 1984), 89.

74. Joseph Eli Kovner, "Route Would Slash Through Residential and Business Districts: Protests Mount," *Eastside Sun,* October 1, 1953, p. 1.

75. Ibid.

161. "Governor's Race, Choice of Two Evils?" *Carta Editorial,* vol. 3, no. 17 (August 10, 1966), p. 3.

162. Ibid.

163. "Some Meanings of the California Elections," *Carta Editorial,* vol. 3, no. 22 (November 30, 1966), p. 1.

CHAPTER 2: "BIRTH OF A NEW SYMBOL"

1. "Man of the Year: The Inheritor," *Time,* January 6, 1967, p. 18.

2. Bernhard M. Auer, "A Letter from the Publisher," *Time,* January 6, 1967, p. 11.

3. Helen Rowan, "A Minority Nobody Knows," *Atlantic,* June 1967, p. 47.

4. Governor's Commission on the Los Angeles Riots. "Violence in the City — An End or a Beginning?" In *The Los Angeles Riots,* ed. Robert M. Fogelson, (New York: Arno Press; New York: New York Times, 1969), 5.

5. Transcript of Los Angeles Commission on Human Relations meeting, March 21, 1966, p. 28, Oscar Zeta Acosta Papers, University of California at Santa Barbara, Department of Special Collections.

6. Organizing among Mexican American youth was not new; it had happened throughout the twentieth century. The best example of this phenomenon was the Mexican American Movement (MAM) of the 1940s and 1950s. This Los Angeles–based group focused on educational reform but never included a large following. Like the Brown Berets, it too emerged from a youth conference (sponsored by the YMCA). For more on MAM, see George J. Sánchez, *Becoming Mexican American: Ethnicity, Culture, and Identity in Chicano Los Angeles, 1900–1945* (New York: Oxford University Press, 1993).

7. Program for Fourth Annual Camp Hess Kramer Leadership Conference for Mexican-American Youth, April 3–5, 1966, p. 1 (in author's possession).

8. Victoria Castro, interview by author, tape recording, Los Angeles, May 24, 1993.

9. Castro, interview; Gerald Paul Rosen, *Political Ideology and the Chicano Movement: A Study of the Political Ideology of Activists in the Chicano Movement* (San Francisco: R & E Research Associates, 1975), 73.

10. "Transcript of the John B. Luce testimony before the Los Angeles County Grand Jury," p. 397, Oscar Zeta Acosta Papers, Department of Special Collections, University of California at Santa Barbara.

11. Ibid., p. 440.

12. CSO, "Community Service Organization: 25th Anniversary Program" (Los Angeles: Community Service Organization, 1972), 8.

13. Ibid., 8–9.

14. "Transcript of the John B. Luce testimony before the Los Angeles County Grand Jury," pp. 396–405, Oscar Zeta Acosta Papers, Department of Special Collections, University of California at Santa Barbara.

15. Castro, interview.

16. Ruben Salazar, "Brown Berets Hail 'La Raza' and Scorn the Establishment," *Los Angeles Times,* June 16, 1969, sec. 1, p. 24.

17. "It's Happening," *La Raza* (newspaper), January 15, 1968, p. 2.

18. *La Raza* (newspaper), November 15, 1967, p. 6.

19. "Sheriff's Harass," *La Raza* (newspaper), January 15, 1968, p. 1.

20. Cruz (Olmeda) Becerra, interview by author, tape recording, Alhambra, California, 15 May 1993.

21. David Sánchez, "The Birth of a New Symbol," pp. 1–2, Richard and Gloria Santillán Collection, University of California at Berkeley, Chicano Studies Library. For more on the Black Panthers' rhetoric, see Phillip S. Foner, ed., *The Black Panthers Speak* (New York: J. B. Lippincott, 1970); for Malcolm X, see Malcolm X with Alex Haley, *Autobiography of Malcolm X* (New York: Ballantine Books, 1965), and David Gallen, ed., *Malcolm X: The FBI File* (New York: Carroll and Graf Publishers, 1991). Here, too, the first glimpses of the Berets' masculinist and nationalist ideology first emerged. The document concretely shows Anne McClintock's notion that all nationalisms are gendered and invented (for more on this, see Anne McClintock, *Imperial Leather: Race, Gender, and Sexuality in the Colonial Contest* [New York: Routledge, 1995]). Sánchez's ideas also reflect historian George Mosse's ruminations that "the ideal of manliness" is "basic to the national ideology" (see George Mosse, *Nationalism and Sexuality: Middle-Class Morality and Sexual Norms in Modern Europe* [Madison: University of Wisconsin Press, 1985], 23). We can read Sánchez's words as his attempt to construct a new society in which the young Chicano man would be the representative subject. Thus, in his "imagined community," men are privileged and indeed are metonymic to the idea of nation.

22. Sánchez, "The Birth of a New Symbol," 2.

23. Ibid.

24. Sánchez, "The Birth of a New Symbol," 3.

25. "Brown Berets: Serve, Observe, and Protect," *La Raza* (newspaper), June 7, 1968, p. 13. According to Cruz (Olmeda) Becerra, the structure implied by the titles never took hold and existed only on paper (Becerra, interview).

26. In Sánchez's conception of the organization, as expressed in "The Birth of a New Symbol," the Berets ideally were young men that would change the course of, and indeed, create a new history. The colonial manifestation of community would be reconstituted and a new imaginary would emerge. The role of men within the document is reminiscent of Mosse's notion of masculinity in the early modern era in Europe. He states, "The ideal of manliness was basic both to the self-definition of bourgeois society and to the national ideology. Manliness was invoked to safeguard the existing order against the perils of modernity, which threatened the clear distinction between what was considered normal and abnormality" (see Mosse, *Nationalism and Sexuality,* 23). So, too, was manliness invoked as a safeguard against the normal and the abnormal in Sánchez's rendering of society. The Brown Beret would act as prophet and bring about the "true" nature of Chicano nationalism and identity — the normal — and safeguard it against the infringement of Anglo society — the abnormal.

Chela Sandoval's model of "differential consciousness." According to Sandoval, "The differential mode of social movement and consciousness depends on the practitioner's ability to read the current situation of power and self-consciously choosing and adopting the ideological stand best suited to push against its configurations, a survival skill well known to oppressed peoples." It "requires grace, flexibility, and strength: enough strength to confidently commit to a well-defined structure of identity for one hour, day, week, month, year." Sandoval goes on to say: "Differential consciousness re-cognizes and works upon other modes of consciousness in opposition to transfigure their meanings: they convert into repositories within which subjugated citizens either occupy of throw off subjectivity, a process that simultaneously enacts yet decolonizes their various relations to their real conditions of existence."[8]

The recent presidential election, with its charges of voter fraud that disenfranchised everyday people, especially African Americans, should make us realize that new tactics are needed in order to make America truly democratic.[9] People of color, especially, need a politics that will truly empower and go beyond the narrow-mindedness that existed within the Chicano movement. As this study has shown, the Chicano movement attempted to deal with the intermingling of race and class, yet was not successful in this endeavor.[10] Though subversive activities on the part of local and federal government agencies hindered the insurgency's attempts to change the status quo, the Chicano movement also failed to achieve its goals because of its essentialist imaginings of community driven by an ideologically bankrupt cultural nationalism. Even CASA could not get away from nationalism's protean grip.

Ultimately, the Chicano movement's inadequacy points to a multifaceted and fractured ethnic Mexican community in the United States. Consequently, trying to shape a mass movement like that which Chicano activists' attempted to create will bring more problems rather than solve the current woes of Mexican America. Thus, the only way to achieve empowerment is to rethink the status and place of ethnic Mexicans in the United States, understand the group's history, and forge alliances that will truly empower everyday people. A step toward this reality can be achieved by keeping in mind that the Chicano insurgency was a specific historical production that cannot be resurrected and instead must be reflected upon and serve as a learning tool — a usable past. Thus, in order to move forward we must acknowledge the past but not be bound by it. Only by constantly redefining the boundaries of identity, community, and citizenship can true change occur. Let us build a just future.

Notes

INTRODUCTION: "THOSE TIMES OF REVOLUTION"

1. Frederic Jameson, "Periodizing the 60s," in *The 60s Without Apology,* ed. Sohnya Sayres, Anders Stephanson, Stanley Aronowitz, and Frederic Jameson (Minneapolis: University of Minnesota Press, 1984), 181.

2. David G. Gutiérrez, *Walls and Mirrors: Mexican Americans, Mexican Immigrants, and the Politics of Ethnicity* (Berkeley: University of California Press, 1995), 38.

3. I use the idea proposed by James R. Barret and David Roediger to describe the experience of Polish, Italians, and how other European immigrants became white. Though the experiences of Mexican Americans are different, they are also "in-between." See Barret and Roediger, "In-between People: Race, Nationality, and the 'New Immigrant' Working Class" (unpublished paper, 1997).

4. For more on this, see Tomás Almaguer, *Racial Fault Lines: The Historical Origins of White Supremacy in California* (Berkeley: University of California Press, 1994).

5. For more on this, see Neil Foley, *The White Scourge: Mexicans, Blacks, and Poor Whites in Texas Cotton Culture* (Berkeley: University of California Press, 1997); and David Montejano, *Anglos and Mexicans in the Making of Texas, 1836–1986* (Austin: University of Texas Press, 1987).

6. For New Mexico, see Deena J. González, *Refusing the Favor: The Spanish-Mexican Women of Santa Fe* (New York: Oxford University Press, 1999); also see Robert J. Rosenbaum, *Mexicano Resistance in the Southwest: The Sacred Right of Self-Preservation* (Austin: University of Texas Press, 1981).

7. Neil Foley, "Becoming Hispanic: Mexican Americans and the Faustian Pact with Whiteness," in *Reflexiones 1997: New Directions in Mexican American Studies,* ed. Neil Foley (Austin: University of Texas–Center for Mexican American Studies, 1997), 66.

67. Ibid.

68. Sánchez, *Expedition Through Aztlán,* 174–81.

69. For more on AIM's invasion of Alcatraz, see Paul Chaat Smith and Robert Allen Warrior, *Like A Hurricane: The Indian Movement from Alcatraz to Wounded Knee* (New York: The New Press, 1996).

70. Sánchez, *Expedition Through Aztlán,* 174–81.

71. Ibid.; and Al Martinez, "Judge Asks Berets to Leave — They Do: Chicano Group Quits Catalina Without Incident," *Los Angeles Times,* September 23, 1972, sec. 2, p. 1.

72. "National Brown Beret Organization Termination Notice," ca. October 22, 1972, Centro de Acción Social Autónomo [hereafter CASA] Papers, M325, box 25, folder 9, Stanford University Library, Department of Special Collections.

73. Dale Torgenson, "Brown Beret Leader Quits, Dissolves Units," *Los Angeles Times,* November 2, 1972, p. 9; and Memorandum to the Acting Director, March 29, 1973, Brown Beret file, no. 105-178715-273, U.S. Department of Justice, Federal Bureau of Investigation.

74. Two previous works point to the gendered nature of Chicano nationalism by surveying literary works, but they do not provide case studies of specific political groups: see Angie Chabram-Dernersesian, "I Throw Punches for My Race, but I Don't Want to Be a Man: Writing US — Chica-nos (Girl Us)/Chicanas — into the Movement Script," in *Cultural Studies,* ed. Lawrence Grossberg, Cary Nelson, and Paula A. Treichler (New York: Routledge, 1992), 81–95; and Ramón A. Gutiérrez, "Community, Patriarchy, and Individualism: The Politics of Chicano History and the Dream of Equality," *American Quarterly* 45, no. 1 (March 1993): 44–72.

75. The case of the Brown Berets upholds Elleke Boehmer's notion that the male role in the nationalist scenario is typically "metonymic," i.e., men are contiguous with each other and with the nationalist whole. She goes on to argue that "the idea of nationhood bears a masculine identity" (see Boehmer, "Stories of Women and Mothers: Gender and Nationalism in Early Fiction of Flora Nwapa," in *Motherlands: Black Women's Writings from Africa, the Caribbean and South Asia,* ed. Suheila Nasta [New Brunswick, N.J.: Rutgers University Press, 1992], 6).

76. *La Causa,* April 1971, pp. 10–11.

77. "Chicanos at UCLA Blow-it," *La Causa,* August 29, 1970, p. 4.

78. "Brown Berets: To Serve . . . Observe . . . Protect," *La Causa,* December 16, 1969, 7.

79. Gloria Arellanes, "Palabras Para La Chicana," *La Causa,* July 10, 1969, p. 6.

80. Mosse, *Nationalism and Sexuality,* 23.

81. "The Adelitas Role En El Movement," *La Causa,* February 1971, p. 10.

82. For more on women in the Brown Berets, see Dionne Espinoza, "Pedagogies of Gender and Nationalism: Cultural Resistance in Selected Practices of Chicana/o Movement Activists, 1967–1972" (Ph.D. diss., Cornell University, 1996).

83. "Declaration of Robert Acosta," Los Angeles, December 1978, Oscar Zeta Acosta Papers, Department of Special Collections, University of California at Santa Barbara.

84. The FBI file contains 1,934 pages on the organization, of which 1,260 were made available to me through the Freedom of Information Act.

85. Memorandum, W. R. Wannall to W. C. Sullivan, March 26, 1968, Brown Beret file, no. 105-178715, U.S. Department of Justice, Federal Bureau of Investigation.

86. Memorandum, FBI Director to SAC [special agent in charge], Denver, March 2, 1976, Brown Beret file, no. 105-178715-299, U.S. Department of Justice, Federal Bureau of Investigation.

CHAPTER 3: "CHALE NO, WE WON'T GO!"

1. Rosalio Muñoz, interview by author, tape recording, Los Angeles, January 27, 1987.

2. John T. Parker, "Chicano Student Leader Muñoz Refuses Induction," *Daily Bruin,* September 30, 1969, p. 2.

3. Muñoz, interview.

4. Ramsés Noriega, interview by author, tape recording, Los Angeles, February 29, 1992.

5. John T. Parker, "Chicano Student Leader Muñoz Refuses Induction," *Daily Bruin,* September 30, 1969, p. 2.

6. Frank Del Olmo "Moratorium Unit Blames Violence on 'Repression' " *Los Angeles Times,* January 29, 1971, p. 1.

7. That appointment was subsequently postponed yet again — until November 1970 — the end result being that Muñoz was never drafted.

8. Jerry Applebaum, "Chicano Leader Charges U.S. with Genocide," *Los Angeles Free Press,* September 19, 1969, p. 2.

9. Muñoz, interview.

10. The Mexican Study Project was initiated in 1963 with funding from the Ford Foundation and the College Entrance Examination Board. It undertook a "comprehensive study of the socioeconomic position of Mexican Americans in selected urban areas of the five southwestern states." The study was completed in 1968 and the results were published in 1970. For more information, see Leo Grebler, Joan W. Moore, and Ralph C. Guzmán, eds. *The Mexican American People: The Nation's Second Largest Minority* (New York: The Free Press, 1970).

11. Ralph Guzmán, "Mexican American Casualties in Vietnam," *La Raza Magazine,* March 1970, p. 12.

12. Ibid.

13. U.S. Bureau of the Census, *Statistical Abstract of the United States: 1970* (Washington D.C.: Government Printing Office, 1972), 331.

14. Reynaldo Macías et al., *A Study of Unincorporated East Los Angeles* (Los Angeles: Aztlán Publications, Chicano Studies Center, University of California at Los Angeles, 1973), 57.

15. California Advisory Committee to the U.S. Commission on Civil Rights, *Police–Community Relations in East Los Angeles, California: A Report of the California Advisory Committee to the United States Commission on Civil Rights* (Los Angeles: The Committee, 1970), 23.

16. "Sheriff Riot on Whittier Boulevard," *La Raza Magazine,* August 1970, p. 7.

17. Frank Del Olmo, "Moratorium Unit Blames Violence on 'Repression,'" *Los Angeles Times,* January 29, 1971, p. 1.

18. Muñoz, interview.

19. Muñoz, interview; and Pat Jamieson, "Rosalio Muñoz Begins Hunger Strike," *Daily Bruin,* November 13, 1969, p. 6.

20. Letter, Ernesto Vigil to Ernesto Chávez, April 21, 1992, in author's possession.

21. Noriega, interview.

22. Letter, Ernesto Vigil to Ernesto Chávez, April 21, 1992, in author's possession; and Roberto Elias, "Draft Conference," *El Gallo,* January 1970, p. 3.

23. "Chicano Moratorium," *La Raza Magazine,* March 1970, p. 5.; and Chicano Moratorium flyer, ca. December 1969, Devra Weber Collection, Chicano Studies Research Center Library, University of California at Los Angeles.

24. Della Rossa, "Chicanos Protest Murder," *Los Angeles Free Press,* March 6, 1970, p. 12; and *La Causa,* February 28, 1970, p. 12.

25. Chicano Moratorium Committee, pamphlet, p. 3, Chicano Moratorium File, Southern California Library for Social Studies and Research, Los Angeles.

26. Della Rossa, "Chicanos Protest Murder," *Los Angeles Free Press,* March 6, 1970, p. 12.

27. "Chicano Moratorium," *La Raza Magazine,* March 1970, p. 5.

28. Frank Del Olmo, "Moratorium Unit Blames Violence on Repression," *Los Angeles Times,* January 29, 1971, pp. 3, 19.

29. Ibid.; Noriega, interview.

30. Muñoz, interview; Noriega, interview; Jacobo Rodríguez, interview by author, tape recording, Alhambra, California, February 13, 1992; letter, Ernesto Vigil to author, April 21, 1992.

31. "National Chicano Moratorium Goes Sour in Last Moratorium Effort!!!" *La Causa,* August 29, 1970, p. 5.

32. Jacobo Rodríguez, interview by author, tape recording, Los Angeles, March 10, 1992.

33. Noriega, interview.

34. William J. Drummond, "How East Los Angeles Protest Turned into Major Riot," *Los Angeles Times,* September 16, 1970, p. 1.

35. "It's Not Called Laguna Park Anymore," produced by Victor Vásquez, August 19, 1974, no. BC2020b, Pacifica Radio Archives, North Hollywood.

36. "Chicano Moratorium," *La Raza Magazine,* September 1970, pp. 21–26; and Mark Lane, "At the Chicano Moratorium," *Los Angeles Free Press,* September 4, 1970, p. 12.

37. William J. Drummond, "How East Los Angeles Protest Turned into Major Riot," *Los Angeles Times,* September 16, 1970, p. 1.

38. San Francisco Chicano Moratorium Flyer, ca. July 1970, Devra Weber Collection, Chicano Studies Research Center Library, University of California at Los Angeles.

39. "It's Not Called Laguna Park Anymore," produced by Victor Vásquez, August 30, 1970, no. B2020b, Pacifica Radio Archives, North Hollywood. Ironically, Laguna Park's name was later officially changed — to Ruben Salazar Park.

40. My retelling of the incident at the Green Mill Liquor Store is compiled from a variety of sources: "Chicano Moratorium," *La Raza Magazine,* September 1970, p. 27; "It's Not Called Laguna Park Anymore," produced by Victor Vásquez, August 30, 1970, no. B2020b, Pacifica Radio Archives, North Hollywood; California Advisory Committee to the U.S. Commission on Civil Rights, *Police–Community Relations in East Los Angeles,* 14–15; and "At the Chicano Moratorium," *Los Angeles Free Press,* September 4, 1970, p. 13.

41. "At the Chicano Moratorium," *Los Angeles Free Press,* September 4, 1970, p. 13.

42. California Advisory Committee to the U.S. Commission on Civil Rights, *Police–Community Relations in East Los Angeles,* 14–15.

43. "It's Not Called Laguna Park Anymore," produced by Victor Vásquez, August 30, 1970, no. B2020b, Pacifica Radio Archives, North Hollywood.

44. "Chicano Moratorium" *La Raza Magazine,* September 1970, p. 27.

45. Roldolfo Acuña, *Occupied America: A History of Chicanos,* 3d ed. (New York: Harper and Row, 1988), 368.

46. "At the Chicano Moratorium," *Los Angeles Free Press,* September 4, 1970, p. 13.

47. For more on Salazar, read his articles from the *Los Angeles Times,* which have been compiled by Mario T. García in *Border Correspondent: Selected Writings, 1955–1970* (Berkeley: University of California Press, 1995). Among them are "Chicanos vs. Traditionalists," from the March 6, 1971 edition, and "Maligned Word: Mexican," from the April 17, 1970 edition.

48. The "myth of Salazar" was created soon after his death, as was evident by the actions of the Los Angeles County Board of Supervisors, who renamed Laguna Park "Ruben Salazar Park" on September 17, 1970 (see "Supervisors Vote to Rename Park in Salazar Honor," *Los Angeles Times,* September 18, 1970, p. 3).

49. "It's Not Called Laguna Park Anymore," produced by Victor Vásquez, August 30, 1970, no. B2020b, Pacifica Radio Archives, North Hollywood.

50. Ibid.

51. Teletype, Los Angeles Bureau to the Director, August 29, 1970, Chicano Moratorium Committee file, no. 100-459861-16, U.S. Department of Justice, Federal Bureau of Investigation; memorandum, R. D. Cotter to C. D. Brennan, September 2, 1970, Chicano Moratorium Committee file, no. 100-459861-22, U.S. Department of Justice, Federal Bureau of Investigation; and teletype, Los Angeles Bureau to the Director of San Diego Bureau, September 2, 1970, Chicano Moratorium Committee file, no. 100-459861-24, U.S. Department of Justice, Federal Bureau of Investigation.

52. I have tried to obtain the transcript of the Salazar inquest but was told by the Los Angeles County Coroner's office that the document has been lost and therefore would not be available for my use.

53. Paul Houston and Dave Smith, "Mexican American Observers Walk Out of Salazar Inquest," *Los Angeles Times*, September 10, 1970, p. 3.

54. Ibid.

55. Ibid.

56. These outbursts constitute moments of "diva citizenship." According to literary critic Lauren Berlant, "Diva Citizenship . . . is a moment of emergence that marks unrecognized potentials for subaltern political activity." She further argues that: "Diva Citizenship occurs when a person stages a dramatic coup in a public sphere in which she does not have privilege. Flashing up and startling the public, she puts the dominant story into suspended animation: as though recording an estranging voice-over to a film we have already seen, she renarrates the dominant history as one that the abjected people have once lived sotto voce, but no more; and she challenges her audience to identify with the enormity of the suffering she has narrated and the courage she has had to produce, calling on people to change the social and institutional practices of citizenship to which they currently hold" (see Lauren Berlant, *The Queen of America Goes to Washington City: Essays on Sex and Citizenship.* [Durham, N.C.: Duke University Press, 1997], 223).

57. Jorge Rodríguez, interview.

58. *La Raza Magazine,* November 1970, p. 8.

59. Dave Smith and Paul Houston, "His Honesty Doubted, Chicano Editor Says," *Los Angeles Times,* September 18, 1970, p. 3.

60. "Chicanos React," *Los Angeles Free Press,* October 16, 1970, p. 2.

61. "Why Rally on the 31st," *La Causa,* February 1971, p. 6.

62. Sue Marshall, "East L.A. Riots, Harassment," *Los Angeles Free Press,* November 20, 1970, p. 2. Although I was able to obtain 406 pages of FBI documents through the Freedom of Information Act, which suggested that the Intelligence Division of the Los Angeles County Sheriff's Department, as well as the Special Operations Conspiracy Squad of the Los Angeles Police Department, had carried on their own investigations of the Moratorium Committee, both of those agencies denied my request for information. The Sheriff's Department indicated that there never was such an investigation, while the LAPD simply said that any such documents had been destroyed.

63. In January 1972, Eustacio "Frank" Martínez revealed that, working as an undercover agent for the Treasury Department's Division of Tobacco, Alcohol, and Firearms, he had infiltrated the Chicano Moratorium Committee. He also disclosed that he was responsible for carrying a shotgun in front of the Moratorium Committee office on November 14, 1971, which resulted in an LAPD raid later that evening (see Frank Del Olmo, "Provoked Trouble for Lawmen, Chicano 'Informer' Claims," *Los Angeles Times,* February 1, 1972, p. 1; and Frank J. Donner, *The Age of Surveillance* [New York: Alfred A. Knopf, 1980], 346–48).

64. Sue Marshall, "East L.A. Riots, Harassment," *Los Angeles Free Press,* November 20, 1970, p. 2.

65. "National Chicano Moratorium Committee," *La Causa,* December 1970, p. 6.

66. Ibid.

67. Chicano Moratorium Committee flyer, ca. January 9, 1971, Devra Weber Collection, Chicano Studies Research Center Library, University of California at Los Angeles.

68. Dial Torgerson, "Downtown L.A. Cleans up after Violent Spree by Protesters," *Los Angeles Times,* January 11, 1971, sec. 1, p. 1.

69. Barrio Defense Committee, "Police Attack Chicano Moratorium Protesters," *La Raza Magazine,* March 1971, p. 12; Della Rossa, "Police Meet Nonviolence with Brutality," *Los Angeles Free Press,* January 15, 1971, p. 2.

70. Dial Torgerson, "Downtown L.A. Cleans up after Violent Spree by Protesters," *Los Angeles Times,* January 11, 1971, sec. 1, p. 20.

71. "Won't Change Plan for January 31 March, Chicano Leader Says," *Los Angeles Times,* January 12, 1971, sec. 1, p. 3.

72. Chicano Moratorium Committee flyer, January 1971, Devra Weber Collection, Chicano Studies Research Center Library, University of California at Los Angeles.

73. Paul Houston and Ted Thackrey Jr., "Man Slain as Violence Erupts in East L.A. After Chicano Rally," *Los Angeles Times,* sec. 1, pp. 1, 3, 16.

74. Sue Marshall, "Who was to Blame? Militant Chicanos Provoke Police; Death and Violence Result," *Los Angeles Free Press,* February 5, 1971, p. 3.

75. Dial Torgenson, "Chicano Violence Laid to Mob that Ignored Monitors," *Los Angeles Times,* February 2, 1971, sec. 1, p. 1; and Paul Houston, "Man Killed in Rioting was Curiosity Seeker," *Los Angeles Times,* February 4, 1971, sec. 1, p. 1. Frank "Eustacio" Martínez revealed that he threw the rocks and bottles at law enforcement officers that provoked the violence of January 31 (see Frank Del Olmo, "Provoked Trouble for Lawmen, Chicano 'Informer' Claims," *Los Angeles Times,* February 1, 1972, p. 1; and Donner, *The Age of Surveillance,* 346–48).

76. Dial Torgenson, "Chicano Violence Laid to Mob that Ignored Monitors," *Los Angeles Times,* February 2, 1971, sec. 1, p. 1.

77. Ibid., sec. 1, pp. 1, 3.

78. Ibid.

79. Paul Houston, "Pitchess Blames East Riot on 'Hoodlums' in Community," *Los Angeles Times,* February 3, 1971, sec. 1, pp. 1, 20.

80. Ron Einstoss, "Charges Filed Against 49 in East L.A. Riot," *Los Angeles Times,* February 5, 1971, sec. 1, p. 21.

81. Ted Thackrey Jr., "Pitchess Fires Three Deputies After Beating of Riot Prisoners," *Los Angeles Times,* February 5, 1971, sec. 1, pp. 1, 20.

82. Noriega, interview.

83. Ricardo Pérez, "La Marcha de la Reconquista," *Regeneración,* September 1971, pp. 10–11.

84. Ibid.

85. Ibid. In addition to the local and state authorities present, the FBI was also keeping a watchful eye on the protesters activities, as evidenced by a report sent to the Los Angeles Bureau from Sacramento (Airtel, Sacramento to Los Angeles, August 7, 1971, Chicano Moratorium Committee file, no. 100-459861, U.S. Department of Justice, Federal Bureau of Investigation).

86. Deganawidah was the name of the American Indian chief who formed the Iroquois Federation, while Quezalcoatl was an Aztec leader, deified after his death. According to legend, the Aztecs believed that Hernán Cortez, the Spanish conqueror of Mexico, was Quezalcoatl incarnate (see *Regeneración,* ca. January 1971, p. 17).

87. Noriega, interview.

88. Ibid.

89. Memorandum from the SAC [special agent in charge], Los Angeles, to the Director, September 3, 1971, Chicano Moratorium Committee file, no. 100-459861-103, U.S. Department of Justice, Federal Bureau of Investigation.

CHAPTER 4: "THE VOICE OF THE CHICANO PEOPLE"

1. Richard A. Martínez, interview by Carlos Vásquez, 1990, oral history interview conducted by the UCLA Oral History Program, for the California State Government Oral History Program, p. 110.

2. Ignacio García, *United We Win: The Rise and Fall of La Raza Unida Party* (Tucson: University of Arizona, Mexican American Studies and Research Center, 1989), 37–39.

3. García, *United We Win,* 37–39.

4. Ibid., 39–40.

5. Ibid., 40.

6. Ibid., 40.

7. Ibid., 40–41.

8. Ibid., 44.

9. Ibid., 50–54.

10. Antonio Camejo, ed., *La Raza Unida Party in Texas: Speeches by Mario Compeón and José Angel Gutiérrez* (New York: Pathfinder Press, 1970), 3.

11. Ibid.

12. Antonio Camejo et al., *Why A Chicano Party? Why Chicano Studies?* (New York: Pathfinder Press, 1970), 3

13. Camejo, *La Raza Unida Party in Texas,* 6.

14. California Advisory Committee to the U.S. Commission on Civil Rights, *Political Participation of Mexican Americans in California* (Washington, D.C.: Government Printing Office, August 1971), 49.

15. Richard A. Santillán, interview by Carlos Vásquez, 1989, oral history interview conducted by the UCLA Oral History Program, for the California State Government Oral History Program, p. 60.

16. "MAPA and La Raza Unida Party" (ca. January 1971), Bert Corona Papers, M248, box 1, folder 17, Stanford University Library, Department of Special Collections.

17. Ibid.

18. Ibid.

19. Ibid.

20. "Raza Unida Party," *La Causa,* March 1971, pp. 3, 6.

21. Santillán, interview by Carlos Vásquez, p. 256.

22. "Young Chicanos Actively Recruit for New Party: La Raza Unida Members Go Door-to-Door Seeking Place on '72 State Ballot," *Los Angeles Times,* August 30, 1971, pp. 3, 22, 23.

23. "Young Chicanos Actively Recruit for New Party: La Raza Unida Members Go Door-to-Door Seeking Place on '72 State Ballot," *Los Angeles Times,* August 30, 1971, p. 3.

24. Martínez, interview, p. 113.

25. "Partido de La Raza Unida: 48th Assembly Race," *La Raza Magazine,* January 1973, p. 10.

26. Martínez, interview, pp. 114–15; and Reynaldo Macías et al., *A Study of Unincorporated East Los Angeles* (Los Angeles: Aztlán Publications, Chicano Studies Research Center, University of California at Los Angeles, 1973), 93.

27. Martínez, interview, pp. 116–17.

28. Santillán, interview by Carlos Vásquez, p. 65

29. Ibid., pp. 66–71.

30. Olga Rodríguez, "Raza Unida Makes Good Showing in Los Angeles," *The Militant,* November 5, 1971, p. 6.

31. Olga Rodríguez, "Raza Unida Confronts Muskie in L.A. Barrio," *The Militant,* November 19, 1971, p. 24.

32. Martínez claims that the Republican Party hired the gunman in order to induce sympathy (see Martínez, interview, p. 128).

33. Frank del Olmo, "Chicano Party Says It Defeated Alatorre in 48th District," *Los Angeles Times,* November 18, 1971, sec. 2, p. 1.

34. Olga Rodríguez, "L.A. Race Shows Raza Strength," *The Militant,* December 17, 1971, p. 10.

35. "We Did It: La Raza Unida," *La Raza Magazine,* January 1972, p. 18.

36. Martínez, interview, pp. 133–37.

37. Vincent Cárdenas, Letter to the Editor, *Los Angeles Times,* January 1, 1972, sec. 2, p. 4.

38. "Resolutions," La Raza Unida Los Angeles Conference, November 26–28, 1971, p. 3, Centro de Acción Social Autónomo [hereafter CASA] Collection, M325, box 26, folder 6, Stanford University Library, Department of Special Collections.

39. Santillán, interview by Carlos Vásquez, pp. 161–62.

40. Ibid.

41. "Resolutions Passed," La Raza Unida Party California State-Wide Conference, San Jose, California, April 8 and 9, 1972, CASA Collection, M325, box 26, folder 6, Stanford University Library, Department of Special Collections; Cruz (Olmeda) Becerra, personal papers, Alhambra, California.

42. Santillán, interview by Carlos Vásquez, pp. 170–71.

43. García, *United We Win,* 114–16.

44. La Raza Unida Party Organizing Committees Southern Region, "On the Status of La Raza Unida Party in Califas, Aztlán: A Position Paper," August 21, 1972, p. 1, CASA Collection, M325, box 26, folder 6, Stanford University Library, Department of Special Collections.

45. Ibid., p. 3.

46. "La Raza Unida Party," *La Raza Magazine,* February 1973, pp. 4–5.

47. Ibid., 7–8.

48. Ibid., 7–8

49. Ibid., 8.

50. Cruz (Olmeda) Becerra, interview by author, tape recording, Alhambra, California, May 15, 1993; and "Furniture Workers Win Strike," *El Obrero,* November 1972, pp. 3–4, CASA Collection, M325, box 26, folder 7, Stanford University Library, Department of Special Collections.

51. "Mejian Workers Triumph Over Bosses: Raza Unida Labor Committee," *La Raza Magazine,* September 1972, p. 18.

52. "Class Approach to Chicano Struggle" (editorial), *La Raza Magazine,* February 1973, p. 2.

53. Richard A. Santillán, interview by author, tape recording, Alhambra, California, August 1, 1999.

54. "Incorporation or Annexation" (editorial), *La Raza Magazine,* February 1974, p. 2.

55. Macías, *A Study of Incorporated East Los Angeles,* 19–26.

56. This change ensured that the representative subject in this national imaginary would once again be a U.S. citizen.

57. James José Raigoza, "The Ad Hoc Committee to Incorporate East Los Angeles: A Study of the Socio-Political Orientations of Mexican American Incorporation Advocates" (Ph.D. diss., University of California at Los Angeles, 1977), 68.

58. Ray Zeman, "Supervisors OK Election on Incorporation for East L.A.," *Los Angeles Times,* June 14, 1974, sec. 2, p. 1.

59. Frank Del Olmo, "Next 5 Weeks Crucial in Campaign to Incorporate East L.A. Into a City," *Los Angeles Times,* September 29, 1974, sec. 2, p. 1.

60. Frank Del Olmo, "Far Less Than Forecast Is Spent in East L.A.'s Cityhood Campaign," *Los Angeles Times,* November 4, 1974, sec. 1, p. 24.

61. Ibid.

62. Frank Del Olmo, "Next 5 Weeks Crucial in Campaign to Incorporate East L.A. Into a City," *Los Angeles Times,* September 29, 1974, sec. 2, p. 1.

63. Jorge García, "Forjando Ciudad: The Development of a Chicano Political Community in East Los Angeles" (Ph.D. diss., University of California at Riverside, 1986), 263.

64. Santillán, interview by Carlos Vásquez, p. 246.

65. Leo Grebler, Joan W. Moore, and Ralph C. Guzmán, *The Mexican American People: The Nation's Second Largest Minority* (New York: The Free Press, 1970), 565. This was before the Twenty-sixth Amendment to the U.S. Constitution (1971) lowered the voting age to 18.

66. Macias, *A Study of Unicorporated East Los Angeles,* 105.

67. In May 1973 La Raza Unida Party, along with other minor parties, filed a suit challenging the constitutionality of third-party requirements. The case, along with others, eventually reached the U.S. Supreme Court, which decided to send

it back to the Federal district court, which in 1976 ruled that the California legislature, not the courts, should work on changing the stipulations. Since the Republican and Democratic parties made up a majority in the California legislature, no action occurred (see Santillán, interview by Carlos Vásquez, pp. 257-62).

68. Becerra, interview; and García, *United We Win,* 147.

CHAPTER 5: "UN PUEBLO SIN FRONTERAS"

1. "History of CASA", p. 6, CASA Collection, M325, box 1, folder 5, Stanford University Library, Department of Special Collections.

2. Ibid., p. 5.

3. Jacobo Rodríguez, "Casa de Carnalismo," *La Raza Magazine,* January 1972, p. 60.

4. "The Case of Los Tres and the U.S. Involvement in Drug Traffic," Committee to Free Los Tres, May 1973, p. 5, CASA Collection, M325, box 37, folder 8, Stanford University Library, Department of Special Collections.

5. Ibid.; and "The Government Drug Conspiracy and the Case of Los Tres," Committee to Free Los Tres (ca. March 1974), CASA Collection, box 37, folder 8, Stanford University Library, Department of Special Collections.

6. "The Government Drug Conspiracy and the Case of Los Tres," Committee to Free Los Tres (ca. March 1974), CASA Collection, box 37, folder 8, Stanford University Library, Department of Special Collections.

7. Ibid.; and Miguel Pendas, "L.A. Chicano Activists Appeal for New Trial," *The Militant,* January 12, 1973, p. 17.

8. "The Government Drug Conspiracy and the Case of Los Tres," Committee to Free Los Tres (ca. March 1974), CASA Collection, box 37, folder 8, Stanford University Library, Department of Special Collections; and Miguel Pendas, "L.A. Chicano Activists Appeal for New Trial," *The Militant,* January 12, 1973, p. 17.

9. George C. and Adriana Roberts posted part of the bail for Alberto and all of the bail for Rodolfo. A noted member of the Communist Party USA in Los Angeles, Rose Chernin, posted the remaining bail for Rodolfo as well as the bail for Juan. Chernin used five $1,000 treasury bonds for this purpose on November 2, 1973 (CASA Collection, box 37, folder 13, Stanford University Library, Department of Special Collections).

10. Draft of flyer written by Carlos Chávez (ca. April 1974), CASA Collection, box 37, folder 8, Stanford University Library, Department of Special Collections; U.S. District Court, Central District of California document dated November 6, 1973, CASA Collection, box 37, folder 13, Stanford University Library, Department of Special Collections).

11. Draft of flyer written by Carlos Chávez (ca. April 1974), CASA Collection, box 37, folder 8, Stanford University Library, Department of Special Collections.

12. "Los Tres vs. Fascist Court," *Sin Cadenas,* August 1974, p. 4.

13. California State College at Los Angeles became California State University at Los Angeles in September 1972.

14. Membership applications for the Committee to Free Los Tres, April

1974, in author's possession; also "History of CASA," p. 19, CASA Collection, M325, box 1, folder 2, Stanford University Library, Department of Special Collections. Because the members were veterans of Chicano activism and had been guided by cultural nationalism, the organization represents what the cultural critic Homi Bhabha argues is an "'in-between' space, [which] provide[s] the terrain for elaborating strategies of selfhood — singular or communal — that initiate new signs of identity, and innovative sites of collaboration, and contestation, in the act of defining the idea of society itself" (see Homi Bhabha, *The Location of Culture* [New York: Routledge, 1994], p. 1).

15. "The Government Drug Conspiracy and the Case of Los Tres," publication of the Committee to Free Los Tres, Los Angeles (ca. 1973), p. 12, CASA Collection, M325, box 37, folder 8, Stanford University Library, Department of Special Collections; and Alfred McCoy, *The Politics of Heroin in Southeast Asia.* (New York: Harper and Row, 1972).

16. "The Government Drug Conspiracy and the Case of Los Tres," pp. 9, 14; and "The People Have the Right to Destroy the Forces Which Threaten Their Survival," publication of the Committee to Free Los Tres (ca. 1973), both in CASA Collection, M325, box, 37, folder 8, Stanford University Library, Department of Special Collections; Carlos Chávez and Arturo Chávez, interview by author, tape recording, Los Angeles, August 2, 1992; and Alfred W. McCoy, *The Politics of Heroin in Southeast Asia* (New York: Harper and Row, 1972).

17. "Principles of the National Committee to Free Los Tres," published by the Committee to Free Los Tres (ca. 1973), pp. 1–3, CASA Collection, M325, box 37, folder 8, Stanford University Library, Department of Special Collections.

18. Ibid., pp. 6–7.

19. "What is True National Consciousness?" *Sin Cadenas,* January/February 1975, pp. 5–6.

20. "Libertad," *Sin Cadenas,* August 1974, p. 1.

21. "Aprender es Luchar," published by El Comité Estudiantil del Pueblo (ca. February 1975), in author's possession.

22. "Women Organize Against Hospital Abuses," *Sin Cadenas,* January/February 1975, p. 2.

23. "Students Issue A Call to Action," *Sin Cadenas,* January/February 1975, p. 3.

24. Ibid.

25. Arturo Chávez, telephone conversation with author, April 27, 1999.

26. Ibid.

27. "Articles of Incorporation," CASA Collection, M325, box 1, folder 1, Stanford University Library, Department of Special Collections.

28. "History of CASA," p. 14, CASA Collection, M325, box 1, folder 5, Stanford University Library, Department of Special Collections; Pedro Arias, "Reagan Compite Con La Migra en Racismo," *La Raza Magazine,* January 1972, pp. 50–53; and Bert Corona, *Bert Corona Speaks* (New York: Pathfinder Press, 1972).

29. "History of CASA," p. 20, CASA Collection, M325, box 1, folder 5, Stanford University Library, Department of Special Collections.

30. Evidence of this can be found in the correspondence schedule entitled "Correspondencia a Rodolfo y Juan," CASA Collection, M325, box 37, folder 8, Stanford University Library, Department of Special Collections.

31. Ibid.

32. "Analysis of CASA and the NCTFLT," Committee to Free Los Tres (ca. April 1975), p. 3, CASA Collection, M325, box 37, folder 9, Stanford University Library, Department of Special Collections.

33. "Propuesta del Comité de Los Tres Para La Integración a CASA–HGT" (ca. March 7, 1975), CASA Collection, M325, box 37, folder 9, Stanford University Library, Department of Special Collections.

34. "Preliminary Report of the National Meeting of CASA Which took Place July 5 to July 12, 1975 in Los Angeles," July 23, 1975, CASA Collection, M325, box 20, folder 10, Stanford University Library, Department of Special Collections.

35. Ibid.

36. "CASA–HGT: The ideological Development of the Organization as Manifested in the Evolution of the Our Political Line" (ca. July 1975), p. 1, Jorge Rodríguez, personal papers, Alhambra, California.

37. CASA, "Reglamento," c. 1975, p. 1, Jorge Rodríguez, personal papers, Alhambra, California.

38. Ibid., p. 6.

39. "Greeley Resignation Letter," October 1975, Jorge Rodríguez, personal papers, Alhambra, California.

40. August Twenty-Ninth Movement, *Fan the Flames: A Revolutionary Position on the Chicano National Question* (Los Angeles: August Twenty-Ninth Movement, 1976). Among the authors of the pamphlet were Cruz Olmeda Becerra and William Flores (see Cruz [Olmeda] Becerra, interview by author, tape recording, Alhambra, California, May 15, 1993).

41. August Twenty-Ninth Movement, *Fan the Flames,* 15–17.

42. William L. Van Deburg, *New Day in Babylon: The Black Power Movement and American Culture, 1965–1975* (Chicago: University of Chicago Press, 1992), 153.

43. Ibid., 171–72.

44. Bruce Michael Tyler, "Black Radicalism in Southern California, 1950–1982" (Ph.D. diss., University of California at Los Angeles, 1983), 338.

45. Elaine Brown, *A Taste of Power: A Black Woman's Story* (New York: Pantheon Books, 1992), 166–67.

46. "Internal Document Regarding Attacks of CASA from the August Twenty-Ninth Movement" (ca. 1976), p. 1, CASA Collection, M325, box 25, folder 8, Stanford University Library, Department of Special Collections.

47. "The Rodino Bill: Against the Right of Workers," CASA pamphlet (ca. 1975), CASA Collection, M325, box 31, folder 14, Stanford University Library, Department of Special Collections; "Thousands Oppose Rodino Bill," *Sin Fronteras,* November 1975, p. 1.

48. "United Front Against Rodino Bill," *Sin Fronteras,* September 1975, p. 1. For more on the coalition against the Rodino bill, see David G. Gutiérrez, *Walls and Mirrors: Mexican Americans, Mexican Immigrants, and the Politics of Ethnicity.* (Berkeley: University of California Press, 1994).

49. "Teatros Address Workers," *Sin Fronteras,* November 1975, p. 4.

50. "CASA–HGT: The Ideological Development of the Organization as Manifested in the Evolution of Our Political Line" (ca. July 1977), CASA Collection, M325, box 1, folder 2, Stanford University Library, Department of Special Collections; and "Rodino Bill Stalled," *Sin Fronteras,* January 1976, p. 9.

51. Antonio Rodríguez, "The Lessons of Bakke — A Call to Struggle," *Sin Fronteras,* February 1977, p. 9.

52. "The Bakke Decision Threatens Special Admissions Programs in California, Maybe Nation," special supplement to *Sin Fronteras,* February 1977, pp. 1–2.

53. Ibid.

54. Ibid.

55. Ibid.

56. *Regents of California v. Bakke,* 438 U.S. 265 (1978).

57. "Solidarity with José Medina: Political Asylum Now," flyer (ca. December 1977), Jorge Rodríguez, personal papers, Alhambra, California; and Carlos Chávez and Arturo Chávez, interview by author, tape recording, Los Angeles, August 2, 1992.

58. "Solidarity with José Medina: Political Asylum Now," flyer (ca. December 1977), Jorge Rodríguez, personal papers, Alhambra, California; and Carlos and Arturo Chávez, interview.

59. "CASA–HGT: The Ideological Development of the Organization as Manifested in the Evolution of Our Political Line" (ca. January 1978), pp. 12–14, CASA Collection, M325, box 1, folder 2, Stanford University Library, Department of Special Collections.

60. Memorandum to SACs [special agents in charge], February 18, 1975, Committee to Free Los Tres file, no. 105-34112, U.S. Department of Justice, Federal Bureau of Investigation.

61. Memorandum from SAC, Los Angeles, to Director, August 30, 1974; memorandum from SAC, Los Angeles, to Director, October 31, 1974; memorandum from SAC, Los Angeles, to Director, December 31, 1974, all in CASA file, no. 105-31729, U.S. Department of Justice, Federal Bureau of Investigation.

62. Airtel memorandum from SAC, Los Angeles, to Director, January 29, 1975, p. 3, CASA file, no. 105-31729, U.S. Department of Justice, Federal Bureau of Investigation.

63. Ibid.

64. Memorandum from Director to Los Angeles Bureau, July 21, 1976, CASA file, no. 105-31729, U.S. Department of Justice, Federal Bureau of Investigation.

65. Ibid.

66. Airtel from the Director to the ADIC, Los Angeles, August 8, 1976, CASA file, no. 105-31729, U.S. Department of Justice, Federal Bureau of Investigation.

67. Memorandum from Attorney General to Director FBI, November 16, 1976, CASA file, no. 105-31729, U.S. Department of Justice, Federal Bureau of Investigation.

68. Letter, Carlos Vásquez to CASA National Coordinating Committee,

December 26, 1977, CASA Collection, M325, box 2, folder 9, Stanford University Library, Department of Special Collections.

69. Ibid.; and Carlos and Arturo Chávez, interview.

70. Document on the "13," by CASA membership (ca. November 1978), Jorge Rodríguez, personal papers, Alhambra, California.

AFTERWORD: "WHY ARE WE NOT MARCHING LIKE IN THE '70S?"

1. Luis Alfaro, "Chicanismo" (video), 1997 (in author's possession).

2. This turn toward electoral politics is evident in the respective bids to represent the 14th district in the Los Angeles City Council in 1983 and 1985 by former Brown Beret leader David Sánchez and CASA head Antonio Rodríguez . California Assembly member Richard Alatorre eventually won that seat. For more on this issue, see Janet Clayton, "Latino Endorsements Split 14th District," *Los Angeles Times,* March 31, 1983, sec. 2, p. 1; and Frank del Olmo, "14th District is No Place for Shifty Politics," *Los Angeles Times,* September 26, 1985, sec. 2, p. 5.

3. David G. Gutiérrez, "Significant to Whom?: Mexican Americans and the History of the American West," *Western Historical Quarterly* 24, no. 4 (November 1993): 527.

4. The Los Angeles County supervisor is Gloria Molina, a former California Assembly and Los Angeles City Council member whose 1992 victory was hailed as a vindication of Edward Roybal's 1958 loss in his bid for a seat on that body. The city councilmen are Nick Pacheco, Mike Hernández, and Alex Padilla. Hernández will soon leave the city council.

5. Gilbert Cedillo, an Assembly member representing East Los Angeles, was also a member of CASA and the Comité Estudiantil del Pueblo.

6. Dornan accused Sánchez of election fraud, claiming that a number of Mexican immigrant, non–U.S. citizens voted for her, a House committee investigated the charges. The panel eventually certified Sánchez's election, and she easily defeated Dornan in the 1998 election. Sánchez, who became the darling of the Democratic National Committee (DNC), emerged in 1999 as the second most productive Democratic party fundraiser — behind only Vice President Al Gore, according to Federal Election Commission records. Yet, when she decided to host a fundraising event for her own Political Action Committee (Hispanic Unity USA, which seeks to promote the political interest of Latinos) at Los Angeles's Playboy mansion, she was quickly urged to change the venue due to the site's promotion of a "lifestyle" that the DNC did not believe best represented the values of the party. When Sánchez refused to move the event, some Democratic leaders who had previously described her as "tenacious" and "bold" now labeled her "defiant" and "stubborn" and yanked her as a speaker at the Democratic National Convention in Los Angeles. Sánchez eventually gave in to party pressure and moved the event to a less highly charged atmosphere. The DNC's treatment of Sánchez makes clear the precarious position held by Latinos in national politics (see Jean O. Pasco and Richard Simon, "Sanchez Fund-Raiser is Moved to City Walk Site," *Los Angeles Times,* August 12, 2000, p. A1).

7. For more on the 2000 census, see the *Los Angeles Times*'s special report, "Census 2000" (*Los Angeles Times,* March 30, 2001, p. U1).

8. Chela Sandoval, *Methodology of the Oppressed* (Minneapolis: University of Minnesota Press, 2000), pp. 59, 62.

9. For the Congressional Black Caucus charges of voter fraud and details of their protest at the certification of the electoral vote, see Eric Lichtblau, "Objections Aside, A Smiling Gore Certifies Bush," *Los Angeles Times,* January 7, 2001, p. A1.

10. Katha Pollitt has recently argued about the importance of looking at race and class together (see Pollitt, "Race and Gender and Class, Oh My!" *The Nation,* June 8, 1998, p. 9).

Bibliography

Archival Sources

MANUSCRIPTS AND SPECIAL COLLECTIONS

Becerra, Cruz (Olmeda), Personal Papers, Alhambra, California
California State University at Los Angeles, Department of Special Collections

    Edward Roybal Papers

Pacifica Radio Archives, North Hollywood, California
Rodríguez, Jorge, personal papers, Alhambra, California
Southern California Library for Social Studies and Research, Los Angeles

    Chicano Moratorium File

Stanford University Library, Department of Special Collections

    Centro de Acción Social Autónomo (CASA) Collection, M325

    Bert Corona Papers, M248

    Ernesto Galarza Papers, M224

    Eduardo Quevedo Papers, M349

    Manuel Ruiz Papers, M295

University of California at Berkeley, Chicano Studies Library

    Richard and Gloria Santillán Collection

University of California at Los Angeles

    Edward R. Roybal Papers, Department of Special Collections

    Devra Weber Collection, Chicano Studies Research Center Library

University of California at Santa Barbara

    Oscar Zeta Acosta Papers, Department of Special Collections

    Colección Tloque Nahuaque, Pamphlet Collection

GOVERNMENT DOCUMENTS AND PUBLICATIONS

California Assembly. Fact-Finding Committee to the Fifty-sixth California Legislature. *Second Report on Un-American Activities in California.* Sacramento, 1945.

California. Governor's Commission on the Los Angeles Riots. *Violence in the City: An End or A Beginning?* Los Angeles, 1965.

California Advisory Committee to the U.S. Commission on Civil Rights. *Police–Community Relations in East Los Angeles, California: A Report of the California Advisory Committee to the United States Commission on Civil Rights.* Los Angeles: The Committee, 1970.

———. *Political Participation of Mexican Americans in California.* Washington, D.C.: Government Printing Office, 1971.

U.S. Bureau of the Census. *United States Census of Population, 1950. Special Reports. Persons of Spanish Surname.* Washington, D.C.: Government Printing Office, 1953.

———. *U.S. Census of Population and Housing: 1960. Census Tracts, Final Report. PHC (1)-82.* Washington D.C.: Government Printing Office, 1962.

———. *U.S. Census of Population: 1960; Subject Reports. Persons of Spanish Surname. Final Report PC (2)-1B.* Washington D.C.: Government Printing Office, 1963.

———. *U.S. Census of Population and Housing: 1970. Census Tracts, Final Report. PHC (1)-82.* Washington D.C.: Government Printing Office, 1972.

U.S. Commission on Civil Rights. *Mexican Americans and the Administration of Justice in the Southwest.* Washington, D.C.: Government Printing Office, 1970.

U.S. Department of Justice. Federal Bureau of Investigation.

    Brown Beret file, no. 105-178715

    CASA file, no. 105-31729

    Chicano Moratorium Committee file, no. 100-459861

    Committee to Free Los Tres file, no. 105-34112

NEWSPAPERS AND PERIODICALS

Atlantic, 1967
Belvedere Citizen, 1949–63
Carta Editorial, 1963–69
La Causa, 1969–72
Chicano Student Movement, 1968
Chicano Student News, 1968
Con Safos, 1972

Daily Bruin, 1969–70
Eastside Journal, 1949–63
Eastside Sun, 1949–63
Frontier, 1954
El Gallo, 1970
La Gente de Aztlán, 1972
Inside Eastside, 1968–69
Los Angeles Daily News, 1949–54
Los Angeles Free Press, 1969–78
Los Angeles Herald-Examiner, 1949–70
Los Angeles Mirror, 1949–54
Los Angeles Times, 1949–2001
Mexican Voice, 1939
The Militant, 1969–78
The Nation, 1970–98
The New Yorker, 1966
New York Times, 1969, 2001
Perspectives: American Historical Association Newsletter, 1997
El Popo, 1970
La Raza (newspaper), 1967–70
La Raza Magazine, 1970–77
Regeneración, 1969–71
Sin Fronteras, 1974–78
Time, 1967

INTERVIEWS

Becerra, Cruz (Olmeda). Interview by author. Tape recording. Alhambra, California, May 15, 1993.
Castro, Victoria. Interview by author. Tape recording. Los Angeles, May 24, 1993.
Chávez, Arturo, and Carlos Chávez. Interview by author. Tape recording. Los Angeles, August 2, 1992.
Martínez, Richard A. Interview by Carlos Vásquez. 1990. Oral history interview conducted by the UCLA Oral History Program, for the California State Government Oral History Program.
Muñoz, Rosalio. Interview by author. Tape recording. Los Angeles, January 27, 1987.
Noriega, Ramsés. Interview by author. Tape recording. Los Angeles, February 29, 1992.
Rodríguez, Jacobo. Interview by author. Tape recording. Los Angeles, March 10, 1992.
Rodríguez, Jorge. Interview by author. Tape recording. Alhambra, California, February 13, 1992.
Santillán, Richard A. Interview by Carlos Vásquez. 1989. Oral history interview

conducted by the UCLA Oral History Program, for the California State Government Oral History Program.

Santillán, Richard A. Interview by author. Tape recording. Alhambra, California, August 1, 1999.

Other Sources

Acosta, Oscar Zeta. "The East L.A. 13 vs. the L.A. Superior Court." *El Grito* 3, no. 2 (winter 1970): 12–18.

———. *The Revolt of the Cockroach People.* San Francisco: Straight Arrow Publishing, 1973.

Acuña, Rodolfo. *A Community Under Siege: A Chronicle of Chicanos East of the Los Angeles River, 1945–1975.* Los Angeles: UCLA Chicano Studies Research Center Publications, no. 11, 1984.

———. *Occupied America: A History of Chicanos.* 3d ed. New York: Harper and Row, 1988.

Allsup, Carl. *The American G.I. Forum: Origins and Evolution.* Austin: University of Texas, Center for Mexican American Studies, 1982.

Almaguer, Tomás. *Racial Fault Lines: The Historical Origins of White Supremacy in California.* Berkeley: University of California Press, 1994.

American Civil Liberties Union. *Day of Protest, Night of Violence: The Century City Peace March.* Los Angeles: Sawyer Press, 1987.

Anderson, Benedict. *Imagined Communities: Reflections on the Origin and Spread of Nationalism.* New York: Verso Press, 1991.

(The) August Twenty-Ninth Movement. *Fan the Flames: A Revolutionary Position on the Chicano National Question.* Los Angeles: August Twenty-Ninth Movement, 1976.

Bakhtin, Mikhail. *Speech Genres and Other Late Essays.* Austin: University of Texas Press, 1986.

Barrera, Mario, and Carlos Muñoz. "La Raza Unida Party and the Chicano Student Movement in California." *Social Science Journal* 19, no. 2 (April 1982): 101–20.

Benjamin, Walter. *Illuminations: Essays and Reflections.* Edited with an introduction by Hannah Arendt, translated by Harry Zohn. New York: Schocken Books, 1968.

Berlant, Lauren. *The Queen of America Goes to Washington City: Essays on Sex and Citizenship.* Durham, N.C: Duke University Press, 1997.

Bernal, Dolores Delgado. "Grassroots Leadership Reconceptualized: Chicana Oral Histories and the 1968 East Los Angeles Blowouts." *Frontiers* 19, no. 2 (1998): 113–42.

Bhabha, Homi. *The Location of Culture.* New York: Routledge, 1994.

Boehmer, Elleke. "Stories of Women and Mothers: Gender and Nationalism in Early Fiction of Flora Nwapa." In *Motherlands: Black Women's Writing from Africa, the Caribbean and South Asia,* ed. Suheila Nasta. New Brunswick, N.J.: Rutgers University Press, 1992.

Briegel, Kaye Lynn. "The History of Political Organizations Among Mexican-Americans in Los Angeles since the Second World War." Master's thesis, University of Southern California, 1967.

Brown, Elaine. *A Taste of Power: A Black Woman's Story.* New York: Pantheon, 1992.

Burns, Stewart. *Social Movements of the 1960s: Searching for Democracy.* Boston: Twayne Publishers, 1990.

Camejo, Antonio, ed. *La Raza Unida Party in Texas: Speeches by Mario Compeón and José Angel Gutiérrez.* New York: Pathfinder Press, 1970.

Camejo, Antonio, et al. *Why A Chicano Party? Why Chicano Studies?* New York: Pathfinder Press, 1970.

Chabram-Dernersesian, Angie. "I Throw Punches For My Race, but I Don't Want to Be a Man: Writing US — Chica-nos (Girl Us) / Chicanas — into the Movement Script." In *Cultural Studies,* ed. Lawrence Grossberg, Cary Nelson, and Paula A. Treichler, 81–95. New York: Routledge, 1992.

Chávez, Marisela Rodríguez. "Living and Breathing the Movement: Women in el Centro de Acción Social Autónomo, 1975–1978." Master's thesis, Arizona State University, 1997.

Chicano Liberation Youth Conference. "El Plan Espritual de Aztlán" (1969). In *Major Problems in the History of the American West: Documents and Essays,* ed. Clyde A. Milner II, 493–95. Lexington, Mass.: D. C. Heath and Company, 1989.

Committee of Concerned Asian Scholars. *The Opium Trail: Heroin and Imperialism.* Somerville, Mass.: New England Free Press, 1972.

Corona, Bert. *Bert Corona Speaks.* New York: Pathfinder Press, 1972.

Cuellar, Alfredo Jr. "A Theory of Politics: The Idea of Chicano Revisionism." Ph.D. diss., Claremont Graduate School, 1976.

DeBenedetti, Charles. *An American Ordeal: The Antiwar Movement of the Vietnam Era.* Syracuse: Syracuse University Press, 1990.

Dickstein, Morris. *Gates of Eden: American Culture in the Sixties.* New York: Basic Books, 1977.

Echols, Alice. *Daring to be Bad: Radical Feminism in America, 1967–1975.* Minneapolis: University of Minnesota Press, 1989.

Escobar, Edward J. "Dialectics of Repression: The Los Angeles Police Department and the Chicano Movement, 1968–1971. *Journal of American History* 79 (March 1993): 1483–1514.

Espinoza, Dionne. "Pedagogies of Gender and Nationalism: Cultural Resistance in Selected Practices of Chicana/o Movement Activists, 1967–1972." Ph.D. diss., Cornell University, 1996.

Evans, Sarah. *Personal Politics: The Roots of Women's Liberation in the Civil Rights Movement and the New Left.* New York: Vintage Books, 1980.

Farber, David. *Chicago '68.* Chicago: University of Chicago Press, 1988.

Fitzgerald, Robin Scott. "The Mexican-American in the Los Angeles Area, 1920–1950: From Acquiescence to Activity." Ph.D. diss., University of Southern California, 1971.

Fogelson, Robert M., ed. *The Los Angeles Riots.* New York: Arno Press; New York: New York Times, 1969.

Foley, Neil. "Becoming Hispanic: Mexican Americans and the Faustian Pact With Whiteness." In *Reflexiones 1997: New Directions in Mexican American Studies,* ed. Neil Foley. Austin: University of Texas, Center for Mexican American Studies, 1997.

——. *The White Scourge: Mexicans, Blacks, and Poor Whites in Texas Cotton Culture.* Berkeley: University of California Press, 1997.

Foner, Phillip S., ed. *The Black Panthers Speak.* New York: J. B. Lippincott, 1970.

Fraser, Ronald, ed. *1968: A Student Generation in Revolt, An International Oral History.* New York: Pantheon Books, 1988.

——. "Significant to Whom?: Mexican Americans and the History of the American West." *Western Historical Quarterly* 24, no. 4 (November 1993): 519–39.

García, F. Chris, ed. *La Causa Politica: A Chicano Politics Reader.* Notre Dame, Ind.: University of Notre Dame, 1974.

——. *Latinos and the Political System.* Notre Dame, Ind.: University of Notre Dame Press, 1988.

García, Ignacio. *United We Win: The Rise and Fall of La Raza Unida Party.* Tucson: University of Arizona, Mexican Studies and Research Center, 1989.

——. *Chicanismo: The Forging of a Militant Ethos Among Chicanos.* Tucson: University of Arizona Press, 1997.

García, Jorge. "Forjando Ciudad: The Development of a Chicano Political Community in East Los Angeles." Ph.D. diss., University of California at Riverside, 1986.

García, Mario. *Mexican Americans: Leadership, Ideology, and Identity, 1930–1960.* New Haven: Yale University Press, 1989.

——. *Memories of Chicano History: The Life and Narrative of Bert Corona.* Berkeley: University of California Press, 1994.

García, Richard A. "The Chicano Movement and the Mexican American Community, 1972–1978: An Interpretive Essay," *Socialist Review* 8, no. 4/5 (July/October 1978): 117–41.

——. *Rise of the Mexican American Middle Class, San Antonio, 1929–1941.* College Station: Texas A & M University Press, 1991.

Gerstle, Gary. *Working-Class Americanism: The Politics of Labor in a Textile City, 1914–1960.* New York: Cambridge University Press, 1989.

Gilroy, Paul. *The Black Atlantic: Modernity and Double Consciousness.* Cambridge, Mass.: Harvard University Press, 1993.

Gitlin, Todd. *The Sixties: Days of Hope, Years of Rage.* New York: Bantam Books, 1987.

Gómez-Quiñones, Juan. *Mexican Students Por La Raza: The Chicano Student Movement in Southern California.* Santa Barbara: Editorial La Causa, 1978.

——. *Chicano Politics: Reality and Promise, 1940–1990.* Albuquerque: University of New Mexico Press, 1990.

González, Deena J. *Refusing the Favor: The Spanish Mexican Women of Santa Fe.* New York: Oxford University Press, 1999.

Gosse, Van. *Where the Boys Are: Cuba, Cold War America, and the Making of the New Left.* New York: Verso, 1993.

Grebler, Leo, Joan Moore, and Ralph C. Guzmán. *The Mexican American People: The Nation's Second Largest Minority.* New York: The Free Press, 1970.

Gutiérrez, David G. "CASA in the Chicano Movement: Ideology and Organizational Politics in the Chicano Community, 1968–1978." Working paper series, no. 5, Stanford Center for Chicano Research, 1984.

———. "Ethnicity, Ideology, and Political Development: Mexican Immigration as a Political Issue in the Chicano Community." Ph.D. diss., Stanford University, 1988.

———. *Walls and Mirrors: Mexican Americans, Mexican Immigrants, and the Politics of Ethnicity.* Berkeley: University of California Press, 1994.

Gutiérrez, José Angel. *The Making of a Chicano Militant: Lesson From Cristal.* Madison: University of Wisconsin Press, 1998.

Gutiérrez, Ramón A. "Community, Patriarchy, and Individualism: The Politics of Chicano History and the Dream of Equality." *American Quarterly* 45, no. 1 (March 1993): 44–72.

Guzmán, Ralph. "The Political Socialization of the Mexican American People." Ph.D. diss., University of California at Los Angeles, 1970.

Hall, Stuart. "Ethnicity: Identity and Difference." *Radical America* 23, no. 4 (October–December 1989): 9–20.

Hobsbawm, Eric J. *Nations and Nationalism Since 1780: Programme, Myth, and Reality.* Cambridge: Cambridge University Press, 1990.

Inda, Juan Javier. "La Comunidad En Lucha: The Development of the East Los Angeles High School Blowouts." Working paper series, no. 29, Stanford Center for Chicano Research, 1990.

Juárez, Alberto. "The Emergence of El Partido de la Raza Unida: California's New Chicano Party." *Aztlán* 3, no. 2 (fall 1972): 177–204.

Katsiaficas, George. *The Imagination of the New Left: A Global Analysis of 1968.* Boston: South End Press, 1987.

Laclau, Ernesto. *Emancipation(s).* New York: Verso, 1996.

Macías, Reynaldo, Guillermo Vicente Flores, Donaldo Figueroa, and Luís Aragón. *A Study of Unincorporated East Los Angeles.* Los Angeles: Aztlán Publications, Chicano Studies Research Center, University of California at Los Angeles, 1973.

Malcolm X, with Alex Haley. *The Autobiography of Malcolm X.* New York: Ballantine Books, 1965.

Marable, Manning. *Race, Reform, and Rebellion: The Second Reconstruction in Black America, 1945–1982.* Jackson: University of Mississippi Press, 1984.

Marín, Marguerite. "Protest in an Urban Barrio: A Study of the Chicano Movement." Ph.D. diss., University of California at Santa Barbara, 1980.

Matusow, Allen J. *The Unraveling of America: A History of Liberalism in the 1960s.* New York: Harper Torch Books, 1984.

McAdam, Doug. *Political Process and the Development of Black Insurgency, 1930–1970.* Chicago: University of Chicago Press, 1982.

———. *Freedom Summer.* New York: Oxford University Press, 1986.

McClintock, Anne. *Imperial Leather: Race, Gender, and Sexuality in the Colonial Contest.* New York: Routledge, 1995.

McCoy, Alfred. *The Politics of Heroin in Southeast Asia.* New York: Harper and Row, 1972.

Miller, James. *Democracy Is in the Streets: From Port Huron to the Siege of Chicago.* New York: Simon and Schuster, 1987.

Montejano, David. *Anglos and Mexicans in the Making of Texas, 1836–1986.* Austin: University of Texas Press, 1987.

Morales, Armando. *Ando Sangrando — I Am Bleeding: A Study of Mexican American–Police Conflict.* La Puente, Calif.: Perspectiva Publications, 1972.

Mosse, George L. *Nationalism and Sexuality: Middle-Class Morality and Sexual Norms in Modern Europe.* Madison: University of Wisconsin Press, 1985.

———. *The Image of the Man: The Creation of Modern Masculinity.* New York: Oxford University Press, 1996.

Muñoz, Carlos. *Youth, Identity, Power: The Chicano Movement.* New York: Verso Press, 1989.

Navarro, Armando. *Mexican American Youth Organization: Avant Garde of the Chicano Movement in Texas.* Austin: University of Texas Press, 1995.

———. *The Cristal Experiment: A Chicano Struggle for Community Control.* Madison: University of Wisconsin Press, 1999.

O'Neil, William L. *Coming Apart: An Informal History of America in the 1960s.* New York: Times Books, 1971.

O'Reily, Kenneth. *Racial Matters: The FBI's Secret File on Black America, 1960–1972.* New York: The Free Press, 1989.

Oropeza, Lorena. "La Batalla Está Aquí!: Chicanos Oppose the Vietnam War." Ph.D. diss., Cornell University, 1996.

Parson, Don. "'This Modern Marvel': Bunker Hill, Chavez Ravine, and the Politics of Modernism in Los Angeles." *Southern California Quarterly* 75, no. 3/4 (fall/winter 1993): 333–50.

Pérez-Torres, Rafael. "Reframing Aztlán." *Aztlán* 22, no. 2 (fall 1997): 15–41.

Pycior, Julie Leininger. *LBJ and Mexican Americans: The Paradox of Power.* Austin: University of Texas Press, 1997.

Raigoza, James José. "The Ad Hoc Committee to Incorporate East Los Angeles: A Study of the Socio-Political Orientations of Mexican American Incorporation Advocates." Ph.D. diss., University of California at Los Angeles, 1977.

Ramos, Henry A. J. *The American G.I. Forum: In Pursuit of the Dream.* Houston: Arte Público Press, 1998.

Rorabaugh, W. J. *Berkeley at War: The 1960s.* New York: Oxford University Press, 1989.

Rosen, Gerald Paul. *Political Ideology and the Chicano Movement: A Study of the Political Ideology of Activists in the Chicano Movement.* San Francisco: R & E Research Associates, 1975.

Rosenbaum, Robert J. *Mexicano Resistance in the Southwest: The Sacred Right of Self-Preservation.* Austin: University of Texas Press, 1981.

Ruiz, Vicki L. *From Out of the Shadows: Mexican Women in Twentieth-Century America*. New York: Oxford University Press, 1998.

Salazar, Ruben. *Border Correspondent: Selected Writings, 1955–1970,* edited with an Introduction by Mario T. Garcia. Berkeley: University of California Press, 1995.

Sánchez, David. *Expedition Through Aztlán*. La Puente, Calif.: Perspectiva Press, 1978.

Sánchez, George J. "Becoming Mexican American: Ethnicity and Acculturation in Chicano Los Angeles, 1900–1943." Ph.D. diss., Stanford University, 1989.

———. *Becoming Mexican American: Ethnicity, Culture, and Identity in Chicano Los Angeles, 1900–1945*. New York: Oxford University Press, 1993.

Sandoval, Chela. *Methodology of the Oppressed*. Minneapolis: University of Minnesota Press, 2000.

Santillán, Richard A. "The Politics of Cultural Nationalism: El Partido de La Raza Unida in Southern California, 1969–1978." Ph.D. diss., Claremont Graduate School, 1978.

Saxton, Alexander. *The Indispensable Enemy: The Anti-Chinese Campaign in California*. Berkeley: University of California Press, 1966.

Sayres, Sohnya, Anders Stephanson, Stanley Aronowitz, and Frederic Jameson, eds. *The '60s Without Apology*. Minneapolis: University of Minnesota Press, 1984.

Smith, Anthony D. *Nationalist Movements*. London: Macmillan Press, 1976.

Smith, Paul Chaat, and Robert Allen Warrior. *Like A Hurricane: The Indian Movement from Alcatraz to Wounded Knee*. New York: The New Press, 1996.

Thompson, Hunter S. "Strange Rumblings in Aztlan." In *The Great Shark Hunt: Strange Tales from a Strange Time*. New York: Warner Books, 1979.

Tirado, Miguel David. "Mexican American Community Political Organizations: The Key to Chicano Political Power." *Aztlan* 1, no. 1 (spring 1970): 53–78.

Tyler, Bruce. "Black Radicalism in Southern California, 1950–1982." Ph.D. diss., University of California at Los Angeles, 1983.

Underwood, Katherine. "Pioneering Minority Representation: Edward Roybal and the Los Angeles City Council, 1949–1962." *Pacific Historical Review* 65, no. 3 (August 1997): 399–425.

Urrutia, Liliana. "An Offspring of Discontent: The Asociación Nacional Mexico-Americana, 1949–1954." *Aztlán* 15 (spring 1984): 177–84.

Van Deburg, William L. *New Day in Babylon: The Black Power Movement and American Culture, 1965–1975*. Chicago: University of Chicago Press, 1992.

Vigil, Ernesto. *The Crusade for Justice: Chicano Militancy and the Government's War on Dissent*. Madison: University of Wisconsin Press, 1999.

Villa, Raúl H. *Barrio-Logos: Space and Place in Urban Chicano Literature and Culture*. Austin: University of Texas Press, 2000.

Weschler, Louis F., and John F. Gallagher. "Viva Kennedy." In *Cases in American National Government and Politics,* ed. Rocco J. Tresolini and Richard T. Frost. Englewood Cliffs, N.J.: Prentice Hall, 1965.

Williams, Raymond. *Problems in Materialism and Culture*. 1980; Reprint, New York: Verso, 1997.

Index

Acevedo, John, 33
Acosta, Oscar Zeta, 69, 72
Acosta, Robert, 59–60
Aguilar, Fred, 85
Ainsworth, Tracy, 30
Alatorre, Richard, 44, 87–89
Alfaro, Luis: "Chicanismo," 117
Alinski, Saul, 12
Alvarez, John, 105f.
American Civil Liberties Union (ACLU), 15
American Council on Race Relations (ACRR), 12
Americanism, 11, 12
ANMA. *See* Asociación Nacional México Americana (ANMA)
anticommunism, 11–12, 14, 20
antiwar protests, 17, 55–56, 61–64, 65–66. *See also* August 29 demonstration
Arechiga, Manuel and Arvina, 29
Arellanes, Gloria, 59
Asociación Nacional México Americana (ANMA), 10–11, 14–18, 41; FBI investigation of, 18; involved in police abuse cases, 25; issues, 15; political ideas of, 15–17; women's participation in, 17–18
assimilation: Americanization campaigns, 11, 12, 30; challenges to, 96–97
August 29 demonstration, 68–69; controversy over, 70–71; Green Mill Liquor Store incident, 69–70, 137n.40; investigation of, 71–72

August Twenty-Ninth Movement (ATM), 109
autobiographical comments, 3–4

Bakke decision, 112
"Bato Loco Yesterday," 58f.2
Belvedere Junior High, 30
Berlant, Lauren, 138n.56
Bernabe, Lucio, 33
Bernal, Esmeralda, 53
Bhaba, Homi, 144n.14
bilingual education demand, 49
Biscailuz, Eugene W., 24
Black Panther Party, 109–10
Blanco, Gilbert, 84
Boehmer, Elleke, 5–6, 134n.75
Bowron, Fletcher, 19, 20
Boyle Heights district, 21, 103; freeway construction through, 25–26; medical facilities proposed for, 21–28
Boyle-Hollenbeck anti–Golden State Freeway Committee, 25–26
Brown, Edmund G. ("Pat"), 33, 36, 41
Brown Berets, 6, 42, 58f.3 and f.4, 78; Chicano nationalism and, 42, 45, 131nn.21, 26; class ideology and ethnic nationalism intermingled, 57–58; differing political views, 50; FBI investigation of, 60; internal tensions, 57, 59; involved in student boycotts, 47–49; National Headquarters Central Committee, 57;

Brown Berets *(continued)*
protest against Reagan and firesetting, 51–54; social and medical services run by, 44, 55; "Ten Point Program," 49. *See also La Causa;* Young Citizens for Community Action (YCCA)
Bueno, Anthony G., 37
Bunker Hill district, 26
Bureau of Narcotics and Dangerous Drugs, U.S., 99
Bustillos, Máximo, 24

California Assembly, campaigns for, 37, 86–89, 92–93, 119
California Eagle, 15
California Highway Commission, 25
California State College at Hayward, 82–84
California Supreme Court, 112
"Campo Tecolote," 56–57
Carta Editorial, 40–41
Casa Carnalismo, 99
CASA. *See* Centro de Acción Social Autónomo (CASA)
Castelan, Julio, 33
Castro, Fidel, 3. 113
Castro, Fred, 33
Castro, Vickie, 43, 45
Catalina Island incident, 56–57
Catholic Church, 7, 12–13, 44
Cátolicos Por la Raza, 6–7
Causa, La: Brown Berets newspaper, 51, 54–55, 59, 73, 84; denouncing the Chicano Moratorium Committee, 66, 68; recruitment illustrations, 58f.2 and f.3; on the War in Vietnam, 55–56. *See also* Brown Berets
Cebeda, Christopher, role in "Nuevas Vistas" fire, 52, 53–54
Census Bureau, U.S., 9–10, 119
Centro de Acción Social Autónomo (CASA), 6, 83, 106–7, 118; disintegration of, 116; FBI infiltration of, 113–15; Greeley chapter, 108–9; internal tensions, 115–16; Marxist-Leninist philosophy of, 98–99, 107, 116; merger with Comité, 104–7; National Congress, 108; opposition to the Rodino bill, 110–11; organizational structure, 108–9; political alliances, 113; "Reglamento" (rule book), 107–8; "¡Resistencia!" poster, 111f.; supporting political asylum for

Medina, 112–13; tensions with other groups, 109–10
Chale con el Draft, 62–63
Chávez, Arturo, 104
Chávez, César, 39, 44
Chávez, Dennis, 35
Chávez, Gloria, 72
Chávez, Isabel Rodriguez, 107
Chávez Ravine district, 26, 28; removal for baseball stadium, 28–29
Chicanismo, 5. *See also* Chicano movement in Los Angeles
Chicano, term, 8, 127n.101
Chicano identity, 6, 119, 121n.3, 144n.14, 148n.10. *See also* Chicano nationalism; class ideology
Chicano Moratorium Committee (CMC), 118; antiwar demonstrations, 6, 65–66, 68–69; broadening of issues, 77, 84; disbanding of, 78–79; internal disputes, 66, 68; "Marcha de la Reconquista," 77–78; "Marcha por Justica" and resulting violence, 74–77; protesting police abuse, 72, 73. *See also* August 29 demonstration; National Chicano Moratorium
Chicano movement in Los Angeles, 3, 5, 6–7, 109, 117–20; Chicano nationalism and, 42–43, 45; collapse of, 7, 117; Marxism and 4, 50; roots of, 1–2. *See also* Brown Berets; Centro de Acción Social Autónomo (CASA); Chicano Moratorium Committee (CMC); Committee to Free Los Tres (CTFLT); Marxism; Marxism-Leninism; Mexican-American history; Mexican American Political Association (MAPA); Sixties
Chicano nationalism, 5, 65, 120; birth of in the Sixties, 42–43, 45. *See also* masculinism and Chicano nationalism; proto-nationalism
Chicano Student News, 48
Chicano Youth Liberation Conference, 66
Cinco de Mayo, 31
City Council, Los Angeles. *See* Los Angeles City Council
City Housing Authority, Los Angeles, 19
City Terrace Chapter, of La Raza Unida, 91–92, 93
Ciudanos Unidos (United Citizens), 82
Civilian Police Review Board (demanded), 49
civil rights issue, 15

class ideology: ethnic identity and, 57–58, 104, 116, 120, 148n.10; Marxism, 102–3; Marxist-Leninism, 4, 50, 98–99, 107, 116. *See also* Mexican Americans, socio-economic status of

CMC. *See* Chicano Moratorium Committee (CMC)

Cochino Rodino (play), 110–11

Cold War era, 16, 17, 30, 41; anticommunism, 11–12, 14, 20; postwar Second World War period, 10–11. *See also* Korean War; Vietnam War

collective identity, 1; and the Chicano movement, 6, 119, 121n.3, 144n.14, 148n.10

Comité de Estudiantil del Pueblo, 103

Comité de Festejivos Patrios, 31–32

Comité. *See* Committee to Free Los Tres (CTFLT)

Committee to Free Los Tres (CTFLT), 98, 101f., 102; campaign against sterilization, 103–4; class ideology and ethnic nationalism intermingled, 104; effort to serve working class people, 104–5; emphasis on Marxism, 102–3; merger with CASA, 104–7; "Principles" of, 103; *Sin Cadenas* (Without Shackles), 103. *See also* Los Tres; *Sin Fronteras*

Committee to Save Chávez Ravine for the People, 28–29

Communist Party (CP), 104

Community for Bario Betterment, 81

Community Opposing Incorporation Now (COIN), 95

Community Redevelopment Agency, 26–30

Community Service Organization (CSO), 10, 41, 44; campaign for Roybal in 9th district, 12–14, 18; involved in police abuse cases, 25, 40

Compeán, Mario, 81

Congreso de Pueblos de Haba Español, El 2–3

Congress of the Puerto Rican Socialist Party, 113, 114

Congress of Spanish-Speaking Peoples, 2–3

Corona, Bert, 14, 32, 36, 83–84, 106

Coroner's Office, LA County, 71–72

Corpus Christi, Texas, 2

Crusade for Justice, 64, 84

Cruz, Roberto, 76

CSO. *See* Community Service Organization (CSO)

Cuba, CASA delegation to, 113

cultural development, autonomous, 16

cultural nationalism, 30, 60, 120. *See also* Chicano nationalism

cultural work, 110–11, 111f.

Davenport, Edward, 20–21

Davis, Edward, 74

Deganawidah-Quezalcoatl University (D.Q.U.) incident, 78–79

"Democratic centralism," 108

democratic Party, 32–33, 92, 95

deportations, 17, 77, 112–13

"¡Despierta Chicano, Defiendo Tu Hermano!" Conference, 104, 105f., 107

Díaz, Angel Gilberto, 70

discrimination, 16

District Attorney, LA County, 72

"Diva citizenship," 138n.56

Downtown Community Association, 27

drug trade, U.S. authorities and, 102

East Los Angeles, efforts to incorporate as a city, 36, 94–96

East Los Angeles Chapter of La Raza Unida, 93–94; police monitoring and harassment in, 64

East Los Angeles Property Owners Association, 36

Eastside Sun, 21, 26, 36; Mendez's column in, 30–32

Eaton, Geraldine, 23–24

Educational Issues Coordinating Committee (EICC), 6

Educational Opportunity Programs (EOPs), 77

"8 Points of Attention" (Sánchez), 51

electoral politics, 117, 118, 119; campaigns for California Assembly, 37, 86–89, 92–93, 119; contemporary turn toward electoral politics, 117, 147n.2; targeting areas, 81–82; voter registration drives, 13, 35, 85–86, 92–93. *See also* La Raza Unida Party (LRUP); Mexican American Political Association (MAPA); Roybal, Edward R.

Elias, Robert, 84

Esparza, Moctesuma, 43, 45

ethnicity: Chicano or Latino, 119, 121n.3,

ethnicity (continued)
    144n.14; ethnic/cultural nationalism and
    class ideology intermingled, 57–58, 104,
    116, 120
Evaluation Task Force, CASA, 116
evictions, 29

Federal Bureau of Investigation (FBI),
    239n.85; ANMA investigation, 18;
    Brown Beret investigation, 60; infiltra-
    tion of CASA, 113–15; investigation of
    the Chicano Moratorium Committee,
    71. See also police monitoring/infiltration
    of Chicano movement activities
feminism, 119–20
Fernández, Juan, 99. See also Los Tres
Fifties, Los Angeles Mexican-American
    community in, 9–10, 29–30. See also
    Cold War era; urban renewal
Flores, Elsa, 111f.
40th Assembly District, 92–93
48th Assembly District, 86–89
Fourteenth Amendment, 112

Gallegos, Herman, 33
García, Alex, 92
García, Hector, 34, 35
gender. See masculinism and Chicano
    nationalism; women and the Chicano
    movement
Golden State Freeway, 25–26
Gonzales, Henry, 35
Gonzales, Rodolfo ("Corky"), 64, 69, 71, 91
Great Depression, 10
Green Mill Liquor Store incident, 69–70,
    137n.40
Gutiérrez, David G., Walls and Mirrors, 1–
    2, 119
Gutiérrez, José Angel, 81, 91
Guzmán, Ralph C., 35, 63–64

Hagan, Peter F., 74
Hall, Stuart, 6
Healey, Dorothy, 104
Hermandad Mexicana, 119
Hidalgo, David, 24
"History of Los Angeles, The" (perform-
    ance), 30
House of Brotherhood, 99
Housing Act (1949), 27
housing issues: evictions, 29; housing con-
    ditions, 63; housing discrimination, 19–

20, 39; public housing, 15, 19–21; urban
    renewal projects, 26–30, 49
Huerta, Dolores, 39
Human Relations Commission, LA
    County, 43

identity. See Chicano identity
immigration, 10. See also population,
    Mexican American
immigration issues, 15; deportations, 17,
    77, 112–13
Immigration and Naturalization Service,
    U.S., 77, 112–13
"in-between" space (Chicano ethnicity),
    121n.3, 144n.14
inquest into the death of Ruben Salazar,
    70, 71–72, 86
institutional racism, 2. See also ethnicity;
    racism

Jameson, Frederic, 1
Javier, Gonzolo, 74
Johnson, Lyndon, 43
Juárez, Benito, 31

Kennedy, Robert, 35
King, Martin Luther, 46
KMEX (Spanish-language TV station),
    68
Korean War, 17. See also military service

Laclau, Ernesto, 7
LAPD. See Los Angeles Police Department
    (LAPD)
League of United Latin American Citizens
    (LULAC), 2
Licón, George, 43, 45
Lindsay, Gilbert, 38
López, Gilbert, 92–93
López, Henry: campaign for secretary of
    state, 32–33
López, Ignacio, 33
López, Roger, 84
Los Angeles City Council: 9th district
    council seat, 12–14, 18, 38, 117–18;
    public housing contract, 19–21
Los Angeles City Government: City
    Housing Authority (CHA), 19;
    Community Redevelopment Agency,
    26–30
Los Angeles Committee to Stop Forced
    Sterilizations, 103–4

Los Angeles County: Coroner's Office, 71–72; District Attorney, 72; Human Relations Commission, 43; Urban Affairs Department, 63

Los Angeles Police Department (LAPD): Chicano picket of and violent response, 72, 73–74; chiefs of, 21, 74; police-community relations, 25, 49; role in August 29 event and aftermath, 69–70, 71. *See also* Police monitoring/infiltration of Chicano movement activities; Police violence against Mexican Americans

Los Angeles Superior Court, 37, 41

Los Angeles Times, 28, 70

Los Lobos, "Revolution," 1

LRUP. *See* Raza Unida Party, La (LRUP)

Luce, John B., 44–45, 71–72

Lydick, Lawrence, 100

McCarran Act, 17, 18

McCarthyism, 14

McCone Commission, 43

McCoy, Alfred: *The Politics of Heroin in Southeast Asia,* 102

McWilliams, Carey, 15

Malcolm X, 46, 47

Maoism, 50

MAPA. *See* Mexican American Political Association (MAPA)

"Marcha de la Reconquista," 77–78

"Marcha por Justica", 74–77

Martínez, Frank, 73

Martínez, Richard A., 80, 85, 88

Marxism, 102–3; purge of leftists, 38–39

Marxism-Leninism: the Chicano movement and, 4, 50; in organizational politics, 98–99, 107, 116

masculism and Chicano nationalism, 5–6, 47, 134nn.74, 75; in the Brown Berets, 57–59, 131nn. 21, 26

Medina, Jacques, 112–13

Mendez, John F: "Pan American Panorama" column in the *Eastside Sun,* 30–32

Mescalaros, 78

Mexican American (term), 8

Mexican-American history, 1–3, 5; the contemporary turn to electoral politics, 117, 147n.2; the fifties and the protonationalist phase, 5, 6, 9–11, 30, 42; the Sixties/seventies and Chicano nationalism, 5, 42–43, 45, 42–43, 45, 65, 120. *See also* Chicano movement; electoral politics

Mexican-American literature, 127n.101

Mexican American Movement, 11

Mexican American Political Association (MAPA), 38–39, 83–84, 117–18; campaign for East Los Angeles cityhood, 36; city and state political efforts, 36–39, 40–41, 42; ethnic identification and, 33–34, 40; part of a national political alliance, 34–35; purge of leftists in, 38–39; Robert Kennedy campaign activism, 35–36; women's participation in, 33

Mexican-American reform activism, 2–3. *See also* Asociacíon Nacional Mexico-Americana (ANMA); League of Latin American Citizens (LULAC)

Mexican Americans, socioeconomic status of, 10, 15, 121n.3. *See also* class ideology

Mexican-American voting behaviors study, 96, 135n.10

Mexican American Youth Leadership Conference, 43–44

Mexican American Youth Organization (MAYO), 81–82

Mexican Chamber of Commerce, 20

military service: impact on Mexican Americans, 17, 55–56, 61, 63–65. *See also* Korean War; Vietnam War

"¡Mi Raza Primero!" poster, 3

Molina, Gloria, 147n.4

Montag, Gustav Jr., 75

Montes, Carlos: initial disappearance of, 52–53; role in "Nuevas Vistas" fire, 52, 53–54

Moreno, John, 37

Mosse, George: *Nationalism and Sexuality,* 131nn.21, 26

Muñoz, Rosalio: antiwar activism, 61–64, 69; cochair of Chicano Moratorium Committee, 65; in controversy over "Marcha por Justica" violence, 74, 75–77

Muskie, Edmund, 87

National Chicano Moratorium, 67f.; picket of Los Angeles Police Department and resulting violence, 72, 73–74

nationalism. *See* Chicano nationalism; protonationalism

Naturalization act of 1790, 2

Nava, Julian, campaign for school board, 43–44

New American Movement, 104

Ninth Circuit Court of Appeals, U.S.,
    100–101
Noriega, Ramsés, 62, 64; antiwar protest
    organizer, 66; involvement with the
    Chicano Moratorium Committee, 72,
    78–79
"Nuevos Vistas" and fire, 51, 52, 53–54

Ochoa, Rachel, 43, 45
Office of Economic Opportunity (OEO),
    43, 44
Olivares, John, 84
Olmeda, Cruz, 47, 50
"Operation Wetback," 17
Ortiz, Alberto, 99. See also Los Tres
Ortiz, Juan, 43, 54
Oxnard group, 78–79

Partida Communista Mexico, 113
Parker, Bobby, 99, 100
Parker, William, 21
Parsons, Johnny, 46
Partido Socialista Puertoriqéño, 113, 114
Paz, Frank, 33
peace movement. See antiwar protests
Pimental, Rosemary, 85
Pinkston, Thomas W., 71
"Piranya, La" (coffeehouse), 44–45
Pitchess, Peter, 70–71, 76
police-community relations, 25, 49. See also
    Los Angeles Police Department (LAPD);
    Sheriff's Department
police monitoring/infiltration of Chicano
    movement activities, 138nn.62, 63; of
    the Brown Berets, 52–53, 59–60; of the
    Chicano Moratorium Committee, 70–
    71, 73–74; in East Los Angeles, 64; in
    Los Tres case, 99–102. See also Federal
    Bureau of Investigation (FBI); Los
    Angeles Police Department
police violence against Mexican Americans,
    44; Bloody Christmas episode, 23–24;
    Bustillos accusation, 24; Hidalgo law-
    suit, 24; Los Angeles Police Department
    role in August 29 event, 69–70; National
    Chicano Moratorium picket of Los
    Angeles Police Department, 72, 73–74;
    Ríos-Ulloa incident, 22–23
Political Association of Spanish-Speaking
    Organizations (PASSO), 34–35
politics, electoral. See electoral politics

population, Mexican American, 9–10, 43,
    119–20
postwar era, 10–11
Priest, Ivy Baker, 40–41
Property Owners Committee (Boyle
    Heights), 28
Proposition 14, 39
Proposition X, 94–96
protonationalism, 5, 9, 30, 42. See also
    Chicano nationalism
public housing, 15, 19–21
"Pueblo Sin Fronteras, Un." See Sin
    Fronteras

Quevedo, Eduardo, 33, 38–39

racism, 2, 16
radicalism, 15
Ramírez, Gloria, 85
Ramírez, Ralph, 43, 47; role in "Nuevas
    Vistas" fire, 52, 53–54, 73
Raza, La newspaper, 45, 86; coverage
    of Brown Berets in, 48–49, 50–51;
    on the failure of a third party strategy,
    92
Raza Unida Party, La (LRUP), 6, 80–82,
    96–97, 118; California party, 82–85;
    effort to incorporate East Los Angeles
    as a city, 94–96; City Terrace Chapter,
    91–92, 93; East Los Angeles Chapter,
    93–94; internal tensions and fragmenta-
    tion of, 89, 90–92; organizational struc-
    ture, 89–90; political races involved in,
    86–89, 92–93; San Fernando Chapter,
    95–96; Southern California Organizing
    Committee, 91–92; third-party ballot
    requirements discouraging, 96, 142–
    43n.67; third party strategy of, 82–85,
    92–93, 96–97
Reagan, Ronald, 41, 52, 77
real estate lobby, 20
reapportionment, 37
reform. See Mexican American reform
    activism
Republican Party, 86
residual culture, 5, 9
Ríos, Anthony, 22–23
Rodino, Peter: and the Rodino bill, 110–11
Rodríguez, Alvaro, 23
Rodríguez, Antonio, 116
Rodríguez, Jorge ("Cokie"), 71

Ross, Fred, 12–13
Roybal, Edward R.: active in referendum opposing baseball stadium, 29; campaign for 9th district council seat, 12–14, 18, 29, 117–18; campaign for state lieutenant governor, 32–33; elected to and serving in the U.S. Congress, 37–38, 41, 110; involved in police abuse cases, 23, 24, 25; opposing the "Subversive Registration Ordinance," 18–19; opposition to freeway construction through Mexican-American district, 26; Robert Kennedy campaign activism, 35–26
Ruiz, Raúl, 72, 95; campaign for assembly, 86–89
Rumford Act, 39

Salazar, Ruben: columnist for the *Los Angeles Times,* 70, 137n.48; death and subsequent inquest, 70, 71–72, 86
Sánchez, David, 43, 45, 46, 131nn.21, 26, 147n.6; arrest of, 46; "Birth of a New Symbol, The," 46–47, 131n.21; on Chicano participation in student boycotts, 48; disbanding the Brown Berets, 57; editor of *La Causa,* 51, 57; involvement with Chicano Moratorium Committee, 65, 78–79
Sánchez, George I., 36
Sánchez, Josefina, 38
Sánchez, Leopoldo, 37, 41
Sánchez, Loretta, 119
Sánchez, Rodolfo, 99. *See also* Los Tres
Sandoval, Chela, 120
San Fernando Chapter of La Raza Unida, 95–96
Santillán, Richard A., 84–85, 86
Second World War, 3, 11
sheriff's department, 24, 59–60, 70–71, 73–74, 76; dismissing deputies, 77. *See also* police violence against Mexican Americans
Sin Fronteras, 98, 107
Sixties, 7, 42–43. *See also* Chicano nationalism
Smith Act, 17
Solis, Hortencia, 33
Soto, Mary, 33
Soto, Philip, 37
Southern California Organizing Committee of La Raza Unida, 91–92

State Assembly. *See* California Assembly
Stockholm Peace Appeal, 17
student boycotts, 47–49
Suarez, Mario, 127n.101
"Subversive Registration Ordinance," 18–19
Sumaya, Fernando, 52, 53–54
Supreme Court. *See* U.S. Supreme Court

Tafoya, Richard, 37–38
Taft-Hartley Act, 17
"Teatro Movemento Primavera," 110–11
Texas: La Raza Unida Party (LRUP) founded in, 80–82; Mexican-American activism in, 2, 35
third-party ballot requirements, 96, 142–43n.67
To Hell with the Draft, 62–63
tokenism, 36
Treaty of Guadalupe Hidalgo, 15, 49
Tres, Los, 99–101, 106. *See also* Committee to Free Los Tres (CTFLT)
Tubbs, Marie, 25

UCLA Mexican-American Study Project, 96
UFWA. *See* United Farm Workers Association (UFWA)
Ulloa, Alfred, 22–23
undocumented workers, 104
United Democrats for Incorporation, 95
United Electrical Workers, 15
United Farm Workers Association (UFWA), 39, 40, 84
United Slaves (US), 109–10
United States. *See* by organization
United States Attorney, 100
United States government: Bureau of the Census, 9–10, 119; Bureau of Narcotics and Dangerous Drugs, 99; Department of Justice (*See* Federal Bureau of Investigation [FBI]); foreign policy of, 16–17, 102
United States Ninth Circuit Court of Appeals, 100–101
United States Supreme Court: Bakke decision and, 112; Los Tres case appeal and ruling, 100, 101, 105
Unruh, Jesse, 33
Urban Affairs Department, LA County, 63
urban guerillas, 46

urban renewal projects, 26–30, 49

Valdez, Armando, 83
Vásquez, Carlos, 113, 115
Vietnam War, 6, 61, 79. *See also* antiwar
    protests; military service
violence against Mexican Americans, 21–25
"Viva Kennedy Clubs," 35
voter registration drives, 13, 35, 85–86, 92–
    93

¡Wake Up Chicano, Defend Your Brother!
    Conference, 104, 105f., 107
War on Poverty, 43, 44
Watts rebellion, 40

Waxman, Henry A., 88
Williams, Raymond, 5, 9
women and the Chicano movement, 25,
    33, 39, 43, 85; Brown Berets and, 58–59;
    Comité's outreach to, 103–4; contribu-
    tions to CASA, 107, 111; participation in
    ANMA, 17–18. *See also* masculism and
    Chicano nationalism
World Federation of Trade Unions Con-
    ference on Youth, 113
World War II. *See* Second World War

Young Citizens for Community Action
    (YCCA), 43–45. *See also* Brown Berets
Younger, Evelle, 72

Compositor: BookMatters
Text: 10/13 Galliard
Display: Galliard
Printer and Binder: Sheridan Books, Inc.